D1239166

VOLUME 4

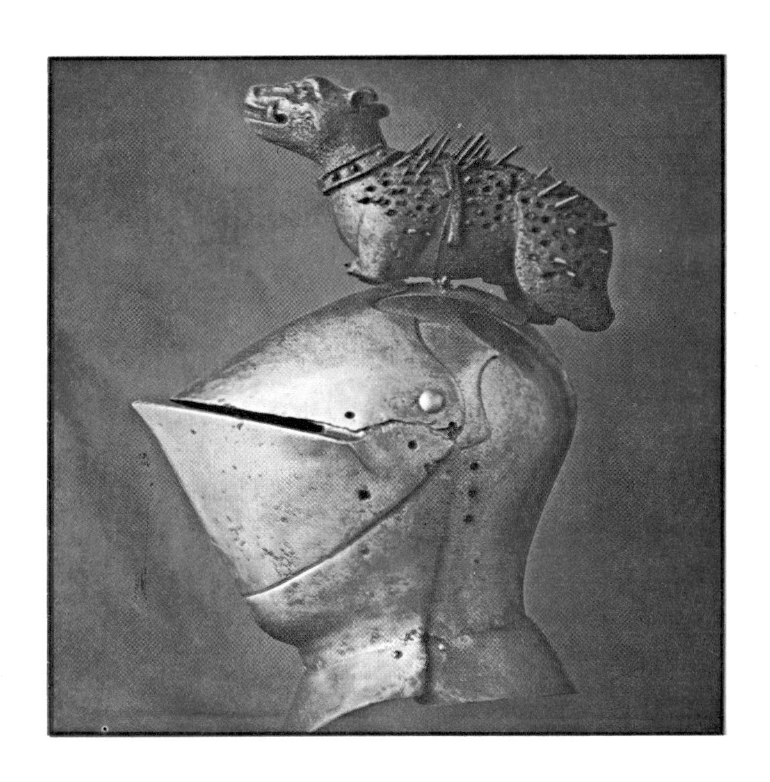

DISCOVERING ANTIQUES

THE STORY OF WORLD ANTIQUES

GREYSTONE PRESS/NEW YORK · TORONTO · LONDON

This superb full-color work is brought to you in its entirety from the original publisher, The British Publishing Corporation. Only the arrangement has been slightly altered. In fact, rather than disturb the text in any way, you will find the English monetary system used throughout the set. Here is a handy conversion table showing the value of a Pound (£) in terms of U.S. dollars.

DATES	U.S. Dollars equal to one Pound (£)
1939	$3.92 to 4.68
1940 to Sept. 1949	4.03
Sept. 1949 to Nov. 1967	2.80
Nov. 1967 to Aug. 1971	2.40
Aug. 1971 to June 1972	2.60
June 1972 to present	2.45 (floating rate)

20 shillings = one Pound (£)
21 shillings = one guinea

In February, 1971, the guinea was taken out of circulation.

TITLE PAGE PHOTO CREDIT: *Philip Sidney's Helmet* by kind permission of Viscount de L'Isle, V.C., P.C., Penshurst Place, Kent.

Published by the Greystone Press
225 Park Avenue South
New York, N.Y. 10003

Library of Congress Catalog Card Number: 72-90688

Cover Design: Harold Franklin

MANUFACTURED IN THE UNITED STATES OF AMERICA.

Contents

Edward Pinto

Elizabethan Tableware

Fig. 1 ***The Cobham Family,*** *attributed to Hans Eworth (active in England c.1545–74). The Elizabethan era was an age of domestic peace and prosperity, as can be seen from this happy family gathering.*
(Collection of the Marquess of Bath.)

In considering the Elizabethans at table, due account must be taken of the great disparity between the table appointments and food of royalty and the nobility, and that of the cottager, with the gentry and yeoman farmer falling between. Moreover, there were also vast differences between the semi-medieval conditions at the beginning of the great Queen's wise and inspiring rule of forty-five years and the prosperous state in which she left the realm.

William Harrison, rector of Radwinter in Essex, has left us a remarkably clear account of changes which took place between the years 1577–87 in his *Description of England.* After describing improvements in house building, particularly the increase in the number of chimneys and in the standard of sleeping accommodation as recalled by the older men, he goes on to say:

> *The third thing they tell of, is the exchange of (vessell, as of) treene platters into pewter, and woodden spoones into siluer or tin. For so*

1

J. Freeman

Fig. 2 At first sight, there does not appear to be much connection between a wooden trencher and a part-song with a refrain. Roundels are the connecting link. Thin, circular trenchers, usually of sycamore, they were decorated on one side with verses in gilded and brightly painted ornamental borders and the roundelays or 'poesies' were recited or sung at the end of the meal. After the more robust trenchers or platters had been cleared, each guest received a roundel. Plain face up, it was used for marchpanes or candied fruits and then reversed to show the 'poesies', as illustrated; each guest could then sing his or her verse in turn, probably to the accompaniment of a lute. (Victoria and Albert Museum, London.)

J. Freeman

Fig. 3 Carved lever nutcrackers, almost invariably made from strong, tough boxwood, were used on the Continent from medieval times; screw types were probably introduced later. The finest of these lever nutcrackers, decoratively carved with human or animal heads and made chiefly in France, Italy and the Low Countries, found their way to other countries including England, where they were highly valued. The lower jaws are pivoted together by boxwood or iron pins and actuated from the back. All early specimens have jaws only large enough for cobs and filberts, the popular dessert nuts for many centuries; often there is a secondary hollow or oval recess in the levers, large enough for a walnut. Almonds were more commonly used for cooking than dessert. This carved boxwood nutcracker, depicting Hercules astride and breaking the jaws of the Nemean lion, is Italian, date-carved 1570; it is an almost anatomical carving and is probably the finest and earliest dated wood example known. (Pinto Collection, Birmingham Museum and Art Gallery.)

Museum Photo

Museum Photo

Fig. 4 Elizabethan goblets of wood must once have been very common. Having little intrinsic value, such humble vessels were usually discarded when worn or split. Now great rarities, they are highly regarded. The simple treen examples illustrated here are decorated with the typical incised or scratch ornament of their period. The smaller of the two, which is $5\frac{5}{8}$ ins. high, has the characteristics of both a goblet and a loving cup. Vessels of a similar form were also made in pewter. (Pinto Collection, Birmingham Museum and Art Gallery.)

common were all sorts of treen stuffe in old time, that a man should hardlie find foure peeces of pewter (of which one was peraduenture a salt) in a good farmers house . . . .

The main materials of tableware used by the Elizabethans were gold, silver-gilt, silver, pewter, pottery and treen (meaning literally made of tree or wooden). Glass and china tableware were both great rarities.

In great medieval houses, the family and important guests had dined daily at the damask-clothed high table, placed on a dais running across one end of the great hall; lesser guests and retainers had their meals at long tables, placed at right angles to the 'high', in the body of the hall. Whilst in some ancient families this custom was still maintained in Elizabeth's reign, many medium-sized and large houses were now adding family eating parlours to their homes although they might still retain large halls for banquets, dancing and revelling. Seating at table still followed the custom of medieval times. The master, mistress and guests of great importance had chairs; the others used stools and forms. Floors were still rush-strewn, but some fine new eating parlours were carpeted.

From 1582, Elizabeth began to receive from the Continent New Year gifts of rare gold, silver and crystal-handled forks, but these were intended simply for serving candied fruits. Thomas Coryat, writing in 1611 after his return from Italy where he had acquired the habit of eating with a fork, tells how he was jeered at and dubbed *furcifer* when he introduced the custom into England.

Since it was normal practice to eat with the fingers throughout Elizabeth's reign, only a spoon was provided at each place, except at a high table or in the eating parlour of an important family where knives might be furnished. It was usual, however, for everyone to carry a knife in a leather or wooden sheath. It seems, moreover, that in polite society diners carved for themselves and, according to etiquette, ate meat with three fingers of one hand.

It was customary to wash the hands before, after and sometimes during meals. In a noble household, a silver ewer and basin and plenty of towels were provided on a table in proximity to the dining-table; a rose-water dish might be handed round during the meal. Under such conditions, fine damask napkins were also used. By contrast, in the body of a great hall or in a separate servants' hall, a community wooden or pottery bowl and a towel sufficed for hand-washing.

Fig. 5 This lovely Verzelini glass goblet, engraved John and Jone Dier, 1581, is one of the rare pieces of Elizabethan table glass still in existence. Until 1575, when Elizabeth granted Jacomo Verzelini a monopoly for making 'Venice Glasses', there was no fine glass manufacturer in England. Verzelini, a Venetian, came to England from the Netherlands bringing some of his *émigré* compatriots with him and established his glasshouse in Broad Street, London. His fragile but beautiful glasses were fashionable novelties for wealthy Elizabethans, but it is doubtful if his glass seriously challenged the popularity of silver and silver-gilt which, having a solid worth related to money values, could be bequeathed confidently to descendants. (Private Collection.)

Sotheby & Co.

Sotheby & Co.

Fig. 6 Pewter tableware, largely used in Tudor times by those who could not afford silver and disdained treenware, included dishes, platters, spoons, flagons, wine-measures, tankards, beakers, and salts and pepper-pots. Having less intrinsic value than silver, Elizabethan pewter survivals, now patinated to a dull grey, are even rarer. Originally highly polished like silver, the majority of English pewter was plain, like this rare, *c.*1600 half-pint (old English wine standard) wine-measure, but sometimes it was decorated with line engraved designs, resembling those on silver. This measure, of baluster form, 6 ins. high, would originally have been one of a set. (Private Collection.)

Fig. 7 Elizabethans loved pageantry, colour and ornament. This liking for decorativeness extended to food and those who could afford it enhanced gastronomic anticipation with the eye appeal of iced, moulded and pattern stamped confections and other bedecked dishes in great variety. Illustrated are both sides of a finely carved boxwood cake mould, 11½ ins. diameter, made in Nuremberg and date-carved 1567 above the double-headed, crowned eagle. The reverse side shows a stag among foliage. This is a fine art mould; at the lower end of the scale are found crudely carved moulds, some used for the gingerbread which was sold at fairs. (Pinto Collection, Birmingham Museum and Art Gallery.)

Museum Photo

Fig. 8 This Elizabethan service of treen is probably a unique survival, although others were doubtless made. It consists of a number of different purpose components of sycamore. The centre part, a large and a small double cup, may be used either way up. Surmounting the upper cup is a domed lid, which is hollow and contains a spice box. Above this lid-box is a hollow knop handle, made to hold a nutmeg. The cup is held by the rim of the double base, the upper part of which is hollowed out to hold a lemon; the lower part forms a box for ten cedar of Lebanon roundels. The whole complex, when assembled, forms an imposing standing cup, 18 ins. high decorated with typical Elizabethan bands of ornament in sunk relief. (Burrell Collection, Glasgow Art Gallery and Museum.)

Sotheby & Co.

Fig. 9 The standing salt still occupied the place of honour at the Elizabethan table, as in the Middle Ages. It divided master, mistress and honoured guests – the quality 'above the salt' – from less important visitors and retainers below. In the homes of nobility, the finest salts were often masterpieces by great goldsmiths and silversmiths. Some were formed as birds and beasts, with bodies of nautilus shell; others, such as the Gibbon Salt of the Goldsmiths' Company, dated 1576, incorporated rock crystal stems. A favourite outline was the bell salt. This handsome silver-gilt example, engraved with strapwork on a punched ground, 8 ins. high, bears the 1600 maker's mark TS in monogram. As on many salts, the top is detachable, and serves as a pepper castor. (Private Collection.)

Sotheby & Co.

Fig. 10 The Elizabethans had a splendid selection of drinking vessels, of which tankards, goblets and beakers were probably the most popular. Some goblets and standing cups had bodies of rare imported materials, such as coconuts, ostrich eggs, or nautilus shells, mounted in silver. This 7½ ins. high, silver-gilt covered beaker which dates from 1573, is early for an English vessel of this type in silver. It is also an early example of the *chinoiserie* influence. The mixing of motifs and of engraving with *repoussé* work contribute to the rich appearance of this vessel. (Private Collection.)

Sotheby & Co.

Fig. 11 Elizabethan tankards, with and without covers, were made of silver, pewter, Rhenish stoneware and other foreign and English glazed pottery; some had English mounts of silver or pewter added. Wooden tankards, mostly hollowed from birch or maple, and some communal ones of immense size provided with lines of pegs for regulating the individual drinker's draught, were used in Scandinavia. A few Tudor peg tankards of silver and pewter have survived. This 7½ ins. high, strap-work decorated, silver-gilt tankard of 1579 doubtless belonged to a person of high rank. (Private Collection.)

Elizabethans in Miniature

Daphne Foskett

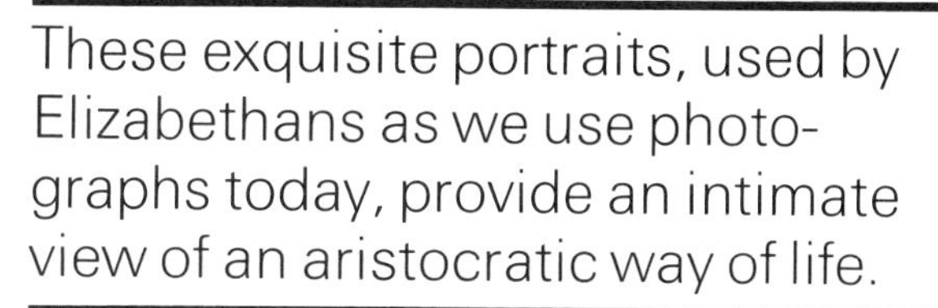
These exquisite portraits, used by Elizabethans as we use photographs today, provide an intimate view of an aristocratic way of life.

Elizabethan portrait miniatures symbolise all that is best in this flamboyant and romantic era. The colourful costumes and jewellery worn by Queen Elizabeth and her Court are shown off to perfection in these small portraits and have left us with a vivid impression of the people who, in their various ways, made England great.

While the word miniature is used nowadays to describe any small object, in painting it is accepted as meaning a portrait executed in any medium, i.e. water-colour, oils, enamel or plumbago, and drawn to such a small scale that it may easily be held in the hand. Originally these small portraits were called limnings, or painting in little, and this name for them survived well into the seventeenth century when the word miniature replaced it. The word is derived from *minium*, the Latin word for red lead, or vermilion, the pigment used to paint initial letters on the illuminated manuscripts of the Middle Ages. The verb *miniare* denotes the process, and the person who did this work was called a 'miniator'. From this we can see that the word miniature refers to the process and not the object.

A. C. Cooper

Fig. 1 ***Portrait of an Unknown Man**, by Laurence Hilliard, 1621. 2 x 1⅝ ins.
Set within a contemporary green enamel locket, from which is suspended a drop pearl, this is an exceptionally fine example of the seventeenth century use of miniatures. Set in jewelled lockets, they were often exchanged as mementoes or love tokens. The cover of the locket or box protected the paints from fading and kept out dirt and damp. As a result, portraits such as this one are in nearly perfect condition.
(Author's collection.)*

Treasured possessions of a flamboyant and romantic era

Many of the artists who worked at this time still remain anonymous and are known only from their works. Fortunately, others such as Nicholas Hilliard left important records and dated works, from which it has been possible to construct the story of their lives and some knowledge of their pupils. The history of portrait miniatures was in its infancy when Queen Elizabeth was born in 1533. Only seven years before, in 1526, Hans Holbein (1497/8–1543), who has always been considered the father of the art, set foot in England for the first time.

Nicholas Hilliard (*c.*1547–1619) was undoubtedly the most important artist of the period and it was due to his influence that the British school of miniature painting was firmly established. Hilliard was born in Exeter in about 1547, the son of Richard Hilliard, an Exeter goldsmith, and his wife Laurence, *née* Wall. Little is known about his early life, but in 1562, following the family tradition, he started his apprenticeship as a goldsmith and jeweller under his future father-in-law Robert Brandon.

Sometime prior to this, Hilliard is said to have studied under Holbein, and from his own words we know that Holbein's style had a great influence upon him. In his *Treatise Concerning the Arts of Limning*, written in 1600, which was published in the *Walpole Society*, Vol. I, from the manuscript in the Edinburgh University Library, Hilliard says, 'Holbeans maner of limning I haue euer imitated and howld it for the best . . .' That he had already begun to paint miniatures before starting his apprenticeship is known from the existence of three portraits of *c.*1560: two self-portraits, and one of Edward Seymour, Duke of Somerset (probably after Holbein).

Combining the illustrator's art with the dexterity of the goldsmith

Hilliard became a freeman of the Goldsmiths' Company in July 1569, and may well have entered the Queen's service about the same time. The most youthful representation of her by him was painted *c.*1569. It is in the collection of the Duke of Portland, and shows Her Majesty dressed in robes of state, crowned, and holding the orb and sceptre. A small diamond is set into the centre of the cross surmounting the orb. Hilliard's earliest known dated miniature of the Queen is in the National Portrait Gallery, London, and is dated 1572.

In July 1576, Hilliard married his first wife Alice, the beautiful daughter of Robert Brandon, at St. Vedast's, Foster Lane. By her he had eight children, of whom Laurence (1581/2–1647/8), followed his father's profession and was his pupil.

Nicholas Hilliard developed his own style in which he succeeded in combining the art of the illuminator with the dexterity of the goldsmith, and his works, many of which are rightly described as masterpieces, obtained for him a reputation as a great artist far beyond the shores of his native land.

His ability to portray the sense of poetry and symbolism which were embodied in the spirit of the Elizabethan age endeared him to the Queen and the Court. Not only was Hilliard the Queen's limner, but in 1584, he was commissioned to make her

Fig. 2 **Richard Sackville, 3rd Earl of Dorset**, *by Isaac Oliver, 1616. 9¼ x 6 ins. One of Oliver's finest full-length portraits, this shows him at the height of his powers although it was executed only a year before his death. The shading lends depth and character to the likeness. (Victoria and Albert Museum, London.)*

J. Freeman

second Great Seal. For this service he was rewarded by being given the lease of certain lands including a twenty-one-year lease of Poyne Manor, Middlesex.

In spite of his popularity and numerous patrons, Hilliard was frequently in financial difficulties. These were never resolved for long in spite of assistance given to him by friends, including Sir Robert Cecil, first Earl of Salisbury and a powerful political figure under Queen Elizabeth.

The absence of shading on Hilliard's miniatures is partly explained in his *Treatise* where he mentions how, on his first meeting with the Queen, she discussed the question of shading, and how she had noted that the Italians did not use any. She then chose to sit for her picture 'in the open ally of a goodly garden, where no tree was neere, nor anye shadowe at all'. This absence of shading is one of the chief differences between the works of Hilliard and those of his gifted pupil Isaac Oliver (d. 1617).

Hilliard and his followers painted on parchment stuck onto card, usually playing-cards, and used opaque pigments, the colours being blended with gum arabic to which sugar was sometimes added. The fact that in many cases Hilliard's carmines have faded, has resulted in the features now appearing rather mask-like.

True to his training as a jeweller, Hilliard gave great attention to detail

True to his training as a jeweller, Hilliard gave great attention to detail and mastered the intricacy of lace and embroidery to perfection. The majority of his works are inscribed in gold against a blue background, giving the sitter's age and the date on which the portrait was painted. He frequently added a symbol or riddling motto, or small flowers placed against the corsage or doublet. Two of his most notable symbolic miniatures are at the Victoria and Albert Museum: *A Youth Leaning against a Tree among Roses* (Fig. 10), painted *c.*1588 and inscribed: *Dat pœnas laudata fides* (My praised faith causes my sufferings); and one of an unknown man painted against a background of flames, supposedly suffering martyrdom at the stake and holding a locket towards his heart which presumably contains a portrait of his mistress.

Hilliard's best and most prolific period was between the years 1572–1600 and his undiminished ability to paint, even towards the latter part of his life, may be seen by examining the miniature of a gentleman thought to be Henry Carey, 2nd Earl of Monmouth (1596–1661), (Fig. 4) painted when Hilliard was seventy years old. This miniature, which is in the collection of the Duke of Portland, is inscribed: *Encores Vn ★ Luit pour moy* (Still one star shines for me) and on a separate card on which the miniature is mounted: *Quadragessimo Ano Dni 1616 Vera Effigigies Ætatis Suæ 20* (Painted on Quadragesima Sunday in the Year of our Lord 1616, a true portrait at the age of 20).

Although Hilliard undoubtedly had a number of pupils who may well have been responsible for many of the replicas which were demanded by his patrons, and which were bestowed so liberally on visiting Royalty and favourites at Court, few of their names are known, and their works remain unidentified.

Fig. 3 *A Lady Called Mrs.* ***Holland,*** *by Nicholas Hilliard, 1593.* $\frac{15}{16}$ *x* $1\frac{15}{16}$ *ins. Like all Hilliard's miniatures, this one is painted on parchment stuck to a piece of card and cut to the appropriate shape. Playing-cards were normally used since they were made of the smoothest cardboard.*
(Victoria and Albert Museum.)

Fig. 4 ***A Gentleman thought to be Henry Carey, 2nd Earl of Monmouth,*** *by Nicholas Hilliard, 1616.* $2\frac{1}{2}$ *x 2 ins.*
A translation of the inscriptions reads, 'Still one star shines for me,' and 'Painted on Quadragesima Sunday in the year of Our Lord 1616, a true portrait at the age of 20.'
(Collection of the Duke of Portland.)

Fig. 5 ***Mrs. Hilliard*** *by Nicholas Hilliard, 1578. Diameter* $2\frac{5}{16}$ *ins. Alice Hilliard was the beautiful daughter of Robert Brandon, Chamberlain of the City of London. The inscription states that she was Nicholas Hilliard's first wife, but no records of her successor have been found.*
(Victoria and Albert Museum.)

Fig. 6 ***Self-Portrait aged 30,*** *by Nicholas Hilliard, 1577. Diameter* $1\frac{15}{16}$ *ins.*
From this and the portrait of his wife (Fig. 5), it is evident that Nicholas and Alice Hilliard were a handsome and well-to-do couple.
(Victoria and Albert Museum.)

Fig. 7 ***Portrait of an Unknown Gentleman,*** *by Nicholas Hilliard, 1593.* $2\frac{3}{4}$ *x* $2\frac{1}{8}$ *ins.*
The son of a goldsmith and a member himself of the Goldsmiths' Company, Hilliard was well qualified to paint the intricate details on armour.
(Collection of the Earl Beauchamp.)

Fig. 8 ***Portrait of an Unknown Gentleman,*** *by Laurence Hilliard (1581/2–1647/8), 1636.* $1\frac{3}{4}$ *x* $1\frac{1}{2}$ *ins.*
Although Laurence Hilliard never achieved the superb quality of his father's work, he practised a similar technique, as is apparent here in the blue background and lack of shading in the face.
(Collection of the Earl Beauchamp.)

9

10

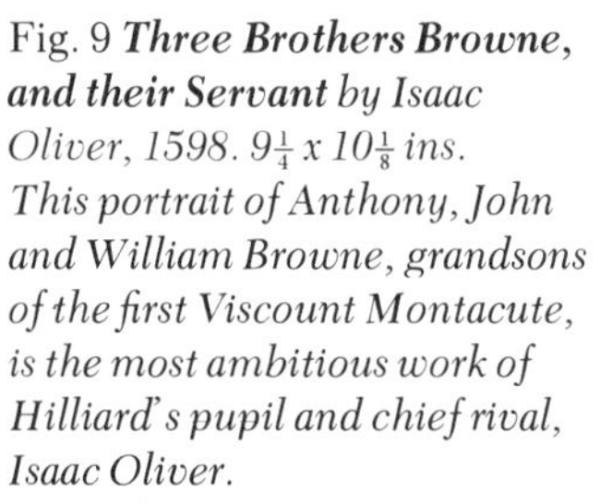

Fig. 9 ***Three Brothers Browne, and their Servant*** *by Isaac Oliver, 1598.* $9\frac{1}{4}$ *x* $10\frac{1}{8}$ *ins.*
This portrait of Anthony, John and William Browne, grandsons of the first Viscount Montacute, is the most ambitious work of Hilliard's pupil and chief rival, Isaac Oliver.
(Burghley House Collection.)

Fig. 10 ***A Youth Leaning against a Tree among Roses*** *by Nicholas Hilliard, c.1588.*
$5\frac{5}{16}$ *x* $2\frac{15}{16}$ *ins.*
The inscription above this forlorn young man's head reads: My praised faith causes my sufferings. *One of Hilliard's best known portraits, it expresses the religious romanticism of the Elizabethan age.*
(Victoria and Albert Museum.)

The majority of Elizabethan miniatures are painted against a plain blue background, but as time went on the occasional curtain or landscape background became popular. The earliest shape was circular, but Hilliard introduced an oval format which has remained popular ever since, with variations of rectangular or even heart-shapes.

Whereas many large portraits show us the sitter dressed to suit the artist, miniatures generally provide us with a much more accurate survey of fashion, particularly with regard to the bodice, doublet, coiffure and jewellery, and were in themselves of great importance at a period when personal adornment was in such demand. The fact that many of the artists were goldsmiths forged an even closer link between the two arts.

'Small pictures which are to be viewed in hand'

These 'small pictures which are to be viewed in hand', to use Hilliard's words, are among the gems of British portraiture. Fortunately not only was Hilliard himself a prolific artist, active for over fifty years, but his most notable pupil, Isaac Oliver, carried on the tradition and was well patronised by the Court and nobility of the day.

Oliver's date of birth remains unknown; he was the son of a Huguenot goldsmith who, in 1568, brought him with his mother to England to escape religious persecution. The date of his apprenticeship to Hilliard is uncertain, and although in his early works Oliver's style followed that of his master, he later developed a greater sense of character using dark grey and black shading, a method disliked by Hilliard. The high esteem in which both artists were held is noted by Henry Peacham, in *The Gentlemans Exercise,* published in 1607, when he says, 'nor must I be ingratefully undmindfull of mine owne Countrieman, who have beene, and are able to equall the best, if occasion served, as old Mr. Hilliard, Mr. Isaac Oliver inferiour to none in Christendome for the countenance in small'.

Oliver executed a number of large history and subject miniatures, only a few of which have survived. Of his large full-length portraits, that of Richard Sackville, 3rd Earl of Dorset, signed: *Isaac Olliuierus fecit, 1616,* in the Victoria and Albert Museum, is a fine example of his work (Fig. 2). His most ambitious miniature is that of the 'Three Brothers Browne, and their Servant' (Fig. 9) which is in the Burghley House Collection. It represents Anthony, John and William Browne, grandsons of the first Viscount Montacute, and is inscribed, signed and dated 1598.

By about this time, Oliver had become a serious rival to Hilliard and was still at the height of his power when he died in 1617. His son Peter Oliver (1594?–1647), followed his father's profession, but was only a child when Queen Elizabeth died, and his work falls into the next period.

Of Hilliard's other pupils, his son Laurence became apprenticed to his father in *c.*1597. He received a good education, and besides being trained as a goldsmith and limner, could speak Spanish. Few signed miniatures by him exist, and although he worked in the manner of his father, he does not as far as we know seem to have attempted anything very ambitious and the quality so apparent in the older man's work is often lacking. An example of Laurence Hilliard's work accessible to the public is at the Victoria and Albert Museum and is of an unknown lady wearing a wide brimmed hat, signed HL. Two other signed miniatures by him are in the collection of the Earl Beauchamp: both are of unknown men, and are inscribed, dated and signed: LH. An unsigned portrait of an unknown man, inscribed and dated: *Ano Dni, 1621 Ætatis*

Fig. 11 ***Portrait of an Unknown Lady in a Masque Costume*** *by Isaac Oliver, c.1610. $2\frac{1}{2}$ x 2 ins. This portrait illustrates the reason for the rivalry between Hilliard and Oliver; the lady's charms and the details of her sumptuous costume are masterfully displayed. (Victoria and Albert Museum.)*

Fig. 12 ***Mrs. Norgate*** *by Edward Norgate, 1617. $2\frac{1}{8}$ x $1\frac{3}{4}$ ins. Norgate was above all an illuminator, but he did paint a few miniatures in the style of Hilliard and Oliver. The mask-like quality of this portrait of Judith,* née *Lanyer, whom he married in 1613, is due to the fading of the carmine, or red paint, used in miniatures. (Victoria and Albert Museum.)*

11 J. Freeman
12 J. Freeman

Fig. 13 ***Queen Elizabeth I, aged 38,*** *by Nicholas Hilliard, 1572. 2 x $1\frac{7}{8}$ ins. This portrait of the Queen was painted shortly after Hilliard entered her service as Court Limner. Although he was only twenty-five at the time, his style was fully developed and his attention to detail was remarkable. (National Portrait Gallery, London.)*

National Portrait Gallery

Suæ, 74. (Fig. 1), and set within a contemporary green enamel locket from which is suspended a drop pearl, is in the collection of the author.

Of the other artists who executed Elizabethan miniatures we know little. Rowland Lockey (active *c.*1581–*c.*1616) was apprenticed to Hilliard in 1581 and painted portraits in oil as well as miniatures. Few works can at present be ascribed to him, and it is probable that some have been wrongly attributed to Hilliard.

The most important miniature attributed to Lockey is the group of Sir Thomas More and his family, painted *c.*1600, and based on a painting by Holbein. This miniature was among the Sotheby Heirlooms, which were sold at Sotheby's in 1955.

Miniatures were not infrequently executed by heraldic draughtsmen, and of these Edward Norgate (*c.*1581–1650) is worthy of attention. He was the son of Dr. Robert Norgate, Master of Corpus Christi College, Cambridge. Norgate is best known as an illuminator, and for his treatise, *Miniatura or the Art of Limning*, published in 1919 from the manuscript in the Bodleian Library, Oxford, and edited by Martin Hardie. Only a few authentic works by him exist; the first to be identified was of his wife Judith, whom he married in 1613. This miniature (Fig. 12) is in the Victoria and Albert Museum and is inscribed and dated on the reverse; the translation reads, 'She has not died: she has departed. Rarest ornament of Modesty, Affection and Beauty. To his most sweet wife, Ed: Norgate'. A replica of this miniature exists, and two others attributed to Norgate, thought to represent John Harrison, jun. and his wife Mary. These are in the collection of Miss Lawson Tancred, a descendant. Harrison was interested in heraldry and may have been related to, or friendly with, Norgate. The miniatures are in superb condition and brilliantly painted, placing the artist high among those who painted 'in little'.

14

Museum Photo

Fig. 14 ***Man Surrounded by Flames*** *by Nicholas Hilliard c.1590. 2¾ x 2⅛ ins. This unidentified gentleman is believed to be suffering martyrdom at the stake. The locket he holds toward his heart presumably contains a portrait of his mistress. Unlike most of Hilliard's works, this symbolic miniature is not painted against a background of solid colour. (Victoria and Albert Museum.)*

He was taken to the Queen's bed-chamber, where she 'opened a little Cabinet wherein were divers little pictures'

There are many instances when miniatures played their part in all the intrigue and flattery which surrounded Queen Elizabeth and her Court; indeed she was probably one of the first persons to own a collection of them, as is testified by Sir James Melville, emissary of Mary Queen of Scots. Writing in his *Memoirs* he described how he was taken to the Queen's bed-chamber, where she 'opened a little Cabinet, wherein were divers little pictures wrapped within Paper, and their Names Written with her own hand upon the papers'.

From the outset, miniatures were always intended to be personal mementoes of the sitters, and were presented as such in gold or silver lockets and frames, many of which were studded with precious stones. Some of the lockets were enamelled, and had a pearl suspended from the base of the oval, and a lid, which covered the portrait to prevent it from fading. Others were set into a wooden or turned ivory box with a lid, and where the miniatures have been kept in this way, they have retained their colours remarkably well.

FURTHER READING

The Elizabethan Image by Roy Strong, London, 1970.

British Portrait Miniatures by Daphne Foskett, London, 1963.

Nicholas Hilliard by Erna Auerbach, London, 1961.

English Portrait Miniatures by Graham Reynolds, London, 1952.

British Portrait Miniatures by Basil S. Long, London, 1929.

MUSEUMS AND COLLECTIONS

Portrait Miniatures of the Elizabethan period may be seen at the following:

Cambridge:	Fitzwilliam Museum
Greenwich:	National Maritime Museum
London:	Victoria and Albert Museum
Richmond:	Ham House

PRACTICAL HINTS

For the collector who can afford to purchase miniatures of this period, or who is knowledgeable and lucky enough to find a bargain, here are a few hints on what to look for and what to avoid:

1. As with all forms of collecting, one must be wary of cleverly painted fakes. It often takes a good deal of experience to detect them, but one tip is to examine any prospective purchase carefully, if possible under a lens. Repainting can usually be detected since the paint is raised above the level of the original pigment.

2. It is important to remember that all Elizabethan miniatures are painted on vellum stuck onto card; ivory was not used until *c.* 1690.

3. Always avoid paying a large sum of money for a miniature unless you are sure of its authenticity or are buying it from a reputable dealer. False signatures and dates are frequently met with, although often the gold is rather too 'hot', or the inscription amateurish.

4. Remember that with the passage of time, many miniatures have deteriorated from exposure to light and damp. But examples may still be of interest even if they are not perfect, whereas with the later periods the collector can afford to be more selective.

5. It is important to be certain that the sitter's costume is correct, for there are many miniatures for sale which are certainly not Elizabethan.

6. It is advisable to study the manner in which the artists painted, and the type of paint they used in order not to be taken in by a cleverly painted print or photograph framed up to deceive.

1

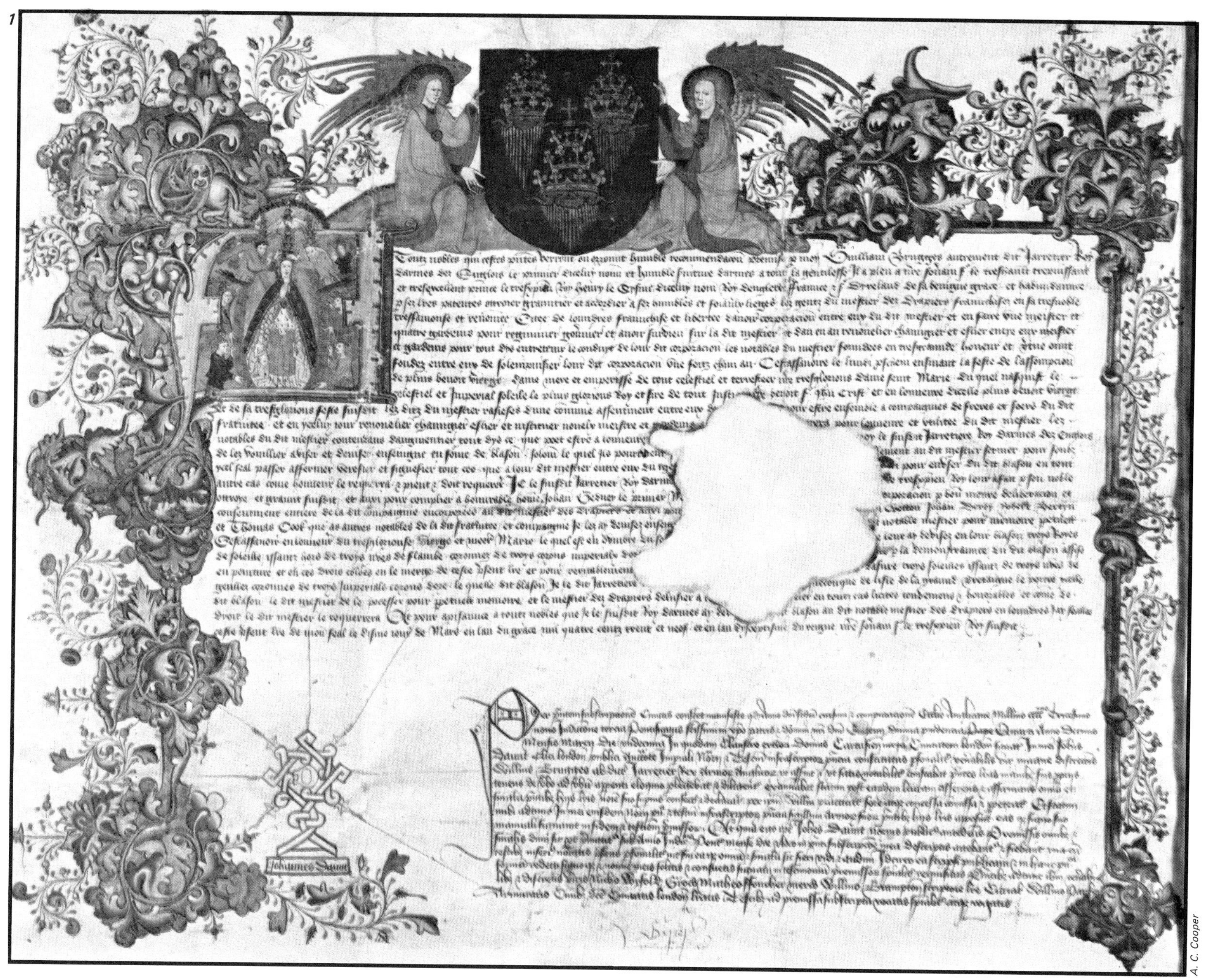

A. C. Cooper

Craftsmen and their guilds

G. W. Whiteman

The craft-guilds, renowned for their halls and splendid art treasures, have long played an important role in English craftsmanship and the pageantry of London

Fig. 1 ***Letters Patent*** *granting arms to the Worshipful Company of Drapers, 10 March, 1438–39. The drapers had been empowered to govern themselves in a charter of 1364, which also gave them control of the cloth trade in London; but it was not until this Patent was granted that they were incorporated as a guild. (The Worshipful Company of Drapers, London.)*

English social life still bears the imprint of the Middle Ages, as we can see in our Common Law and parliamentary systems. There is no more remarkable survival from that era than the Livery Companies of the City of London. There are eighty-four in all, each with its own coat of arms and each cherishing the tradition of some craft or trade even if it has lost any practical connection with it. Worthy city gentlemen even now administer charities, run educational endowments, entertain distinguished guests from overseas and belong to institutions with such titles as the Worshipful Company of Haberdashers, Girdlers, or Painter Stainers, and, almost unbelievably, the Worshipful Company of Armourers and Brasiers.

There are twelve Chief Companies, all incorporated between the years 1327 and 1558, their names suggesting something of the nature and history of the trade guild. Five of them – the Mercers, Drapers, Merchant Taylors, Haberdashers and Clothworkers – relate to the wool and cloth trade; evidence of the major importance of cloth to the economy of England in the Middle Ages. The Skinners represent the traditional rival to cloth, furs. The Fishmongers, Grocers, Salters and Vintners are the food and drink trades guilds. Lastly, though not in order of precedence, come the Goldsmiths and Ironmongers representing the craftsmen and merchants in metal, precious and non-precious. A great many now defunct crafts figure in the names of the Minor City Companies.

Guilds were a feature of medieval social life not only in London but throughout this country and the Continent. The original guild (or gild) was a kind of

2

A. C. Cooper

3

Fig. 3 ***Pair of salts,*** *one with unknown maker, London, 1518, and one with maker's mark a short sword, London, 1522. Silver, parcel-gilt, height 5½ ins. This unusual pair of hour-glass shaped salts may well have been a gift to the Ironmongers' Company, which was incorporated in 1463.*
(The Worshipful Company of Ironmongers, London.)

The Antique Collector

4

The Antique Collector

Fig. 2 ***The Lambard Cup,*** *maker's mark a bird within a shaped shield, probably for John Bird, London, 1578. Silver-gilt, height 12½ ins.*
This superb cup was presented to the Drapers on 4 August, 1578, by Mr. William Lambard. It bears the arms of England, of the Company, and of Sir William Cordell, Master of the Rolls. The inscription reads: A Proctour for the Poore am I & remember theim before thow Dye. 1578.
(The Worshipful Company of Drapers.)

Fig. 4 ***The Arlington Tazza,*** *maker's mark a cup in a shaped shield, London, 1532. Silver, parcel-gilt, height 5 ins, diameter of bowl 9 ins, weight 27 ozs.*
This dish, a secular piece, was probably used to hold sweetmeats and other kinds of food. It was purchased by Goldsmiths' Hall in 1953. The inscription reads: Benedictus Deus in donis suis et sanctis in omnibus.
(The Worshipful Company of Goldsmiths, London.)

industrial union or insurance club among men of the same calling; the *geld* was payment into a common fund as a guarantee. The guild, which had a markedly religious character, with patron saints and religious ceremonies, looked after its members, helped them in distress long before the days of Poor Law, even buried them and cared for their widows. It also trained members by an apprentice system which was legalised in 1562, laid down strict standards of work and sought to gain royal charters, which would give them a monopoly of a particular craft or trade, and oblige anyone in that calling to belong. There was careful supervision of standards and honesty in each craft, the hall-marking of English silver being an outstanding example which still survives.

Gradually, especially through the growth of capitalism in the cloth trade, the English town guilds tended to become merchant-guilds rather than craft-guilds; the cloth merchants, for instance, separated from the tailors and the leather-merchants from the butchers. This left the merchant-guilds and craft-guilds in bitter rivalry for control of trade, a struggle that was eventually won by the craft-guilds through the granting of royal charters and marked by the wearing of distinctive liveries.

Thus in the fourteenth and fifteenth centuries in England there was a measure of middle-class civic rule through the craft-guilds. The wealthy merchants generally accepted their authority and were allowed to join as members, thereby strengthening the craft-guilds still further. Even Edward III and Henry VI took the fashionable step by joining the Armourers' Guild.

By the sixteenth century the wealth and power of the guilds had become a corrupting influence. They often followed narrow protectionist policies, abusing their monopolies and, because of their religious affiliations, they were a target, along with the monasteries, for anti-clericalism. It was inevitable that they should attract the rapacity of Henry VIII and his Court. By 1539 the monasteries had been suppressed and Henry, having spent the vast sums thus expropriated, turned his attention to the guilds. Throughout the provinces their revenues and charities were plundered by a confiscatory act of 1545, and by the end of Edward VI's reign almost all had been liquidated.

Only in London did the Livery Companies survive in strength, their wealth and power being too great even for the forceful Tudor monarchs. Instead the Crown chose to patronise them and London pageants of Elizabethan days were made colourful and glittering by the companies' liveries. Elizabeth I loved to have near her person the companies' 'hanssome' men and 'whifflers' (pipers), especially the Merchant Taylors in their scarlet robes, and river pageants with the decorated barges of the city companies were equally spectacular.

But the companies had their troubles. Exploited

5

R. B. Fleming

Fig. 5 **Map of London** *showing the armorial bearings of the Guilds, by John Norden (d.1593). Scale 4 ins. to 1 mile. Life-size. (Guildhall, London.)*

Fig. 6 **Pewter flagon**, *English, sixteenth century. (The Worshipful Company of Pewterers, London.)*

6

R. F. Michaelis

again and again by Henry VIII and his successors as milch-cows to finance wars and lavish royal expenditures, they often survived only by pawning or melting down their plate. They also had to find men for war service; at the time of the Armada the city companies impressed 10,000 men and were required as well to raise £60,000. But the companies always had the good sense to try to get some mortgage or security, however valueless a piece of land might have seemed at the time. It was the huge increase in the value of such properties over the centuries which enabled the companies to recoup their fortunes in the eighteenth and nineteenth centuries, even after such an overwhelming blow as the Great Fire of London.

They were 'but merchant goldsmiths and had but little knowledge in the science'

If the city companies representing crafts had insisted on reserving their membership to skilled artisans they could not have survived for so many centuries; such companies as the Bowyers (bow-makers), Loriners (bit-makers, spurriers), Horners, and Armourers would have died a natural death. But the desire for craft exclusiveness existed strongly and, in 1529, three working members of the Goldsmiths' Company pleaded to have its membership limited to approved silversmiths. They complained that persons had been wrongly admitted to the Company who were 'but merchant goldsmiths, and had but little knowledge in the science'. One sympathises with any craftsman who takes a proper pride in his work, but the days of the tight craft-guild were already over. The dispute got as far as the Star Chamber, but after a four-year struggle the artisans lost and also lost their own membership of the Goldsmiths' Company.

The wealthy merchants in the guilds were, in fact, the men who supplied the wherewithal for the companies' survival in difficult days, who often provided London with its lord mayors, and who gave the plate and other treasures to the companies which are now among their chief possessions. Certain working goldsmiths themselves rose to be lord mayors and magnates, two of the best known being Sir Martin Bowes (p.110, Fig. 12) and Sir Hugh Myddelton; they gave their names to Tudor cups which are outstanding even among the unique collection of plate of the Goldsmiths' Company.

Today not many members of the livery companies of London have a working knowledge of the trade or craft whose badge they honour, but there are certain companies which still play an important part in their own spheres. The craft of the silversmith is actively promoted by the Goldsmiths; the Saddlers are patrons of the modern saddlery trade at Walsall; the Apothecaries hold professional examinations in pharmacy; the Vintners advise and promote the interests of the wine trade; the

7

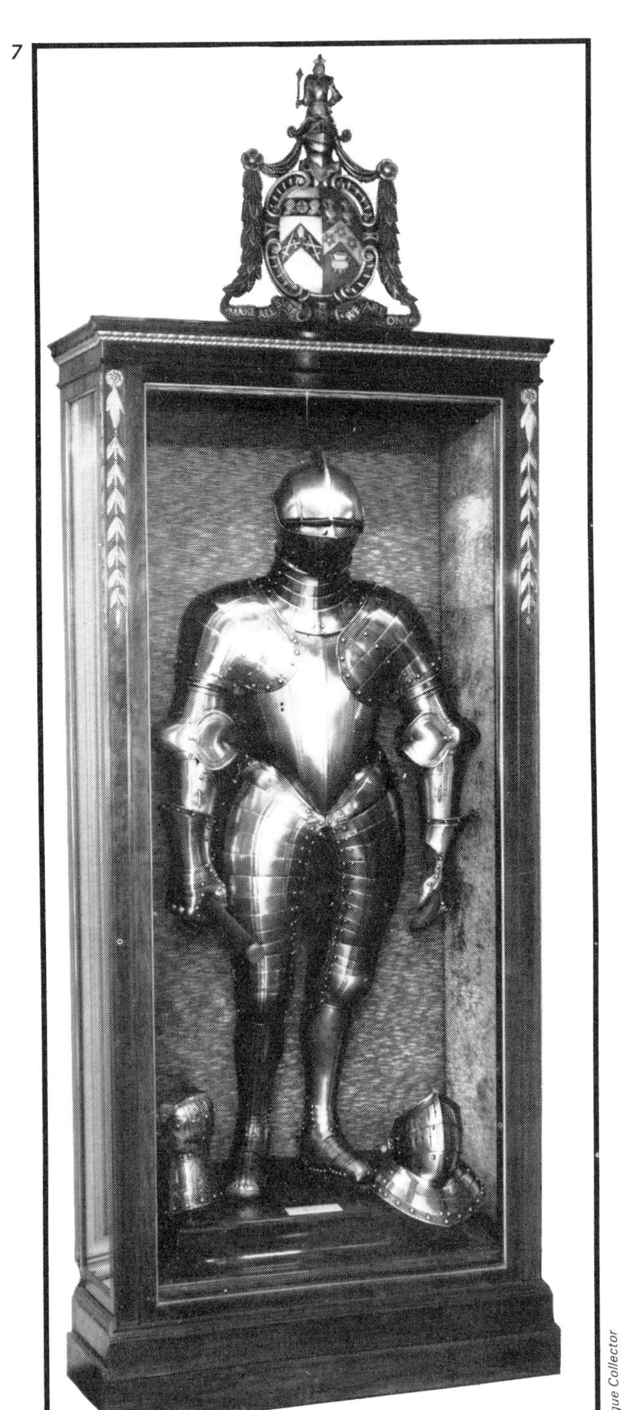

The Antique Collector

Fig. 7 ***The Third Suit of Armour of Sir Henry Lee*** *(1530–1610) by Jacobe Halder of Greenwich, Master of the Greenwich armour factory. Sir Henry was Champion to Elizabeth I until 1590, and Master of the Armories from 1580 to 1610. The suit is engraved with the initials A.V. for Anne Vavasour, his mistress, and weighs sixty-seven pounds. (The Worshipful Company of Armourers and Brasiers, London.)*

Fig. 8 ***Owl Pot,*** *unmarked. Brown stoneware mounted in silver-gilt around the neck and foot, height 7¾ ins. The pot was presented to the Company in 1537, at which time it was valued at 28s 6d. (The Worshipful Company of Armourers and Brasiers.)*

8

The Antique Collector

Clothworkers have actively sponsored textile research. But broadly speaking the original functions of the companies have changed from crafts and trades to those of administering charities, sponsoring schools and colleges and providing hospitality. For those interested in antiques, the companies not only constitute a unique survival themselves from the past but they own art treasures, especially gold and silver plate, of great historic interest and of fabulous present-day value.

From early times the city companies built halls in London as meeting-places for business and feasts. Many beautiful medieval halls were lost in the Great Fire of 1666 and though rebuilt they have often been damaged since by fire and by enemy action in World War II. The Mercers, the first company in order of civic precedence, had their hall burnt down in a fire raid in May 1941. Others whose halls were destroyed or damaged at that time include the Merchant Taylors, the Clothworkers, the Fishmongers and the Skinners. Happily nearly all the movable treasures of the companies were saved. The Grocers' Hall survived both world wars but suffered a disastrous fire in 1965 which also destroyed a number of the Company's historic treasures.

The charters and records of the companies are carefully preserved as are a great number of relatively little-known art treasures. Some of these have come down from earlier times by direct gift, often by Masters; but still more have been acquired in recent times by gifts, bequests or purchases. This is especially true of the gold and silver plate for which the Livery Companies are famous and which is brought out for display at their banquets. Yet even until the early nineteenth century, plate of an earlier age was not admired for its historic interest but looked upon as financial security. When an emergency occurred, it was often melted down. Early designs were regarded as unfashionable, and there were few compunctions even in the Goldsmiths' Company about melting down early plate either to raise funds, as in the Civil War, or merely to follow a more fashionable style.

All the companies, however, preserve certain specially presented pieces; for example, the cup and ewer given by Samuel Pepys to the Clothworkers and the beautifully designed Richmond Cup presented to the Armourers by John Richmond, Master of that Company in 1547–48. The Armourers and Brasiers also possess a unique series of seventy-two seal-top spoons dating from between 1552 and 1627. The collection owes its origin to the requirement that each newly admitted court assistant at that period should present a spoon to the Company.

The collection of early English plate of the Goldsmiths' Company is one of the most important anywhere in the country. A number of pieces have been gifts, like the two Tudor cups already referred to, but the main body of the collection has been built up in more recent times by a policy of careful purchase. Besides keeping meticulous records of its own plate, the Goldsmiths have comprehensive records of the plate of the other city companies.

The chief treasure at the Armourers' Hall, in Coleman Street, is the third suit of armour of Sir Henry Lee, Elizabeth I's champion, which it has been estimated could have been bought in 1718 for about six shillings, so little was early armour regarded at that time. The family associations which often occur in the City companies are well illustrated by the fact that thirteen members of the Pontifex family have been Masters of the Armourers' and Brasiers' Company.

From time to time the London livery companies have been criticised as anachronisms and for their privileges and ownership of property. A royal commission of 1880 cleared them of a number of charges and stimulated them to operate their affairs and charities with greater efficiency. Nearly a century afterwards we see them as a distinctively British institution, with all the colour and historic interest of the past but with new and effective roles in our own time. They fit into our immense range of voluntary societies, provide a flexibility in civic affairs, and foster many worthy causes that escape the net of the welfare state. For the student of antiques they are reminders of how the standards of craftsmanship of the past which we admire so much to-day were built up and strictly maintained.

STUART NEEDLEWORK

Therle Hughes

1

Fig. 1 **Embroidered Box,** c.1670. *Worked in silk threads, height 12½ ins., width 10¼ ins., depth 7 ins. The drawers are filled with tiny contemporary toy animals, such as peacocks made of twisted wire, beads and chenille thread. (Royal Scottish Museum, Edinburgh.)*

Anthony Howarth for 'Treasures of Britain', Drive Publications Ltd.

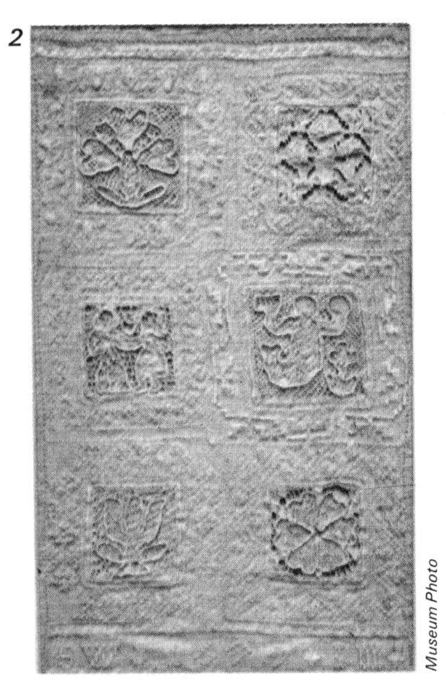

Museum Photo

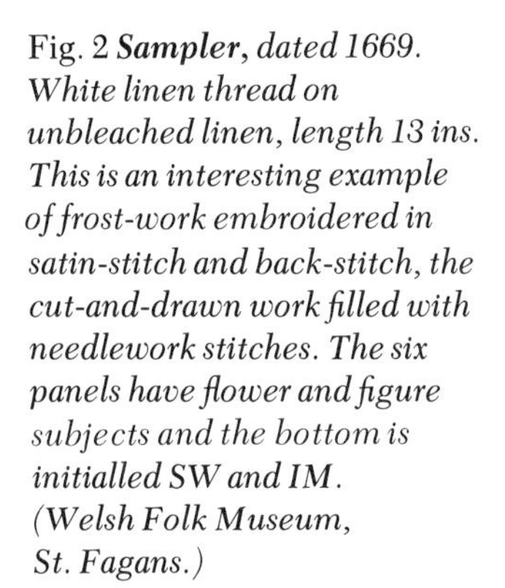

Museum Photo

Fig. 2 **Sampler,** *dated 1669. White linen thread on unbleached linen, length 13 ins. This is an interesting example of frost-work embroidered in satin-stitch and back-stitch, the cut-and-drawn work filled with needlework stitches. The six panels have flower and figure subjects and the bottom is initialled SW and IM. (Welsh Folk Museum, St. Fagans.)*

Fig. 3 **Open Wire Basket,** *c.1670. Satin and threaded coloured beads. Such baskets are thought to have been 'gift wrappings' for wedding and christening presents at a period when the presentation of gifts was of great importance. The beads were threaded on stiff wires, and shaped into elaborate three-dimensional forms. (Lady Lever Art Gallery, Port Sunlight, Cheshire.)*

Gold and silver threads, seed-pearls, wire coils, spangles and beads: all these mingled with the linens, silks and wool of Stuart embroidery to make enduring objects of beauty.

The home embroidery of Stuart days should be seen in the light of its essential usefulness, transformed into beauty by sheer love of the work. Basically, the stitchery extended the serviceability of fabrics that itinerant weavers made from the yarn created by wearisome, endless home spinning. At the same time it was very largely the practical home-maker's substitute for more costly professional work in a range of crafts from tapestry-weaving to tooled leather book-binding, from jewellery to lace.

It is instructive to establish the kind of large and reasonably well-to-do household, brought vividly to life in many Stuart wills, inventories and household accounts, that had time for this type of needlework. These documents record day-to-day activity within the narrow bounds of estate and local township; the rich fabrics purchased and occasional labour hired, of sewing silks and Venice gold stocked by the merchant among his ink-horns and raisins-of-the-sun, of ribbons and laces bought from the hawker at the door.

For this sort of needlework, the mistress of the house had to be a formidable figure, enterprising and versatile. Doubtless she was able to call upon gentlewomen of the household to carry out her schemes and was often aided by the local schoolmaster, perhaps, to draw out a pattern, or by ill-paid poor quilters. More often than not there would be children in plenty, whose sketchy formal education was accompanied from a very early age by a happy intermingling of household crafts. Seasonal work would busy them all in kitchens and dairies, in still-room or herb garden, but there would be long hours, too, among the innumerable hangings and coverlets, cushions and table carpets. These provided warmth, colour and comfort in rambling, draughty rooms, however square and simple the joiner-made furniture, and formed a worthy setting for sumptuous embroidered dress.

The difference in Stuart needlework of 1603 and 1714 is profound, traceable in household furnishings, dress and a range of minor articles from samplers to book-bindings. Sometimes it is easy to see the distinctive work of the professional embroiderer, whether in ceremonial furnishings for the great guilds or in such small but important details as the Lord Chancellor's bag of the Great Seal. But in general, the seventeenth century expected the home embroiderer to reach and even exceed professional standards.

Books specifically for the needlewoman included the famous *Schole-house for the needle* by R. Schorleyker, 1624, containing 'sundry sorts of spots, as Flowers, Birds and Fishes, etc., and will fitly serve to be wrought, some with Gould, some with Silke, and some with Crewell . . .' *The Needle's Excellency* by J. Boler (tenth edition, 1634) contains patterns from various sources but is interesting mainly for a prefatory poem by John Taylor which lists a number of stitches such as 'Tent-worke, Raisd-worke, Laid-worke, Frost-worke, Net-worke, Most curious Purles, or rare Italian Cutworke, Fine Ferne-stitch, Finny-stitch, New-stitch and Chain-stitch'. The work that survives can seldom be identified with printed design, whether in pattern books or among such other obvious sources as works on botany, illuminated documents or printed lining and wallpapers.

The change during the Stuart period is most

4

Fig. 4 ***Detail of a Bedspread*** *signed and dated* Mary Thurston 1694. *Worked in silks. This delightfully delicate pattern is an early example of* chinoiserie *work. An almost identical cover made by Mary Thurston's sister, Sarah, has a different fairytale scene for its centrepiece. (Fitzwilliam Museum, Cambridge.)*

clearly seen, perhaps, in household embroideries. They reflect the advance to more orderly house design for the rich and medium-rich, with loftier rooms planned for specific purposes. Such rooms gave a new height and grandeur to the curtained bed and prompted a new demand for occasional furniture met by lighter, more elegant cabinet-maker's work. Their furnishings demonstrated the ever-widening interests of the seventeenth century as trade reached out beyond the Levant to direct exchanges with India and China; these Europeanized Eastern forms are described by the term *chinoiserie* (Fig. 4). In pattern, style and materials the embroiderer acknowledged the changes just as she accepted the loss of flamboyant Tudor carving in favour of the flatter, more monotonous, early Stuart furniture ornament, which was replaced in due course by late Stuart smooth-surfaced marquetry and exotic, colourful japanning.

The bed served as a tent of warmth and privacy

In almost every Stuart room the bed was the dominant feature, welcome because it offered the only real comfort in the house. At night it served as a tent of warmth and privacy; throughout the day as a declaration of wealth and status. Here, among crest-embroidered cushions, the businessman humbled his petitioner; the new mother received congratulations among her embroidered coverlets; and bereavement found expression in the family's black-draped 'mourning bed'. The late Stuarts discovered the resilient caned day-bed and so began the transition to overstuffed day furniture and hence the segregation of sleeping-chamber from living-quarters.

The Stuart standing bed was an ornate wooden structure hung with valances and curtains and bases (low valances below the bed-stock). A fabric roof was still an alternative to the wooden tester. In very rich houses the headboard might become the basis for high relief embroidery and the whole wooden frame might be covered with costly textiles. James I paid £1,515 for a bed embroidered in gold and silver and two elbow chairs and six stools to match, a change of fashion recorded in inventories of the day.

For travelling there were easily dismantled tent-beds. The Earl of Northampton possessed one in 1614 of purple velvet with its tester, five curtains and single valance 'imbrodred highe with flowers piramides wise', valued at £220. The field-bed itself was worth a mere £4. Valances, which were flat and little handled, might carry pictorial embroidery; the stiff bases had minor flower slips or formal sprig patterns and the four or five lined curtains and accompanying corner pieces were decorated with a more flowing ornament.

Exotic birds are open-mouthed, but screeching, not singing

'Forest work', 'verdure' or 'small leaves', in a heavy Italianate manner, were popular for a long time for hangings on walls and beds. But the growing delight in Indian painted cottons during the seventeenth century, and the ecstatic welcome for Chinese embroideries, prompted the development of a style now called Jacobean. Here a favourite pattern was the so-called Tree-of-life, consisting of slanting tree forms rising from hummocky ground. Each hummock is decorated with a separate motif and the springy curving branches above, bearing leaves, flowers and creatures, are all as restless and fantastic as patterns in lace. The exotic birds are open-beaked, but surely screeching rather than singing.

The basis of such work was a narrow linen or linen-and-cotton twill (pure cotton was used when a strong cotton warp was evolved). The embroidery materials were the cheap weavers' clippings of long-staple worsted known as crewels, worked in a wealth of outline and filling stitches to provide the texture beloved of the needlewoman. To her, restricted to inexpensive materials, they represented escape from the time-consuming monotony of tent- and cross-stitch, that closely covered the fabric, into the freedom of surface decoration. Expense was an important factor, for sewing silk might be seven times the price of crewels, and sewing gold more costly still. A pattern of leaves in dusky greens (now much faded to blue) must have been a particularly welcome contrast to late Stuart glitter, when even the embroiderer felt the impact of Europe's welcome for the bright reds of cochineal resulting from the contact between Spain and distant Mexico.

Here, as elsewhere in Stuart embroidery, the eventual change was to more silken finery. Celia Fiennes in her travels around Britain at the century's end noted, for example, that the Duke of Norfolk had a half-tester bed with crewel embroidery on dimity, and another with 'fine Indian quilting and embroidered with embroidery silk'. By then the worsted crewels tended to be thinner, and silk embroidery was in the delicate spindly manner of much imported Oriental work: in chain-stitch, satin-stitch and French or Peking knots, all making the most of the costly silk upon the surface of the fabric.

'Wrought very finely by Queen Mary and her Maids of Honour'

The handsome new furniture of Restoration England had little use for table-carpets but whole households became involved in embroideries for overstuffed chairs, day-beds and stools. Some were embroidered *en suite* with the bed draperies. Celia Fiennes at Windsor praised the 'hangings, chairs, stools and screen, the same, all of satin-stitch done in worsteds, beasts, birds, images and fruits all wrought very finely by Queen Mary and her Maids of Honour'.

The hard-wearing tufted turkey-work used for much upholstery – often recorded for guildhall furnishings and the like – is knotted rather than stitched and presumably professionally worked. But the tight flower-head patterns that survive were also repeated in much home upholstery embroidery in fine over-and-over tent-stitch and coarser cross-stitch typical of counted-thread embroidery on linen canvas, as contrasted with surface stitches in costly silks. In the early-eighteenth century even the embroiderer's big naturalistic flower heads were often the favourite 'Season' flowers of Chinese work – prunus, peony, lotus and chrysanthemum – on a rich Imperial yellow ground. Other seat furniture towards the end of the period showed upright stitches in the bright zigzag patterns known as flame-stitch, the bands of different coloured silks achieving effects comparable to popular combed marbling on paper and pottery slipware.

On a smaller scale, cushions reflected the same fashions and proved ideal home-made gifts. The underside was bottomed or lined with plain fabric but the top often showed the early Stuart delight in crowded detail, being worked in tent-stitch, cross-stitch, or long-armed cross-stitch with touches of silk among the crewels (Figs. 7 and 8). Some were in appliqué work but the main seventeenth-century contrast to self-effacing tent-stitch, whether in wool or in silk, was flamboyant

5

Museum Photo

Fig. 5 ***Casket*** *with rising lid and two doors, c.1665. Flat couched stitch in coloured floss silks, the handles missing, length 13¾ ins., depth 10¼ ins., height 7 ins. The top of this beautiful casket depicts Isaac and Rebecca, while the door panels show Abraham with the angels. Not visible in the photograph are scenes of Jacob's dream, the sacrifice of Isaac, and a mermaid rising from the sea. (Lady Lever Art Gallery.)*

7

Museum Photo

6

Museum Photo

Fig. 6 ***Detail of a Mirror Frame*** *c.1665. Silver thread, purl, chenille and silks, framed in tortoiseshell. (Lady Lever Art Gallery.)*

8

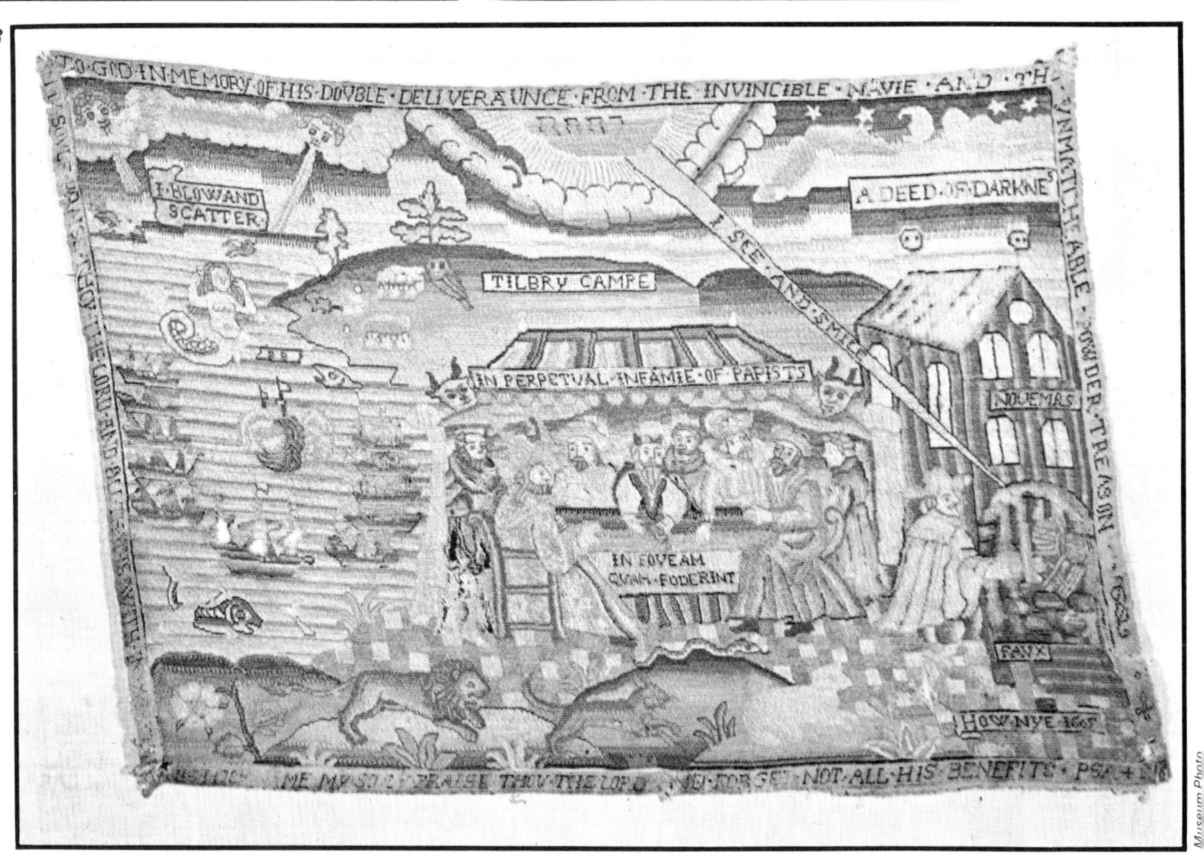

Museum Photo

raised work now known as stump-work, on a base of white satin.

This raised work, which has become extraordinarily attractive to collectors, must be seen as part of a child's education. At first, samplers were intended to some extent as pattern repositories but soon became mere records of adroitness, the narrow strip sometimes three or four feet long including coloured work, white-work, marking alphabets and cut-work. By the end of the period, the sampler had become a schoolroom exercise which a teacher could display both for its decorative presentation in a squarer, bordered shape and for the high moral tone of its increasingly lengthy texts and verses. It is hardly surprising that children scarcely into their teens welcomed the opportunities in raised-work to make ingenious use of their bright clever stitchery, but it must be remembered that this was also one of the great periods for quilting, the quietest expression of the needlewoman's devotion to her craft.

Raised-work may be found mounted on the small mirror-frames (Fig. 6), the flat boxes for lace, gloves and the like and the toilet and jewel caskets that furnished a teenager's dressing-table (Fig. 1). Even the period's sweet bags or perfume sachets might be so enriched – charming 'gift wrapping' alternatives to embroidered purses, bead-threaded wire trays and heavy-gauntleted gloves. As early as 1614, professional examples are described in the Northampton inventory: 'two large sweet bags embroidered with embossed work, of silver, gold and coloured silk and filled up with ovals of divers personages, lined both with coloured satin black, the ground white', valued at £15.

These raised-work pictures have so many similar details that one suspects a common origin either in printed patterns or in white satin sold ready-drawn or printed with the splendid mansion on the skyline below a sun in splendour, the Italianate fountain and fish-pool in the foreground and, in between, the Stuart-costumed figures acting out a familiar Old Testament or Apocryphal story; Jephthah's daughter and Isaac and Rebecca were favourites. Sometimes the figures seem to be the English king and queen, sometimes they represent the four Continents, or Seasons, or Elements, sometimes Orpheus charms the birds or Daphne changes into a laurel, and always the background is crowded with detail.

Our delight today centres on the quality of their stitchery. The rounded-out figures were stitched separately and applied, the faces sometimes covered with silk worked with fine split-stitch. They were then outlined in stem-stitch in the ancient *opus anglicanum* manner. Other details, of apron or flower petal or royal pavilion, might be worked in lace-stitch and almost fully detached.

Small figure portraits in embroidery reflecting a vogue for painted miniatures – such as portraits of Charles I – are entirely different in their flat presentation. Some were worked mainly in tent-stitch, others in a range of cushion stitches, but they were very different from the work of a professional embroiderer such as Edmund Harrison. In the highly professional *Adoration of the Shepherds* from his workshop, now at the Victoria and Albert Museum, the figures' faces are in fine split-stitch but the clothing is principally in horizontal lines of metal threads couched with silk.

This was an important period for work in metal. Silver or silver-gilt wire was flattened and closely wound on cores of white or orange silk, more evenly wound from about the mid-seventeenth century. This kind of work was of great professional importance in dress embroideries, such as the period's bodice fillings known as stomachers. Glinting, rich effects were achieved by working the thread over slight padding or lines of string.

Familiar amateur dress detail in the early-seventeenth century includes delicate black line embroidery. This is noted, for example, on the 'night caps' men used for informal daytime wear when they doffed their hot wigs and in women's coifs and bodices. The patterns suggested delicate pen drawings of coiling stems and familiar flowers lit only with spangles. White-work including drawn and cut thread work, called frost-work (Fig. 2), became an important alternative to the lace-loving Stuarts, but the student of old records has to remember that the term cut-work could refer to the slashing of puffed and padded costume, just as lace could also mean braided work. Indeed, words must often have seemed wholly inadequate to describe the later Stuart dress in its most costly magnificence, when every ribbon might be embroidered and lace-edged.

John Evelyn, describing a fop, suggested that 'a frigate newly rigg'd kept not half such a clatter in a storm as this puppet's streamers did when the wind was in his shrouds'. Even the King's humble rat-catcher had his embroidered costume: that of William Hester, rat-catcher to William and Mary, was of crimson cloth lined with blue serge and edged with blue velvet 'embroidered with their Majesties' WRMR and crowns on back and chest and six Rattes Eating a Wheatsheave on the left shoulder'.

Fig. 7 ***Panel depicting Lot and his family***, *c.1650. Worked in a close tent-stitch of coloured silks which completely conceals the linen ground, 8 x 11½ ins., excluding the braid mount. The story of Lot was a favourite Biblical subject for pictorial panels. On the far right, Lot's wife is already half transformed into a pillar of salt. (Burrell Collection, Glasgow Art Gallery and Museum.)*

Fig. 8 ***Prayer-book Cushion,*** *c.1606. Silk* petit-point *(tent-stitch), 12½ x 18 ins. This intricate cushion was worked to commemorate the defeat of the Armada in 1588 and the discovery of the Gunpowder Plot in 1605. The ships of the Armada are seen on the right approaching Tilbury Camp, where Elizabeth's forces were gathered to repulse them, and a mermaid declares her intention to 'blow and scatter' the enemy. In the centre are seen various foreign potentates including the Pope and a cardinal plotting around a table and prompted by two devils to commit ever more horrible deeds. On the right is Westminster Hall surmounted by two traitors' sculls. A lion chases a fox at the bottom left, symbolic of England's recent great victories over 'the invincible navie and the unmatchable powder treason'. (Lady Lever Art Gallery.)*

MUSEUMS AND COLLECTIONS

Stuart needlework may be seen at the following:

Birmingham:	City Museum and Art Gallery
Cambridge:	Fitzwilliam Museum
Cardiff:	National Museum of Wales
Edinburgh:	The Royal Scottish Museum
Glasgow:	Art Gallery and Museum
London:	Victoria and Albert Museum
Manchester:	Platt Hall Whitworth Art Gallery
Nottingham:	Castle Museum
Oxford:	Ashmolean Museum
Port Sunlight:	Lady Lever Art Gallery

FURTHER READING

English Domestic Needlework, 1560–1860 by Therle Hughes, London, 1961.
Catalogue of English Domestic Embroidery of the sixteenth and seventeenth centuries, 2nd edition, 1950. Also specialised publications on **Samplers, Flowers in English Embroidery, Elizabethan Embroidery,** etc., issued by the Victoria and Albert Museum, London.
English Needlework by A. F. Kendrick, London, 1933.
Needlework Through the Ages by M. Symonds and L. Preece, London, 1928.

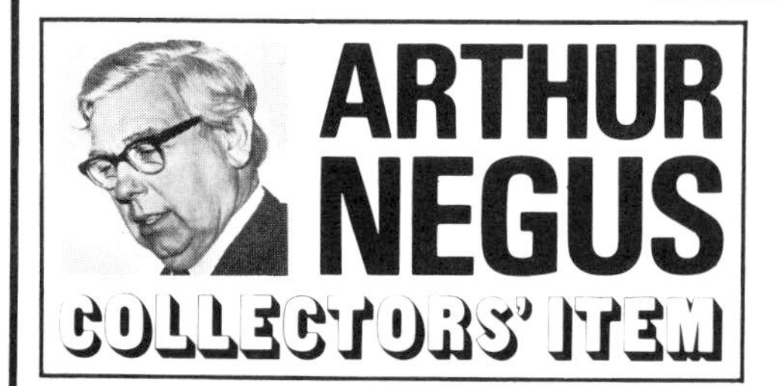

TUNBRIDGE WARE

Celia Fiennes remarked in her diary of 1697 that the 'shoppes' of Tunbridge Wells 'were full of all sorts of curious wooden ware which this place is noted for, neate and thin ware of wood, both white and lignum vitae wood'. This is the earliest reference to Tunbridge Ware. Thereafter, it is frequently referred to by visitors to the town and it seems to have become a popular souvenir brought home for friends by those who had stayed in the Kent town.

The highly decorative wood mosaics which characterise Tunbridge Ware were produced from a solid block composed of thin rods of different coloured woods which had been glued together. A thin cross-section of this block was sawn off and applied to various articles as a veneer. At first, the objects were mainly wooden dishes and trenchers, and these were decorated with geometric mosaic patterns, but throughout the eighteenth and nineteenth centuries the art was elaborated. All kinds of boxes made to contain everything from tea-caddies to handkerchiefs from sealing wax to spices, were produced. Table tops, ink-stands, pipe racks, napkin rings and egg cups; an almost endless list of miscellaneous articles were skilfully decorated.

As time passed, the designs became more elaborate and sophisticated and the squares, diamonds and star patterns were, in the 1840s, followed by minute mosaic work of a representational kind. Flowers were a popular motif and soon afterwards birds and animals were also used. This ware was based on Berlin woodwork of the period and the mosaic pieces (tesserae) were very small, sometimes as minute as needlework stitches.

The introduction of colourful foreign woods combined with the native woods in the 1830s added greater variety – by 1850 about one hundred and eighty different woods were regularly used. Skilful cutting also enlivened the effect and there were subtle contrasts between the horizontal and vertical grains of the wood.

Sadly, the interest in Tunbridge Ware degenerated after the middle of the century and by 1889 all the local factories were closed. Although attempts were made to revive the craft in the 1920s and '30s they were unsuccessful, and this fascinating and often very attractive mode of decoration died out.

Collecting Hints

Work similar in appearance to Tunbridge Ware is still produced in Italy. This Sorrento Ware is immediately recognisable as dyed woods are used and the decoration lacks the rich coloration of the original Tunbridge Ware.

One should also guard against the work made in the 1920s and '30s when there was an attempt to revive the art. It is generally of poor quality and a very limited number of woods were employed.

Names To Look For

Craftsmen can be identified by labels attached to the ware.

The Wise family (firmly established in the seventeenth century), started one of the earliest manufactories. Numerous firms were engaged in this type of decoration during the course of the next two centuries. Fenner and Nye worked independently. Nye was one of the major exhibitors of Tunbridge Ware at the Great Exhibition of 1851.

Another firm was established by the Barton family early in the eighteenth century. It is interesting to note that it was John Barton who invented the circular saw for cutting veneer in 1811.

Earlier on, other makers included K. J. and A. Sharp, James Friend and George Bennett, all of whom produced skilled work.

Where To Buy

Tunbridge Ware is often found in general antique shops.

Prices

Tunbridge Ware comes in many shapes and sizes, from small boxes to complete table top decoration and accordingly the prices vary. But for between £3 and £30 one can buy items which would form a good collection.

Left: *Snuff box in Tunbridge Ware with a decorative geometrical pattern.*

Below left: *Thomas Barton box. The lilies around the box show the use of Tunbridge green wood.*

Below right: *Tudor Cottages at Tenterden, Kent, in an Oxford frame, designed to hang on a wall.*

Opposite: *Stamp box. It depicts the head of Queen Victoria as she appears on 1d. Black and 1d. Red.*

Flavia Petrie Collection: A. C. Cooper

Flavia Petrie Collection: A. C. Cooper

SILVER-MOUNTED WARES

Judith Banister

1

P. Parkinson

Fig. 1 **Ostrich Egg Cup and Cover,** *unmarked, c.1610. Silver-gilt mounts with ostrich motifs, height 20¾ ins. Arms of Exeter College and of Cleve. (Exeter College, Oxford.)*

The fashion for mounted wares in Tudor and early Stuart England was symptomatic of a people with a passionate desire for the exotic whether in the style of the mounts or choice of wares, ranging from ostrich eggs to gourds, horns and coconuts.

Since Anglo-Saxon times at least, the rare, the curious and the valuable have been made more precious and beautiful by the addition of gold or silver mounts. During the medieval and Tudor periods, as the world was shrinking in the path of European mariners and merchants, so the treasure-houses of kings and princes and the cupboards of the wealthy were being filled with new and strange objects from India and China, Africa and the West Indies. There were ostrich eggs and fragile porcelain, mother-of-pearl and nautilus shells, gourds and coconuts. From nearer home came Venetian glass, Baltic amber, stoneware from the Rhineland, the fabulous unicorn's horn (in reality, the tusk or tooth of the narwhal), Turkish coloured pottery and varieties of rock crystal, agate and other hardstones, many of them carved in the workshops of southern Germany and northern Italy. And in England itself there was already a long tradition of working in horn, ivory and the spotted maplewood.

'Pots of earth of sundry colours garnished with silver'

Mounted wares are of two basic types: the decorative and the useful. The latter includes horn cups and beakers, wooden mazers or drinking-bowls and the leather jugs and bottles known as blackjacks, all of them favourite subjects, from medieval times onwards, for mounting with silver or silver-gilt. In addition, the middle of the sixteenth century saw the introduction of mounted stonewares, those 'pots of earth of sundry colours, and moulds, whereof many are garnished with silver' which William Harrison reported in 1587 as being used by all sorts and conditions of people all over the country.

Decorative mounted wares, for the display cupboards of the nobility and for ceremonial use, appeared in a host of lavish and imaginative guises under the inspiration of the renaissance designs which reached England by the second quarter of the sixteenth century. Some, despite their fragility, have survived to form the nuclei of rich royal and national collections. Inevitably, many have been lost, mostly those with fine and heavy mounts. In England, large numbers, especially with gold mounts, were sent to the Mint for disposal by Queen Elizabeth I in 1600 when she needed money. However, some of the less exotic pieces did have a fair chance of survival, for the iconoclasts and the tax-gatherers did not always trouble themselves over mounted wares when there were ample hoards of gold and silver vessels to satisfy them.

Several medieval mazers, the name given to bowls of spotted maplewood, appear to have been converted into all-silver bowls and standing cups during the sixteenth century, while the few that bear Elizabethan hallmarks on their mounts were possibly restored, rather than new pieces. The mazer in the Armourers' and Brasiers' Company Collection is in fact inscribed: 'Everard Frere gave this Mazer garnisht wt. silver 13 ounces wc. was new garnished ano. 1579 for y. Poor . . .' and it has a boss, apparently from an older mazer, presented to the Company by its first Master in 1453. Other mazers perhaps acquired new silver mounts when presented to colleges or companies, but there is no doubt that, while few new ones were made, old mazers were still in use well into the seventeenth century. The so-called Pepys Mazer of 1510 got its name simply from the fact that Pepys recorded drinking from it when he visited the almshouses at Saffron Walden in 1659.

It is, however, among the richer and rarer materials that one can glimpse something of the lost treasures of Tudor times. Ivory, the tusk of the Indian elephant and other tusks of whale or mammoth, were among the most popular exotic materials used in medieval times for carving and mounting (Fig. 11). However, they were gradually going out of favour and only 'oone Salte of Iuerie garnishhid with siluver guilt' appears in the royal inventory of 1574.

The fragility of materials does not seem to have deterred the Elizabethan goldsmith from lavishing rich gold and silver work on them. Among the most prized of medieval imports were ostrich eggs, often

2

3

Fig. 2 **Ostrich Egg Cup and Cover**, *maker's mark a heart over two clubs in saltire, 1584. Silver-gilt mounts, height 14½ ins. (Toledo Museum of Art, Ohio.)*

Fig. 3 **The Gibbon Salt**, *maker's mark three trefoils in a trefoil, London, 1576. Silver-gilt with an irregular five-sided pillar of rock crystal enclosing a silver-gilt figure of Neptune, height 12 ins; weight 57 oz. gross. This extrordinary salt, which was worth about £12 in 1632, is believed to have been given as a bribe to the Goldsmiths. (The Worshipful Company of Goldsmiths, London.)*

called gripe or griffin eggs in early inventories. Strange though the ostrich itself might be, the fabulous griffin, with its eagle's head and lion's body, apparently had greater appeal as creator of these large eggs with their relatively thick, pitted and yellowish shells. Their size was, of course, ideal for standing cups, but obviously most of the rich silver and silver-gilt frames made for them have acquired replacement eggs during the past four centuries.

Of highly sophisticated workmanship is the cup and cover of 1584, now in the Toledo Museum of Art, Ohio (Fig. 2). The vase-shaped stem is flanked by four dolphin brackets, while the shell is enclosed by four alternating male and female caryatid straps in the best renaissance manner. Both the domed foot and the deep lip mount are engraved with fruit motifs between four coats of arms of contemporary date.

The origin of the shells is particularly stressed on one or two surviving cups, notably that of about 1610 at Exeter College, Oxford (Fig. 1). The domed base is chased with ostriches, the stem is formed as four ostrich legs clustered together, while three bold plumes on the tall cover support a finial in the form of an ostrich.

Another fragile and less easily replaceable material much favoured in the sixteenth century was pearl shell, the nacreous substance taken from many kinds of mollusc and known as mother-of-pearl. Ewers of mother-of-pearl feature regularly in the inventories of Queen Elizabeth, none of which appears to have survived. Most mother-of-pearl and other mounted wares bear neither hallmark nor often even maker's mark, so that the decoration and style of the mounts are frequently the only clue to date and country of origin. The pearl is usually arranged like staving and the mounts often have crenellated edges that have been worked to contain the pearl, a practical method used for small bowls and other wares until the middle of the seventeenth century (Fig. 4).

A shell of a very different kind that had tremendous popularity throughout the period was the coconut shell which, when shorn of its rough outer covering and painstakingly polished, and often carved, provided a lustrous dark nut. The pieces merited a place in the royal collections or served as royal gifts, to judge from the coconut cups bearing the Tudor arms. Many of the most splendid coconut cups date from the fifteenth century, and have been treasured over the centuries in the collections of Oxford and Cambridge colleges and the City Livery Companies.

Even in the mid-sixteenth century, rather traditional gothic styles persisted for coconut cups, perhaps to complement the simple form of the shell and its sombre colouring. With few exceptions, even those cups enriched with carving on the shell have a certain simplicity of form. From 1586 dates a fine standing cup (Fig. 8), the nut carved with strap-work and armorials, including the cipher of Elizabeth I and the crest of the Sidney family, designed either for the Earl of Leicester or his nephew Sir Philip Sidney. But, rather like stoneware and pottery, coconut cups tended with time to become less extravagant and less precious examples of the mounter's art, and, indeed, became almost a provincial speciality. Most seventeenth-century cups show York or other provincial marks.

Equally widely made throughout the country

4

Fig. 4 **Mother-of-pearl Bowl,** *unmarked, English c.1610. Silver mounts, diameter 4¾ ins. Note the staving, typical of this period. (Christie's, London.)*

A. C. Cooper

Fig. 6 (opposite) ***Siegburg ware jug*** *with English silver-gilt mounts, unmarked, c.1580, height 8¾ ins.*
Until salt-glaze stoneware came into production in England in the 1670s, a large amount of German pottery was imported. This example is made of the popular greyish-white Siegburg ware. (Sotheby and Co., London.)

Fig. 7 (opposite) ***Tankard,*** *unmarked, English, c.1560. Serpentine mounted in silver-gilt, height 8 ins.*
This tankard was made when green serpentine was popular. (Clare College, Cambridge.)

5

M. R. Dudley

Fig. 8 **Coconut Cup,** *London, 1586. Height 7 ins. Coconut cups were very popular throughout the sixteenth century. The shell was shorn of its rough outer covering and painstakingly polished and often carved to form the body of the cup. The foot and lip were usually linked by means of narrow silver straps. This fine example is carved with Elizabethan strap-work, including Elizabeth I's cipher and the badge of the Sidney family. It was a gift from the Queen to either the Earl of Leicester, or to Philip Sidney. (Henry Huntington Art Gallery, San Marino, California.)*

6

A. C. Cooper

7

Stearn & Sons, Cambridge

8

Museum Photo

Fig. 5 ***Standing Salt*** (left), *maker's mark a swan's head erased, London, 1549. Silver gilt and crystal, height 8 ins. (Trinity College, Oxford.)*

9

K. Hoddle

Fig. 9 ***Wan-Li Ewer*** *with English silver-gilt mounts. Sixteenth or early seventeenth century. Height 10 ins. After the 1520s, a great deal of Ming porcelain was brought to England, where it was regarded as a magnificent luxury, and was often mounted in silver, gold or silver-gilt. (Victoria and Albert Museum, London.)*

10

Museum Photo

Fig. 10 ***Katharine Parr's Jug,*** *the* latticinio, *or milk glass body Venetian, sixteenth century, the silver-gilt mounts with maker's mark, a fleur-de-lis, London 1546. Height 6 ins. On the cover are enamelled the arms of Sir William Parr, Elizabeth's uncle and chamberlain, to whom perhaps she presented the jug. (London Museum.)*

were tigerware jugs. To modern eyes, this German mottled stoneware seems unremarkable, but English pottery at the time was very coarse and usually porous. A variety of German stoneware was imported into Elizabethan England: greyish wares from Cologne and the Westerwald, brownish ones from Raeren, and an interesting white ware from Siegburg (Fig. 6). The majority of wares were, however, the brownish ones known as tigerware (Fig. 15). It has been suggested by Sir Charles Jackson, the authority on English silver, that the name was derived from the German *tiegel*, meaning kiln, but it seems equally possible that it meant speckled, or tabby, like a cat.

'My painted Drinking Glass, with the Silver and Guilte foote'

The import of tigerware pots and jugs into England appears to have dated from about 1540, and large numbers were garnished with silver, especially in the 1570s. It is known that they featured as prizes in the various state lotteries of the period, and this probably accounts for their ubiquity – there are surviving tigerware pots bearing provincial marks. Perhaps because they were popular rather than courtly pieces, the standard of the silver and silver-gilt mounts is not always very high, and the quality of embossing and engraving varies considerably.

One of the most fascinating aspects of sixteenth-century mounted wares is the esteem in which they were held by their owners. In the Armourers' and Brasiers' Company is a stoneware pot with silver mounts in the form of an owl, valued at 28s 6d when it was presented by Julyan, late the wife of William Vineard, in 1537. The rarity of glass in England in the first half of the sixteenth century gave it an importance equal to that of Chinese porcelain, both of which were well-represented in the royal collections of the period. Glasses mounted in gold, ewers of red or morrey glass and of 'purslaine' glass have, understandably, vanished, but one rarity with royal connections is the mounted glass pot known as Katharine Parr's jug (Fig. 10). Made of the milky white striped glass known as *latticinio* (milk) probably imported from Venice, the jug is beautifully mounted with silver-gilt, fully marked in London in 1546. On the cover

16th and early 17th century
English Silver-mounted Wares

Fig. 11 (below) ***The Howard Grace Cup,*** *maker's mark, crossed implements, London 1525. Ivory mounted in silver-gilt, set with pearls and garnets, height 12 ins.*
The mounts of this superb piece mark a transition in English style from the Gothic to the Renaissance; the former is reflected in the rope-work borders and the band of gothic lettering, while the latter is seen in the rich elaboration of renaissance motifs on the foot and cover.
(Victoria and Albert Museum.)

A. C. Cooper

Fig. 12 (top left) ***The Bowes Cup,*** *London, 1554. Silver-gilt and crystal, height 19¾ ins., diameter 7 ins.*
The original owner of this cup was Sir Martin Bowes, Prime Warden of the Goldsmiths, who presented the cup to them in 1561.
(The Worshipful Company of Goldsmiths.)

Fig. 13 **Standing Cup,** *London, 1545. Silver-gilt and rock crystal, height 9¾ ins.*
Crystal was a very popular material for cups in the sixteenth century, especially in royal households, for it was believed that poison would cause crystal to shatter.
(The Worshipful Company of Goldsmiths.)

12

P. Parkinson

13

P. Parkinson

15

A. C. Cooper

Fig. 14 ***The Rogers Salt*** (opposite), *London, 1601. Silver-gilt, rock crystal and painted parchment, height 22 ins. This is one of the last great Tudor mounted salts to be made. The cylinder of crystal contains a parchment roll painted with flowers, the arms of the Goldsmiths' Company, and an escutcheon inscribed: 'Ric. Rogers, Comptroller of the Mint'. (The Worshipful Company of Goldsmiths.)*

Fig. 15 (above) ***Tigerware Jug,*** *maker's mark, a cross between four pellets, English c.1570. Silver-gilt mounts, height 9¼ ins. Note the neat bands of engraving around the neck. (Christie's, London.)*

Fig. 16 (below) ***Rock Crystal Ewer,*** *the crystal Milanese, c.1580, the silver-gilt mounts English, maker's mark E.I., c.1620. Height 6⅜ ins. (Christie's, London.)*

16

A. C. Cooper

are enamelled the arms of Sir William Parr, the Queen's uncle and her Chamberlain, to whom perhaps she presented it. Painted glass was also much esteemed, but few pieces have survived.

Intrepid adventurers who made their way to the Orient returned with such rarities as celadon and, by the 1520s, Ming porcelain. Despite their oriental origin, there was no effort on the part of the English silversmiths to produce mounts in anything but the current European style. Even such popular inscriptions as 'Live to die and live', were used. Monstrous-looking griffin and eagle-head terminals to the spouts of ewers were by renaissance times part of the standard European ornamental repertoire (Fig. 9). Similarly, the mounts on Turkish and other coloured pottery were unmistakeably English in character.

The dark green mottled marking of the serpentine

While potters and artists strove to create hard and brilliant new materials, the gem-carvers and jewellers of renaissance Europe continued to lavish their craftsmanship on both transparent and opaque gem materials such as alabaster, marble, jasper, agate, serpentine and rock crystal. Just as the speckled surface of tigerware appealed to the Elizabethan man-in-the-street, so the dark green mottled marking of the serpentine appealed to the wealthy patron. The mounted 'serpentine pott' bequeathed by Dr. William Butler to Clare College, Cambridge (Fig. 7) is an excellent example. Queen Elizabeth owned dozens of such mounted pieces, including a serpentine collock or barrel, just one of more than a dozen serpentine wares.

Of all the precious mounted materials, however, the most splendid survivors are those of rock crystal. Royal collections no doubt had more than their share of them, for it was thought that the crystal would shatter if poison were placed in it. Queen Elizabeth had more than fifty cups, bowls and ewers of crystal, some set in gold, others in silver-gilt, and more than a dozen salts, including state salts. By tradition, the Bowes Cup of 1554 in the Goldsmiths' Company Collection (Fig. 12) is known as Queen Elizabeth's Coronation Cup, although the owner, Sir Martin Bowes, was not then Lord Mayor, but Prime Warden of the Goldsmiths, to whom he gave the cup in 1561. Here is Elizabethan goldsmithing at its most delightful. The crystal cylinder is supported by four Atlas figures around a globe of crystal and is enclosed by four caryatid straps. Another piece of hemispherical crystal is held within the domed cover which is topped by a graceful female figure bearing a shield with the donor's arms enamelled on it, while the remaining surfaces of the cup from foot to finial are rich with repoussé chasing.

Yet another crystal cup in the same collection, dated 1545, though less exceptional in its quality, has a faceted bowl of rock crystal with three very slender straps holding it between the foot and the cup-shaped engraved lip (Fig. 13). Other recorded cups have faceted bowls and stems, and one, of about 1600 in Yateley Church even has a steeple cover.

The rock crystal cylinder was also used for a number of fine ceremonial salts, many of them enclosing standing figures within the crystal column. Such is the silver-gilt salt of 1549 now at Trinity College, Oxford (Fig. 5) with scrolling caryatids supporting the stone.

Many of the great state salts of the period were of architectural form and none more majestically so than the pillared Gibbon Salt of 1576 (Fig. 3), presented to the Goldsmiths in 1632 after a search had been made through the City for substandard wares. Within the columns, a cylinder of rock crystal contains a figure of Neptune, holding above his head the tiny well for the salt.

Not only rock crystal and silver-gilt, but jewels as well, decorate some salts. The Elizabethans were at times ready to accept grandeur for its own sake, as can be gauged from the records of clock salts and the rare sixteenth-century rock crystal candelabrum which appeared in Christie's, London in 1956.

By 1600, much of the glory that formed the royal and other collections had been dissipated by the needs of war, and hundreds of pieces were sent to the Mint for melting. Here and there, elaborate standing cups and salts were still mounted; the Duke of Bedford's salt at Woburn is dated to about 1610, and a few years later a Milan-carved crystal ewer was mounted in silver-gilt by an English goldsmith (Fig. 16). But the age of grand silver was virtually over with the old century, and it is with a salt of 1601 (Fig. 14), that the story of Tudor mounted wares ends: a cylinder of rock crystal in a restrained and simple setting chased in low relief with formal foliage, its cover topped with a miniature crystal and silver steeple, its cylinder of rock crystal holding a splash of colour in the parchment roll painted with flowers, the arms of the Goldsmiths' Company and an escutcheon inscribed 'Ric. Rogers, Comptroller of the Mint'.

FURTHER READING

Illustrated History of English Plate (2 vols.) by Sir Charles Jackson, London, reprinted 1967.
Investing in Silver by Eric Delieb, London, 1967.
English Silversmiths' Work, Civil & Domestic by Charles Oman, London, 1965.
Old English Silver by Judith Banister, London, 1965.
English Domestic Silver by Charles Oman, 5th Edition, London, 1962.
The Plate of the Worshipful Company of Goldsmiths by J. B. Carrington and G. R. Hughes, London, 1962.

MUSEUMS

Examples of silver-mounted wares may be seen at the following:

Great Britain: British Museum, London
London Museum, London
Victoria and Albert Museum, London
Royal Scottish Museum, Edinburgh

U.S.A. Henry Huntington Art Gallery,
Metropolitan Museum, New York
San Marino, California
Toledo Museum of Art, Ohio

Occasional mounted wares are to be found in many provincial museums and galleries and there are examples in most of the collections of colleges at Oxford and Cambridge and in the London City Livery Companies.

Early English printed books

M. Morton-Smith

Printed books with magnificently tooled and decorated bindings carried the spirit of the Renaissance throughout England.

England entered the sixteenth century in a turmoil of unrest, hunger and unemployment, the results of the Wars of the Roses and the 'Black Death'. English writing was still medieval in character but the main stream of English literature, through Chaucer, Langland and Wycliffe had been halted

Expositio hymnorum totius anni secundum usum Sar diligentissime recognitorum multis elucidationibus aucta. Impressa Londini per Winandum de Worde in parochia sancte brigide in vico anglice nuncupato (the flete strete) ad signum solis commorantem.

Sotheby Photo

Fig. 1 ***The Device of Wynkyn de Worde.*** *Caxton's partner Wynkyn de Worde used an adaptation of Caxton's device on the work he printed. Here it is illustrated with his own name printed on a formalised scroll below.* *(Sotheby and Co., London.)*

and was to be renewed in a different direction. The Renaissance in Italy had inspired princes, prelates and scholars, and the Greek and Latin writings which they admired were spreading over Europe in print; Gutenberg's invention of the hand type-caster, enabling thousands of identical characters to be made, and the development of the printing press, coincided with the sudden increase in demand for books. The 'new learning', combined with a spirit of nationalism fostered by Henry VIII's break with Rome and the competition with Spain to exploit the riches of the New World, resulted in a national literature. Its sources were Italian and classical but were transmuted by the 'humanism' of Linacre and Grocyn, Colet and More, the friends of Erasmus, and by the genius of Elizabethan England.

In 1500 Wynkyn de Worde, Caxton's partner, was printing in London school-books, the lives of the saints in the *Golden Legend*, and Chaucer's *Canterbury Tales*, using adaptations of Caxton's device as his trade mark (Fig. 1). Richard Pynson, who introduced roman type into England, and Julian Notary, who was also a book-binder, were printing the works of Chaucer, Skelton and Lydgate, romances and service books.

Many English books published at this time were illustrated with rather crude, but nevertheless forceful, woodcuts (Figs. 2 and 3). These were more like fifteenth-century Dutch illustrations than the masterly wood engravings being done at the time in Germany, by Albrecht Dürer and Jost Amman, or in Basle and France after the drawings of Hans Holbein the Younger (Fig. 5).

Under an act of 1484, foreign books were imported into England in great numbers and

Books spread the new ideas of the humanists and the Church reformers

continental printers, book-binders, type-cutters and booksellers were encouraged to work there, settling mainly in London. The availability of Italian, French and Swiss books helped to spread rapidly the new ideas of the humanists and the reformers of the church, and the increasing demand for books ensured the growth of the printing trade to the point when, in 1523, an act was passed limiting the employment and apprenticeship of foreigners.

On Christmas Day, 1524, another act came into force making it illegal to buy or sell imported books if already bound, or in quantities of less than a gross. By Queen Mary's Charter of 1556 the Worshipful Company of Stationers was incorporated with powers to make its own laws regulating the printing trade, ostensibly to promote good printing. The Company was also used by the government to control its members: patents were granted to master printers who were members of the Company, giving them the exclusive right to print certain types of books. This led to the monopoly of profitable work being in the hands of a dozen or so of the larger printers, to the impoverishment of the rest of the trade and a consequent decline in the quality of workmanship.

This charter of 1556 regulated the book trade until, in 1586, 'the newe decrees of the Starre

2

Sotheby Photo

Fig. 2 **St. Barbara** *from the* ***Lyfe of the gloryous Vyrgyn and marter Saynt Barbara*** *printed by Julian Notary, 1518. Woodcut. Though charming in its simplicity, this woodcut is crude when compared with the contemporary work of the German woodcutters, such as Dürer.*

Fig. 3 ***A teacher and his pupils*** *from Stanbridge's* ***Paruulorum Institutio*** *(1512-13) printed by Robert Pynson. Woodcut.*

Fig. 4 ***Book binding for Henry VIII*** *probably by* Wootton Deleen, *1545. The binding is elaborately tooled in gilt with renaissance-style ornaments and the arms of Henry VIII.*
(New College, Oxford.)

4

Bodleian Library Filmstrip: English Collections of the earlier 16th century

3

Sotheby Photo

16th century English Printed Books and Book-bindings

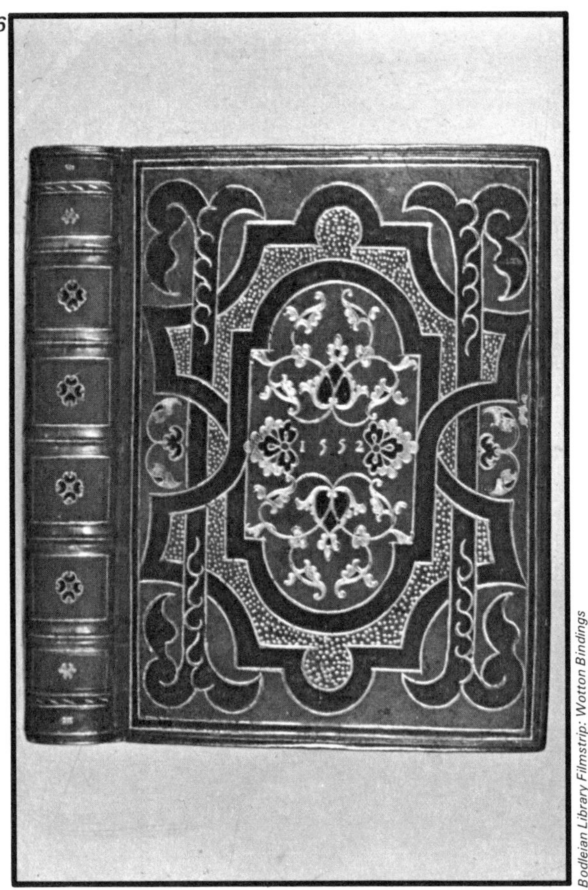

Bodleian Library Filmstrip: Wotton Bindings

Bodleian Library Filmstrip: English Bindings under Elizabeth I and James I

Fig. 6 **Book-binding for Thomas Wotton** *Paris, c. 1552.*
In comparison with this Parisian binding, English bindings (Figs. 4 and 7) are less bold and varied and the tooled work is less competent.
(Astor deposit D3. Bodleian Library, Oxford.)

K. Hoddle

Fig. 5 ***The expulsion of Adam and Eve from the garden of Eden** illustration after Hans Holbein the Younger (c. 1497–1543) for an Old Testament, printed in Lyon 1549.*
The sophistication of Continental woodcutters as compared to the English craftsmen of the same period can be seen on this page from a French Bible.
(Victoria and Albert Museum, London.)

Chamber for orders in printing' restricted all printing to London and the two universities of Oxford and Cambridge, controlling the number of presses in London and requiring the licensing of all books. This was the most important, and restrictive, act concerning printing in Queen Elizabeth's reign.

Book-binding in England continued, at the beginning of the century, to be medieval in style.

Bound in 'crimson satyne' and 'purple velvet written abowte with gold'

Thomas Berthelet, the first English binder to use gold tooling, bound books for King Henry VIII in 'crimson satyne' and 'purple velvet written abowte with gold', calf bindings decorated with fillets and small ornaments stamped in blind and with panels of biblical scenes such as crucifixions and annunciations impressed on the covers. The destruction of the monastic libraries in the 1530s and the consequent distrust of books that looked like Catholic service books, together with the importation of Italian and French styles of binding and type-ornaments, led to new styles of decoration on bindings (Figs. 4 and 7). Henry VIII's coat of arms (with or without the arms of his wives), was also used for 'trade bindings' which, in England, were usually made of calf. German styles of ornamentation with rolls, panels and small tools blind-stamped on the covers, remained common.

John Day (1522–84) began to print with William Seres in London in 1546, issuing a folio edition of the Bible in English in 1549. On Queen Mary's accession, Day went abroad and probably at this time acquired the knowledge and taste that raised the standard of his later work above that of his English contemporaries and to the level of the best continental printers (Fig. 5). Matthew Parker became Archbishop of Canterbury on Queen Elizabeth's accession and encouraged Day to have new types cast and to print the works of the reformers, Thomas Becon, Sleidan, Calvin and Latimer, and, in 1563, Foxe's *Actes and Monuments* (the 'Book of Martyrs'). In 1566 Day printed, at Parker's instigation, *A Testimonie of Antiquitie*, including an Anglo-Saxon homily by Aelfric in the first Anglo-Saxon characters, probably the first new fount of type to have been designed and cut in England since the death of Caxton (Fig. 8). He was also using, by 1574, the finest roman and italic type faces in England.

In the first four decades of the sixteenth century few humanistic texts were printed in

The influence of classical translations was supremely important

England, though Lord Berners' translation of *The Golden Boke of Marcus Aurelius* appeared in 1535, the year in which Henry VIII took on the title of 'supreme Head on earth' of the Church of England. With Thomas Nicoll's translation of Thucydides, 1550, there began a period of translations of classical and continental authors into English that has never been surpassed: Surrey's translation of Virgil, Golding's Ovid, Adlington's Apuleius, Studley's Seneca, North's Plutarch, Young's Boccaccio and Harrington's Ariosto; the list is impressive and because of the influence of these translators on English writers, supremely important. Consequently a new English literature, nourished by these texts, came into being

Many of the best English prose writers emigrated to the Continent when the Reformation was established in England and the Catholic tradition began to disappear, though a translation

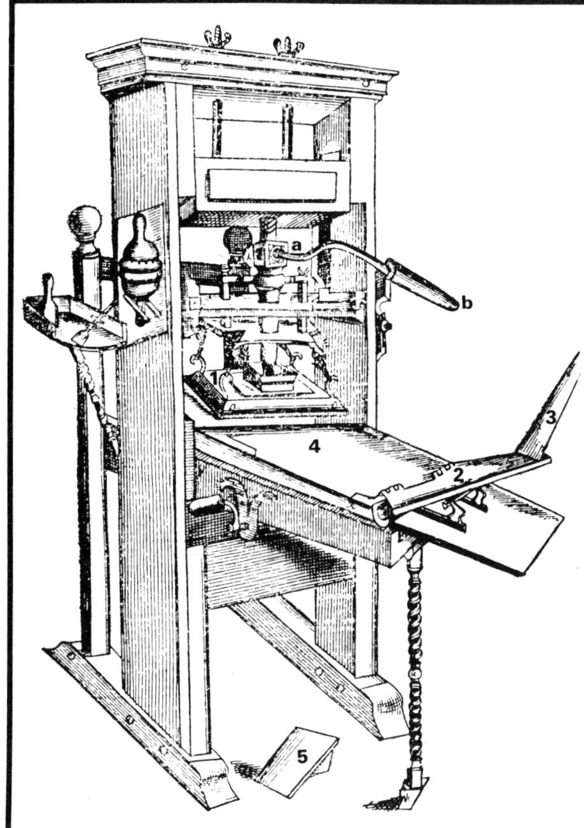

Sotheby Photo

The Hand Printing Press

The operation of the hand press remained substantially the same from the time of Gutenberg in the 1450s until the second decade of the nineteenth century, when, in 1814, *The Times* was printed on a new machine made by Friedrick Köenig.

The original press was made of oak and consisted of a frame within which a plate, or 'platten' (No. 1) was moved up and down to press the sheets of dampened paper on to the type which was locked in a frame on the 'stone' beneath. Two men operated the machine. The 'beater' distributed the ink evenly over the type, and the 'puller' placed the sheet of paper which had been dampened overnight on the 'tympan' (No. 2) and folded the 'frisket' (No. 3) over the sheet to keep it in place. This was then folded over on to the form (No. 4) and slid over the type and under the 'platten'. Placing one foot on the foot rest beneath the press, (No. 5) the 'puller' then pulled the bar (ab) forcing the 'platten' down on to the paper and the type beneath. Releasing the bar the 'puller' could slide the 'tympan' further in and make his second 'pull' to print the second half of the sheet.

The illustration of an old press is reproduced from Joseph Moxon's *Mechanick Exercises on the whole art of Printing*, 1683–84, edited by Herbert Davis and Harry Carter, Oxford University Press, 1962.

Fig. 7 ***Book-bindings for Queen Elizabeth I*** *London c. 1588. This fine binding was probably made for presentation to the Queen. It bears the royal coat of arms and has her initials inserted in the cartouche. It is particularly rare and only two other examples are recorded. (Christ Church, Oxford.)*

8

¶ *The Saxon Caracters or letters, that be moste straunge, be here knowen by other common Caracters set ouer them.*

d.th. th.f. g. i. r. ſ. t. w.

¶ ð. ꝺ. þ. ꝼ. ᵹ. ı. ꞃ. ꞅ. ꞇ. ƿ.

y. z. and. that.

ẏ. ʒ. ⁊ ꝥ.

¶ Æ. Æ. Th Th. E. H. M.

¶ Æ. Ǣ. Ð. Þ. Ɛ. Ꮒ. Ϻ.

S. W. And.

Ꞅ. Ƿ. ⁊.

¶ *One pricke signifieth an vnperfect point, this figure; (which is lyke the Greeke interrogatiue) a full pointe, which in some other olde Saxon bookes, is expressed wyth three prickes, set in triangle wyse thus* ∴

Sotheby Photo

Fig. 8 ***An example of the first Anglo-Saxon type to be cut*** *used by John Day in* A Testimonie of Antiquitie, *1566. Matthew Parker, Archbishop of Canterbury, who took great interest in furthering printing techniques, requested Day to print this work, including an Anglo-Saxon homily by Aelfric. (Sotheby and Co.)*

of More's *Utopia* (originally in Latin) appeared in 1551. But in 1557 the *Songs and Sonnets* ('Tottell's Miscellany') of Henry Howard, Earl of Surrey was printed, to be followed by Gascoigne's *Hundredth sundrie flowres* in 1573, Lyly's *Euphues* in 1578 and, with the publication of Spenser's *Shepheardes' Calender* in 1579, came the full dawn of the English literary Renaissance. Marlowe's *Tamburlaine* was performed in 1587, Sidney's *Astrophel and Stella* and Spenser's *Complaints* were printed in 1591, Shakespeare's *Venus and Adonis*, Sidney's *Arcadia* and works by Drayton, Marlowe, Peele and Hooker in 1593, Shakespeare's *Lucrece* in 1594, and *England's Helicon*, edited by John Bodenham, in 1600.

Patriotic feeling was particularly strong during the Elizabethan era and one of the results was a series of histories of England beginning with Stow's *Summarie of Englyshe Chronicles*, 1565, and Holinshed's *Chronicles*, 1577, which Shakespeare often used as source material for his plays.

The Elizabethan adventurers, Drake, Raleigh and Hawkins, promoted interest in discovery and exploration and books like Hakluyt's *Divers Voyages touching the Discoverie of America*, 1582, and *Voyages into Florida*, 1587, Bigg's *Discourse of Drake's Voyage*, 1588 (the year of the destruction of the Spanish Armada), Raleigh's *Fight about the Azores*, 1591, and *Discovery of Guiana*, 1596, were published.

To prove the antiquity of the doctrines of the Church of England and its true descent from the primitive church, Archbishop Parker published the lives of the Archbishops of Canterbury and the early chronicles of Matthew Paris and Matthew of Westminster. These were the forerunners of a series of excellently edited historical texts, a tradition that was to continue for the next two hundred years.

FURTHER READING

A History of the Old English Letter Founders by Talbot Baines Reed, London, 1952.
Wynken de Worde and his Contemporaries by H. R. Plomer, London, 1925.
Early Illustrated Books: a History of the Decoration and Illustration of Books in the XVth and XVIth centuries by A. W. Pollard, London, 1915.
A Short History of English Printing 1476–1898 by H. R. Plomer, London, 1915.

MUSEUMS AND LIBRARIES

Antiquarian Books may be seen at the following:

London:	The British Museum University of London Library, Senate House, Gower Street, W.C.1 Victoria and Albert Museum
Aberystwyth:	National Library of Wales
Cambridge:	King's College Library Department of Printed Books, University Library
Edinburgh:	National Library of Scotland
Exeter:	Cathedral Library, Bishop's Palace
Oxford:	Department of Printed Books, Bodleian Library

England's first crystal glass

G. B. Hughes

1

K. Hoddle

2

Museum Photo

3

Museum Photo

4

Museum Photo

Fig. 1 **Four Phials of green glass**, *English, seventeenth century. Phials of this type were used to contain medicines and sweet waters. They usually have short necks with flattened rims and high conical necks in the base. Mansell's patent of 1623 refers to 'small violls of green bottle glass'. (Victoria and Albert Museum, London.)*

Fig. 2 **Goblet** *by Giacomo Verzelini, dated 1580. Height $5\frac{1}{8}$ ins. The metal is tinged greyish-black and is slightly bubbly. The letters A and F are engraved on the wide, shallow bowl and joined by a lover's knot. (Victoria and Albert Museum.)*

Fig. 3 **Free-blown Goblet** *from the Broad Street glass-house of Verzelini, dated 1575. The goblet is decorated with diamond-point engraving and shows hounds chasing a deer. The pearwood foot is a replacement. (Corning Museum of Glass, New York.)*

Fig. 4 **Betrothal Goblet** *by Verzelini, dated 1586. Height $5\frac{3}{4}$ ins. The initials of the betrothed couple are linked by a lovers' knot. It is thought that this goblet belonged to a pewterer as it is encircled by the motto of the Pewterer's Company, IN:GOD: IS:AL:MI:TRYVST. (Victoria and Albert Museum.)*

Fig. 5 **Portrait of Verzelini**, *brass rubbing taken from his tomb, 1607. Verzelini was born in Venice in 1522. He emigrated to Antwerp and finally came to England where, despite the vindictive animosity of the native craftsmen who burned down his glass-house, he revolutionised the glass-making industry. (Downe Church, Kent.)*

5

Crown Copyright: National Monuments Record

During the Elizabethan and Stuart periods, a glass-making industry was founded in England which ultimately produced the finest and most durable table-glass ever made.

The Grand Council of the Venetian Republic in the fourteenth century granted liberties to the artist-craftsmen in glass at Murano, verging on those possessed by the nobility. This was in recognition of their development of a fragile, light-weight glass displaying a smoothness and clarity previously unknown. The three-piece drinking-glass, composed of bowl, stem and foot, was evolved and soon every royal table in Europe was graced by exquisite masterpieces of Venetian glass.

An extensive trade was carried on in England during Henry VIII's reign and spasmodic attempts were made to attract Venetian glass-men to England. These were unsuccessful until 1549 when Joseph Cassilari, heading a team of eight glass-men from Murano, set up furnaces in London. Production was well under way when the Venetian Senate demanded their return under penalties ranging from a term in the galleys to death at the hand of a trained assassin.

Carrés furnace was in an old tennis-court

No transparent soda-glass was made in England until 1567 when the French glass-man, Jean Carré, petitioned Queen Elizabeth for a licence to build and operate round glass-houses in the Venetian style. At first this permitted him to make only clear glazing glass similar to the French, which was of finer quality than the English. He was accompanied by several experienced glass-workers and established window glass furnaces at Fernfold in Sussex. Three months later, however, Carré's licence was extended to include the manufacture of *cristallo* in the Venetian style. He obtained possession of the old dining-hall of the Crutched (crouched or crossed) Friars, Aldgate, London, which had been surrendered to the King in 1539 and which had long been used as a tennis-court. The thick stone walls were considered proof against the flames necessary to heat the small open-top melting pots in the furnaces which were fuelled by four-foot billets of charred beech.

The French glass-workers proved unsatisfactory, and the venture was unsuccessful until June 1571, when Carré imported from Antwerp six men fully experienced in the Venetian craft. This group was supervised by Giacomo Verzelini. Carré died less than a year later and the entire project then came under Verzelini's sole control. Carré, however, must be counted as the earliest maker of delicate *cristallo* in England, working nearly a century before Ravenscroft evolved the lead crystal glass that was England's vastly important contribution to the story of elegant table glass.

Verzelini, born at Venice in 1522, emigrated to Antwerp and in 1556 married Elizabeth Vanburen, member of an influential family in that town.

6

Owner's Photo

7

Owner's Photo

8

Museum Photo

Fig. 8 ***Marriage Goblet** by Verzelini, 1578. Height $8\frac{1}{4}$ ins.*
The goblet is engraved with a hunting scene frieze and panels inscribed AT and RT, linked by lovers' knots. (Fitzwilliam Museum, Cambridge.)

Here he became associated with Carré. Under his vigorous personality the Crutched Friars Glass-house was operating profitably by 1575. Contemporary writers praised his *cristallo* as equal to that of Murano.

Verzelini's legal status in England was vulnerable, for, being a 'stranger' and unnaturalised, he possessed no property-owning rights. The fifty or so London glass-sellers, who for long had traded in Venetian glass, combined in an effort to discredit his *cristallo*. So malicious became the glass-sellers that, on the morning of Sunday, 4 September, 1575, while he, his family and workmen were attending a service at St. Olave's Church, his glass-house and home were destroyed by fire.

'Sette uppe within our said cittie one furneys'

The Crutched Friars Glass-house was soon repaired, however, and the Patent Roll of Elizabeth I, dated 15 December in the same year, shows that a monopolistic patent to make fine glass was granted to 'James Verselyne, a Venetian, inhabitinge within oure cittie of London, who hathe sette uppe within our said cittie one furneys and sette on work dyvers and sondrie parsonnes for the makinge of all manner of counterfeyt venyse drinkinge glasses such as be accustomablie made in the town of Morano'.

The patent stipulated that the glassware should be as cheap as or cheaper than any imported; that no similar glasses should be made within the Queen's dominions by other glass-men without a written licence from Verzelini for which he was permitted to charge, and that Englishmen should be instructed in all the arts of its manufacture. The import of foreign glass in the Venetian style was prohibited, thus protecting Verzelini from outside competition. Penalties for infringing the licence were £200 for each furnace – and there might be several in a glass-house – and ten shillings for each glass. Half of the fines were to be appropriated by the Crown and the remainder divided equally between Verzelini and the informer. Verzelini also took the precaution of regularising his legal position by applying for naturalisation: papers were granted on 24 November, 1576.

Demand for Verzelini's glasses became so great that he established a second glass-house in the old hall of the Augustinian Priory in nearby Broad

9

10

Museum Photo

11 12

K. Hoddle

Museum Photo

Figs. 6 and 7 ***The Royal Oak Goblet**, dated 1663.*
Height $5\frac{1}{8}$ ins.
The goblet is made of light and almost colourless metal and weighs only 3 oz. The bucket-bowl stands on a blown knop stem and is engraved with a portrait bust of Charles II in a stylised oak tree. On each side are engraved portraits of the King and Queen and the other view shows the royal coat of arms.
(Formerly in the Bles Collection.)

Fig. 9 ***Flute** of the type made at Sir Robert Mansell's glass-house, London.*
The bowl has a folded foot decorated with diamond-point engraving. The stem is hollow and mould blown into the shape of an urn.
(Victoria and Albert Museum.)

Fig. 10 ***Glass Flask**, late-sixteenth or early-seventeenth century.*
This green glass flask, ribbed and lipped, is a rather more elaborate version of the apothecaries' phials in Fig. 1.
(Victoria and Albert Museum.)

Fig. 11 ***Drinking-glass**, English, dated 1582.*
Engraved with diamond-point the decoration runs in bands around the glass bearing the name of William Smith and heraldic crests.
(Victoria and Albert Museum.)

Fig. 12 ***Goblet** by Sir Jerome Bowes, dated 1602. Height $8\frac{1}{8}$ ins.*
Made by Verzelini's successor, this fine goblet shows traces of gilding on the bowl rim and lower stem. The diamond-point engraving reads BARBARA POTTER 1602.
(Victoria and Albert Museum.)

Street. Eventually he employed about twenty glass-blowers – Thorpe names sixteen Italians working between 1575 and 1594 – with their essential assistants, probably one hundred and fifty men in all. By 1590, he was drawing licence fees from at least fifteen other manufacturers of *cristallo*.

Drinking-glasses made by Verzelini resembled contemporary stemmed goblets in sterling silver. The bowl was developed from the original half-sphere or cup form and fitted with foot and stem, the latter built from several units, one usually a hollow knop. The foot might be plain or edged with a narrow upward fold. The fantastic decorations of Venice were avoided but the stem might be ornamented with masks or mascaroons, small blobs of glass shaped, by stamping while hot, into human or animal faces and applied to the stem. Too fragile for everyday use, these glasses entered the homes of the well-to-do and were protected from damage by wooden display cages.

Several of Verzelini's glasses, elaborately engraved with the diamond point, still exist, carefully preserved as precious evidence of that enterprising period (Figs. 2, 3, 4 and 8). The metal is clouded by innumerable minute bubbles and coloured with various hues such as a pale smoke-grey, greyish-green and pale brown. The engraving is attributed to the London pewter engraver, Anthony de Lysle, in the Liberty of St. Martin's le Grand, an independent decorator from France who became naturalised in 1582. He bought plain glasses from Verzelini and decorated them to commission, usually converting them into personal souvenirs. In several of the existing examples the upper part of the bowl is encircled by a hunting scene, hounds chasing a deer (Figs. 3 and 8). A betrothal glass is engraved with the initials GS linked by a lover's knot, twice dated 1586, and encircled with the motto of the Pewterers' Company – IN : GOD : IS : AL : MI : TRYVST – suggesting that it was originally the property of a London pewterer (Fig. 4). Evidence of gilding is found on the bowls and stems of at least two specimens.

Verzelini made not only goblets but the entire range of useful Venetian glass that had formerly been imported. The Kenilworth Castle inventory of 1588 (*Ancient Inventories*, J. O. Halliwell, 1854) records that the Earl of Leicester possessed three times as many glass bowls as drinking-glasses. Very few glasses of the period have survived and although attributed to Verzelini, these could well be the work of one or another of his licensees.

When Verzelini retired in 1592 he sold his glass-houses to Sir Jerome Bowes, financier and former ambassador to Russia, who retained the glass monopoly for a period of twelve years at an annual fee of two hundred marks. This monopoly patent was duly renewed by James I in 1604. A hint of trouble, however, is given in a clause of Bowes' patent, which extended its scope by allowing him exclusive right to import Venetian glass for noblemen within Her Majesty's realm. Bowes, an ill-tempered individual, realised that his own glass would not meet the necessary requirements and appears to have vented his spleen upon the foreign-born glass-men in his employ, for they resigned in a body. The English replacements did not possess the necessary skills and he was compelled to bring others from Antwerp. Bowes' *cristallo* still sold at Verzelini's prices and output increased, but its quality deteriorated.

The Duke of Rutland's manuscripts record interesting sidelights on the use of fine Anglo-Venetian table glass in wealthy households during the period 1598–1615. Accounts dated 15 August, 1599, include drinking-glasses, four with covers and very long, at 35s 6d. Glass plates with graven rims occur constantly at 6s 2d a dozen, such plates being fashionable dessert table appointments. One entry reads: '4 Julii 1598: Item for sweete meates at dyner when my Lady was there, and hyre of glass plates'. An entry dated 10 June, 1600, records the hire of drinking glasses for a banquet given at the duke's London house at a cost of 11s 6d. The hiring of 'feast vessels' in silver, glass and pewter was a profitable occupation at this period.

The monopoly for 'the sole making of Venice glasses' in 1608 passed to Sir P. Hart and Edward Forcett. Six years later James I granted a twenty-year additional licence to a consortium of financiers from whom he received an annual fee of £1,000; they also contracted to use only Scottish coal. The importation of glass was entirely forbidden.

Vice-Admiral Sir Robert Mansell, with several business associates, came into possession of the glass monopoly in 1618. Within five years, Mansell had eliminated his co-partners and secured a fresh licence giving him complete control of Britain's glass industry with glass-houses in London, Newcastle, Stourbridge, Swansea, Isle of Purbeck, Milford Haven, Newnham-on-Severn, King's Lynn, Awsworth, Wemyss and elsewhere.

This gave him the power to rationalize the industry and in 1624 he employed four thousand men, women and children. The actual blowers were well paid. A government report records that 'the glass-blower might be seen laying aside his cocked hat, dress-coat and sword to prepare for the performance of his daily work'. Fine Venice glasses made at the Broad Street glass-house were highly prized and costly luxuries. Elsewhere Mansell manufactured coarse drinking-glasses and tableware, mirror plate, window glass, bottles and phials (Figs. 1 and 9).

Glass-men discovered making unlicensed ware were imprisoned

Mansell exercised his monopolistic rights to the full. In 1641, for instance, he 'sent Richard Batson into custody without a hearing for buying 129 chests of imported glasses'. At the same time, nobles and merchant princes were permitted to buy glass for their own use direct from Antwerp and Murano. Any glass-man discovered making unlicensed ware was imprisoned and his furnaces confiscated. Mansell retired after the forfeiture of monopolies required by Cromwell, leaving a legacy of sturdy industrial efficiency but little, if any, improvement in the quality of English glass. The manufacture of Venice glass was virtually abandoned during the Commonwealth, but common metals continued to be produced in even larger quantities, prompting Cromwell to impose a glass tax.

During the monopoly regime, bowls were for the most part flower-shaped. Three principal types of Anglo-Venetian drinking glass stems emanated from the Crutched Friars Glass-house.

1. Until 1635 hollow mould-blown stems were usual, often decorated with applied masks or festoons, sometimes both arranged alternately.
2. From about 1590 hollow mould-blown urn-shaped stems might be decorated with vertical bands of ladder patterning.
3. From 1618 to the 1650s blown knops were placed between the solid upper part of the stem which was shorter than formerly, the lower section being slimmer and taller and lacking ornamental moulding.

Within three months of Charles II's arrival in London during 1660, a lime-soda glass known as *christall de roache* or rock crystal was evolved by John de la Cam, a master doctor ordinary to the king of France and friend of the second Duke of Buckingham, 'chymist, fiddler, statesman and buffoon'. The Duke financed Cam to the tune of £6,000 to establish a glass-house in the Charterhouse Yard. Buckingham later financed glass-houses at Greenwich and Vauxhall, his political influence enabling him to accumulate profitable partnerships in several other glass-houses.

Thomas Tilston, a London merchant, was granted in 1663 a 14-year patent for 'makeinge Christall Glasse, a new manufacture not formerly practised in this nation'. This glass was whiter and thicker than anything so far made in England. Profitable export markets were quickly acquired and this glass-house, too, soon came under the control of Buckingham.

The well-known 'Royal Oak' glass (Figs. 6 and 7) is one of the few remaining examples from Buckingham's glass-house. This square-bowled goblet, dated 1663, is elaborately engraved with portraits of Charles II and his queen, and with an expansive royal arms.

The Worshipful Company of Glass Sellers, incorporated in 1664, was given autocratic powers over the glass-houses of London and for seven miles beyond. Members were required to experiment with the object of meeting the needs of the period by producing a 'bright, clear, and whit sound Metall'. Ten years passed without any tangible result. Then George Ravenscroft, operating a glasshouse in the Savoy, notified the Company that he was able to produce 'fine, Chrystalline Glasses in semblance of Rock Cristall for beer, wine and other uses'. Charles II granted him a seven year patent, dating from 16 May, 1674. The Glass-Sellers' Company then agreed to buy his entire output for three years, a contract renewed in 1677.

The new ingredient was calcined flint, prepared from white marble river pebbles imported from Italy, crushed and sifted; instead of soda, Ravenscroft incorporated refined potash from Spain. By the autumn of 1675, with the aid of oxide of lead, he created a new glass of a density and refractive brilliance previously unknown. This glass, tinged with a darkish hue, was easier to work than his former metal. Hollow-ware, if flicked with thumb and finger, emitted a resonant ring that distinguished it from other glass similar in appearance. Ravenscroft announced his glass-of-lead as 'improved flint glass'. This was the metal that for a century and a half dominated the fine table-glass trade of the world.

As the century progressed, flint-glass increased in lustre and clarity and became more durable. By 1695 there were twenty-seven flint-glass houses operating in England, the industry employing about one thousand men, women and children. Even Venice, home of elegant and creative designs, copied the solid, sturdy English shapes, but in fragile soda-glass.

Fig. 13 ***Cider-flute**, early 1660s. Height 14½ ins.*
Flutes were used for serving bottled cider. This elegant example bears the escutcheon of Lord Scudamore and festoons of fruit and flowers. Below this are five trees and the initial S (for Scudamore) repeated three times. (London Museum, formerly in the collection of the Earl of Chesterfield.)

13

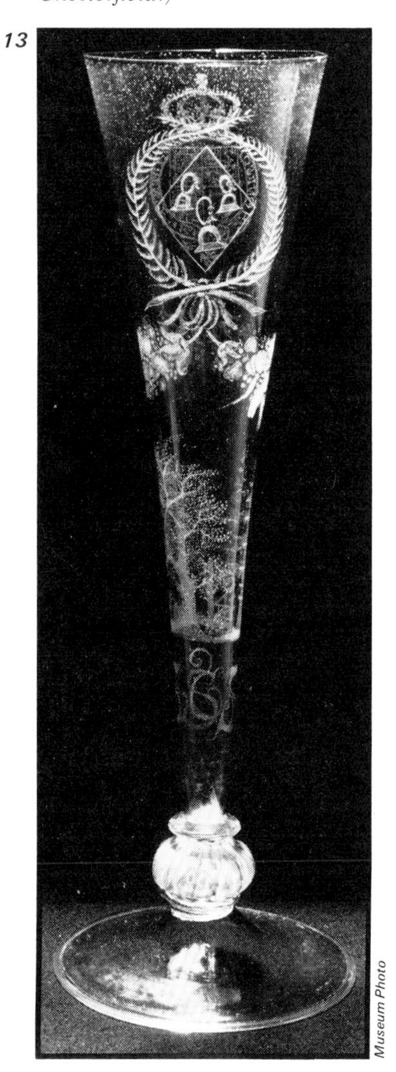

Museum Photo

FURTHER READING

English, Scottish and Irish Table Glass by G. Bernard Hughes, London, 1956.
History of English and Irish Glass by W. A. Thorpe, London, 1929.
History of Old English Glass by F. Buckley, London, 1925.
Old English Glass by A. Hartshorne, London, 1897.

MUSEUMS AND COLLECTIONS

Early English glass is on view at the following:

London:	British Museum Guildhall Museum London Museum Victoria and Albert Museum
Cambridge:	Fitzwilliam Museum
Edinburgh:	Royal Scottish Museum
Lincoln:	Lincoln City and County Museum
Luton:	Luton Museum
Newcastle:	Laing Art Gallery and Museum
U.S.A.	Corning Museum of Glass, New York

PROSPERITY UNDER KING AND COMMONWEALTH

Maurice Ashley

1

James I 1603–25
Charles I 1625–49
Parliamentary Rule 1649–53
Oliver Cromwell 1653–58
Richard Cromwell 1658–59

Stuart England, when a labourer might earn sixpence in a day; when lavish palaces were built but plumbing did not exist; when exquisite works of art were created only to be destroyed by the rampaging Roundhead soldiers.

The royal Court (that is to say the Government) was the lush fount of patronage in seventeenth-century England. Queen Elizabeth I was parsimonious by nature and had preferred to stay in other people's houses rather than to build her own. James I, after he came to England from Scotland in 1603, was wildly extravagant, but his principal hobby was hunting. He devoted most of his life to it when he was not engaged in statecraft or in writing books about witchcraft and theology; his two sons, Prince Henry, who died in 1612, and his brother,

2

Michael Holford Library

3

Fig. 1 (frontispiece) ***Triple portrait of Charles I*** *by Sir Anthony Van Dyck (1599–1641), 1635–36. Oil on canvas, 33¼ x 39¼ ins. Bernini never visited the English Court so the King, determined to own a piece of work by the Italian sculptor, requested Van Dyck to execute this triple portrait which was then sent to Italy as a model for a marble bust of Charles. (By gracious permission of H.M. The Queen.)*

4

5

A. C. Cooper

6

A. C. Cooper

Fig. 2 ***Queen's House, Greenwich,** by Inigo Jones (1573–1652), 1616–35.*
Jones became Surveyor of the King's Works in 1615 and from that date until the outbreak of the Civil War in 1642 he designed the major royal buildings. The Queen's House, built for Queen Anne (wife of James I), was based on an Italian villa plan and was the first strictly classical building in England. Jones' originality is obvious, however, for nowhere in the scheme did he borrow directly from Italian architecture. Slight alterations of proportion and the integration of a variety of classical elements give the house a completely individual quality.

Fig. 3 ***Self-portrait with Sir Endymion Porter** by Sir Anthony Van Dyck. Oil on Canvas.*
Van Dyck (on the right) was a personal friend of Sir Endymion Porter (1587–1649), who was British ambassador to Spain. Like much of the nobility he followed the royal example and took an enthusiastic interest in the arts.
(Prado, Madrid.)

Fig. 4 ***Well staircase**, 1602. Oak.*
This staircase is an important and highly original Jacobean example, only one other of its type existing, and this at Milton Hall, Hunts. The centre pillar (newel post) was constructed separately, an innovation of about 1600.
(Great Fosters, Egham, Surrey.)

Fig. 5 ***Full-blown Jacobean Chimneypiece**, c.1620. Oak.*
The delicately carved cartouches in the central panel are an outstanding feature of this imposing chimneypiece.
(Great Fosters.)

Fig. 6 ***Masquer** by Inigo Jones (1573–1652) for Thomas Campion's* Lord's Maske, *1613. Water-colour.*
Inigo Jones is known not only as an architect but as a designer of sets and costumes for masques which were popular at the Stuart Court. His versatility and imagination can be seen in his sketches for these festivities.
(Chatsworth House, Derbyshire.)

Charles, who succeeded Henry as Prince of Wales, were the leading patrons of the arts. Prince Henry was fond of jewellery, pictures, music and books, and appointed the famous architect, Inigo Jones, as his Surveyor. Charles' secretary, Francis Crane, was the organiser of the Mortlake tapestry works and when Charles became king in 1625, he soon established himself as the most notable connoisseur in Europe.

The nobility followed the royal example. The first Duke of Buckingham, the favourite of James I and Charles I, had a remarkable collection of paintings; Thomas Howard, second Earl of Arundel, arranged for Inigo Jones to be a member of his entourage when he accompanied James' daughter, Elizabeth, to Heidelberg on her marriage to the Elector Palatine; later he brought over to England Wenceslaus Hollar, the Bohemian engraver, to whom we owe so much for depicting England in the Caroline age. Philip Herbert, fourth Earl of Pembroke, was another distinguished patron and collector, who employed John Webb (Inigo Jones' pupil) to rebuild his house at Wilton with its celebrated Double Cube Room.

'No kingdom in the world spent so much on building as we did at this time'

Bishop Goodwin wrote: 'No kingdom in the world spent so much on building as we did at this time'. Gradually the great houses ceased to be built in the style of the Tudor Gothic and assimilated the early renaissance style. Whereas previously a typical nobleman's house would have contained a huge hall, more than a storey high, in which the family, its dependants and servants would all eat together, with sleeping quarters for the family and servants at each end, the hall was now converted into a vestibule or entrance hall, only one storey high. Elaborate staircases were built leading to the great chamber, long gallery and bedrooms and often there were two parlours which became the dining-room and drawing-room.

These houses were taller and more compact than their Tudor predecessors. On the exterior, the gables and mullioned windows disappeared (although there is a fine example of this type of house which was built at Swakeleys, Middlesex, in 1638) and were replaced by rectangular windows, straight unbroken cornices and, in general, less ornate fronts. James I and Charles I both tried to encourage the wider use of brick. Kew Palace and Belton House, Grantham, were both built of Flemish bond brick with alternate rows of what were called 'headers' and 'stretchers'. But brick and glass were expensive and could only be employed in quantity by the well-to-do.

Ordinary town houses were rarely constructed of brick but were wooden or half-timbered with each storey overhanging the one below. The ground floor generally consisted of a shop or workshop in which the master, his family and apprentices lived together. In the country what are now sometimes called seventeenth-century cottages were in fact the farmhouses of yeomen. Some of these houses had glass windows and chimneys to carry away the smoke from the log fires. They were usually built of plaster and timber with thatched roofs, but good use was made of local stone, when, as in Cornwall and the Cotswolds, it was readily available. The actual cottages of the time have largely disappeared. These would have been built of mud, straw and slate and thatched with straw. They would consist of only one room, in which the whole family and sometimes the animals lived, together with a few outhuts.

The farm labourer or cottager earned sixpence to ninepence a day

One must never forget the huge gap that existed between the rich and poor in the seventeenth century. Whereas a duke of Buckingham or earl of Pembroke would spend thousands of pounds on his houses and furnishings, eat enormous meals and even occasionally take a bath, the farm labourer or cottager earned sixpence to ninepence a day and lived on bread, cheese and ale; the only meat he ever saw had probably been poached from the local landowner. John Taylor, known as the 'Water Poet', who died in 1653, wrote of one home he stayed in:

> No meat, no drink, no lodging (but the floor);
> No stool to sit, no lock upon the door.
> No straw to make us litter in the night,
> Nor any candlestick to hold the light.

The furniture in a rich man's house was fairly elaborate. The walls would usually be panelled, the plaster ceilings decorated with heraldic emblems, scrolls, birds and beasts. Wallpaper was virtually non-existent and tapestries or hangings went out of fashion until the Mortlake tapestries came in from 1619 onwards. There were native carpets, but Turkish and Persian carpets were also popular. The East India Company imported porcelain, but glassware was an extravagance. Furniture was more plentiful than in the Elizabethan era, but chairs were still scarce. The most elaborate and expensive feature of a rich man's house was the four-poster bed adorned with gorgeous hangings and testers, or canopies. Such a bed might cost thousands of pounds.

Elizabeth I had a bath once a month, but James I was averse to them

Yet domestic life had its primitive aspects. The beautiful beds were easily infected by bugs. Knives and forks, as well as chairs, were scarce. So were baths. Queen Elizabeth I had a bath once a month, but James I was averse to them. The well-to-do would have close-stools, which were carried about the house, and a cesspool in the cellar. Hygiene and medicine were little known to these ancestors of ours. For the poor, life was short, brutish and nasty. Doctors had two main remedies, bleeding their patients or purging them. Surgery, carried out without anaesthetics, was primitive in the extreme and surgeons were often also barbers. All sorts of old wives' remedies were employed and chests of herbs were kept to cope with illnesses.

Even for the rich, doctors would diagnose illnesses and prescribe remedies by correspondence. Thus the expectation of life was short. The poor had an inadequate and unbalanced diet (potatoes had not been introduced and vegetables were rarely eaten), while the rich were liable to be killed by overeating or, if that did not happen, they might easily be murdered by the ministrations of their doctors. London was exceptionally smoky and smelly.

Though it seems extraordinary, the shortness of life and the frequent suddenness of death induced men to build splendid homes and furnish them extravagantly not for their own enjoyment but for the admiration of posterity.

So a newly-built house, a great bed, an armchair – and, one may add, a lavish funeral – were the status symbols of the time. Pictures and porcelain were collected from abroad by the rich to adorn their houses, for there were few good native painters or craftsmen of outstanding distinction. An exception was William Dobson, a fine portrait painter who flourished at the time of the Civil War in Oxford. But the painters and sculptors who were most steadily patronised were Italians and Flemings. Charles I bestowed his patronage particularly on Rubens and Van Dyck. There was, however, an excellent school of English miniaturists which included Samuel Cooper (who painted a famous portrait of Oliver Cromwell), Peter Oliver and John Hoskins. When Charles I became the most generous patron of the Mortlake tapestry factory he caused Raphael's Cartoons, designed for the Vatican, and Titian's *Supper at Emmaus* to be copied.

7

A. F. Kersting

Fig. 7 ***Double Cube Room** at Wilton House designed by Inigo Jones and executed by John Webb, c.1649. The room was specifically designed to house the portraits of the Pembroke family painted by Van Dyck in the 1630s. It is geometrically constructed, as the name suggests, and has been described as the most beautiful single room in England.*

It is sometimes said that Oliver Cromwell was no patron of the arts, though it was hardly his fault that Charles I's collection of paintings was dispersed. It is true that the Roundhead soldiers were sometimes responsible for the destruction of images in churches, though much more destruction dates from the Protestant Reformation. Not only was Cromwell a lover of organ music and he and his wife the patrons of portrait painters, but he took an active interest in the Mortlake tapestries in their last days. At one stage, he was a member of the committee of enquiry into the tapestry manufacture, and a colleague of his, Sir Gilbert Pickering, was appointed governor. Six hangings were purchased for Cromwell's lodgings at Whitehall when he was Lord Protector.

Undoubtedly the greatest architect of the first half of the seventeenth century was Inigo Jones (1573–1652). The term 'architect' occurs very seldom either in literature or in documents before the seventeenth century; neither Inigo Jones nor Christopher Wren was originally trained as an architect. Comparatively little is known of the career of Inigo Jones and few of his buildings remain. He was born in Smithfield, the son of a clothmaker, and he first became known at Court as a designer of scenery and costumes for masques, of which James I's queen, Anne of Denmark, was inordinately fond. He visited Italy twice, once about 1600 and then in the company of the Earl of Arundel in 1613–14, and became a firm admirer of the early renaissance style which was reflected in his architecture. When he was appointed Surveyor General of the King's Works in 1615 at a salary of £275, many duties were imposed upon him. For example, he continued to collaborate in preparing court masques with Ben Jonson, by whom it was said that he had a domineering and arbitrary temper and who called him Dominus Do-All.

The Stuart monarchy set the example with a fastidious taste in the arts

Inigo Jones supervised building in London, which the monarchy wanted to restrict; he was concerned with brick-making and put in order Charles I's collection of coins and medals. The principal buildings which he designed included the Banqueting House in Whitehall, completed in 1622, the Queen's House at Greenwich, and the church of St. Paul and its piazza in Covent Garden. He also worked on plans for rebuilding St. Paul's cathedral which was then a gothic structure. Unquestionably he was as responsible as any one man for converting English architecture to the renaissance style.

These changes in style were of course gradual and were mainly adapted from foreign models. But the Stuart monarchy set the example with a fastidious taste in paintings, tapestries, classical decoration, coins, medals, miniatures and furniture.

EARLY STUART HOUSES

The following early Stuart houses are open to the public:

London:	Banqueting Hall by Inigo Jones, Whitehall Charlton House, Greenwich Queen's House by Inigo Jones, Greenwich
Derbyshire:	Bolsover Castle
Essex:	Audley End
Hertfordshire:	Hatfield House
Middlesex:	Swakeleys, Ickenham
Norfolk:	Blickling Hall
Surrey:	Dutch House, Kew Palace
Warwickshire:	Aston Hall, Birmingham
Wiltshire:	Double Cube Room by Inigo Jones, Wilton House

Early Stuart and Commonwealth Furniture

Margaret Macdonald-Taylor

Leslie Harris

Fig. 1 **Day bed**, c.1610–20. Plain framework upholstered with crimson velvet. This famous day bed, or couch, is intended for reclining; there is a hinged and cushioned head-rest attached to the arm at each end. A ratchet adjusts the bed to the height desired. Although a great deal of upholstered furniture was made at this time, a piece of this complexity and richness was a rare luxury.
(By kind permission of H.M. Treasury and The National Trust. From the Sackville Collection at Knole.)

Native craftsmanship flourished, rich carving and upholstered work was produced in abundance and luxurious pieces were imported from the Continent.

In the early seventeenth century, before the disturbances of the Civil War, the arts prospered. James I founded the Mortlake tapestry works and his son, Charles I, became a great collector of pictures and the patron of Rubens and Van Dyck. Charles' possessions included some magnificent furniture, much of which was probably of foreign origin. Although Inigo Jones was introducing the new Italian style in interiors of white and gold, most people continued to live in 'Jacobethan' homes, in rooms panelled in oak and hung with tapestries with which contemporary furniture, often inlaid and mostly carved, was in harmony. At Knole, Kent, much of the interior decoration is Jacobean in date but still Elizabethan in character.

Inventories, such as that of the Earl of Arundel's house near London, record a profusion of splendid pieces and decorative details: rooms with coloured hangings, their floors covered with tinted leather; chairs upholstered 'suteable' to the beds and hangings, and various tables, each one with its own cover of coloured leather or 'Turkey carpett'. Chests, two large trunks for linen, several wicker screens (usually beside a fire-place) and two small hanging brass clocks are entered, as well as at least one large looking-glass in an ebony frame. While furniture serving basic needs was evidently made in England, it is known that luxuries like large looking-glasses and fine cabinets were imported.

Native craftsmanship was good; pieces were made carefully, with mortise and tenon joints.

2

3

4

Museum Photo

Fig. 3 ***Farthingale chair***, *c.1645. Oak, covered with Turkey-work. The farthingale chair was left without arms in order not to crush the wide skirts of the period. (Victoria and Albert Museum.)*

Fig. 4 ***X-frame armchair*** *from the Spangle Bedroom, Knole, one of a set of four armchairs, c.1610–20. Red satin with appliquéd gold tissue. There is a portrait of James I at Knole sitting on a similar chair. (Knole, Kent.)*

Fig. 5 ***Armchair***, *mid-seventeenth century. Carved oak with inlaid decoration. (Victoria and Albert Museum.)*

Fig. 6 ***Chair***, *Shropshire, mid-seventeenth century. Walnut with knobbed turning. (Victoria and Albert Museum.)*

7

A. C. Cooper

Fig. 7 ***Dummy-board figure***, *English, c.1620. Cardboard. (Victoria and Albert Museum.)*

During the last twenty years or so before the Restoration, furniture was partially a simplification of the Elizabethan style. Aristocratic patronage was then rare, and Puritan taste discouraged anything savouring of levity; this naturally affected ornamentation.

Richly decorated with silver tissue appliqué motifs

Upholstered pieces existed in quantity in early Stuart times. The upholstered bed, always of prime importance, consisted of a light-weight frame entirely covered and hung with material. One Arundel piece had furnishing of red cloth, another of yellow and green sarcenet, a silk fabric. This furnishing included the canopy overhead as well as curtains, valances and the coverlet. A superb bed from the Spangle Bedroom (Fig. 11) at Knole is entirely furnished with red satin richly decorated with silver tissue appliqué motifs. The armchair and stools are covered 'suteable' to this important bed.

Frames of armchairs were closely covered with fabric, garnished with gold or silk fringes fastened on with gilt nails. Fine examples survive at Knole, including four X-frame armchairs (Fig. 4), some with matching footstool and each with a different cover appliquéd in satin, silver and cream brocade, green or crimson velvet. The straight backs end in finials, egg-shaped and usually banded with gilt nails. The arms, closely upholstered, are set low, curving down forward over the top of the front X-frame. A portrait at Knole of James I shows him in such a chair, much resembling one standing nearby in the same gallery. Other fine seats at Knole, besides stools in this style, include a settee with padded seat and a back with winged 'ear pieces'; also a day bed, rather similar but intended for reclining, since there is a hinged cushioned head-rest attached to the arm at each end (Fig. 1). A ratchet adjusts the couch to the height desired. Both these pieces have a plain framework.

Turning from these luxurious rarities, the amateur of antiques will find much of interest in the wood furniture of the period; the characteristic

Fig. 2 **Draw table,** *c.1600. Inlaid with sycamore and boxwood. The draw table was an Elizabethan innovation for the dining parlour and remained in common use until the Restoration. Two leaves concealed underneath the top could be pulled out to extend the table to about double its length. (Victoria and Albert Museum, London.)*

Fig. 8 **Writing-desk,** *early seventeenth century. Oak. The interior of this portable desk is fitted to hold an ink-pot and sand-box (for blotting). (Victoria and Albert Museum.)*

8

Museum Photo

5

6

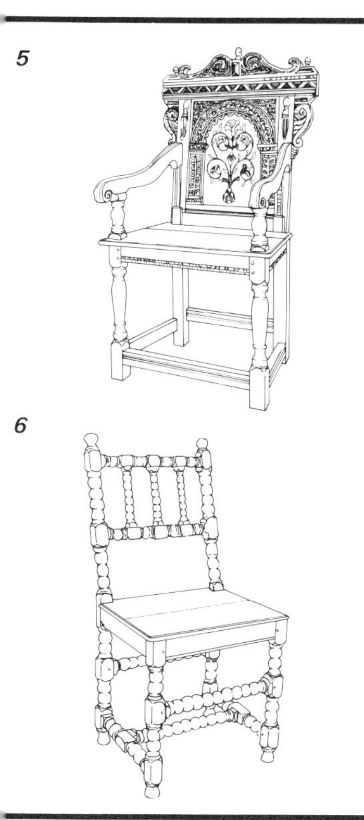

supports, baluster or columnar, or the occasional knobbed turning to seats (Fig. 6) and small tables; the continued presence of the bulb or vase, sometimes called cup and cover, conspicuous on bed-posts and legs of large tables; the various motifs favoured in carved ornament – fluting, gadrooning, strap-work, arcading, lunettes and acanthus or similar foliage. Oak was the chief wood, but elm, beech, birch and walnut are also seen, while bog oak, box, holly, pear and sycamore provided inlaid decoration in chequer patterns or somewhat naïve floral designs.

Like its Elizabethan predecessor, the Jacobean bedstead (Fig. 12) was richly carved, often inlaid, and sometimes painted and gilded, too. The panelled tester, or canopy, with its frieze and cornice, rested on a framed bedhead formed by two tiers of panels. The upper tier was filled with arcading, or on occasion with coats of arms in cartouches. The lower tier, usually concealed by the pile of bed-clothes and pillows, was plain. The two free-standing bedposts, usually crowned with an Ionic capital, stood on rectangular pedestals; the bulb, carved with gadrooning or acanthus, was still a feature. Originally such beds had their full complement of curtains, valances and coverlet of silk, velvet or embroidered linen. The trundle bed, hardly more than a frame on castors, and the settle bedstead, a composite piece, were also in use. Wicker cradles have perished, but discreetly carved oak examples exist.

The panel-back armchair sometimes had a cresting across the top, with a decorative pendant 'ear piece' at each end; the earlier inlaid decoration, usually floral, gave way presently to low-relief carving, often leafy, against a lightly-tooled background. The back, on plain uprights, is attached to the wooden seat, which may have its front and side rails inlaid (earlier) or carved with fluting (later).

The chair-table is another composite object, the oblong back being hinged to tilt forward and rest on the level arms, thus becoming a table-top. The farthingale chair, without arms, was made with a padded seat on columnar front legs, the small padded back was fixed across the plain back uprights, the legs being joined with stretchers. An example at the Victoria and Albert Museum (Fig. 3) is of oak, covered with bright Turkey-work. Forms had baluster legs, canted at an angle for stability, and united by stretchers. Many plain stools were provided as seats at the long dining-table since they could be readily stored beneath it.

Fig. 9 **Coffer,** *late seventeenth century. Pine, covered with leather and studded with brass-headed nails. Travelling trunks known as coffers were used for home storage as well as for luggage in the seventeenth century. They were often fitted inside across one end with a suspended lidded box to hold small objects. They were commonly covered with leather, as is this example, for protection, and the brass-headed nails with their complicated pattern served also to strengthen as well as to beautify the exterior. (Victoria and Albert Museum.)*

9

Museum Photo

Early 17th century English Furniture

Fig. 10 **Armchair**, *mid-seventeenth century. Oak, covered with Turkey-work. Brightly coloured Turkey-work was a popular style of needlework imitated from the hand-knotted carpets imported from Turkey; hence its name. (Victoria and Albert Museum.)*

Fig. 11 **Upholstered bed** *in the Spangle Bedroom, Knole, c.1610–20. Hangings and coverlet of red satin with silver tissue appliqué. This magnificent bed is part of a rare set including stools and chairs. (Knole, Kent.)*

Long tables of oak, or perhaps elm, chiefly used for meals, were supported on four, six, or eight legs, as length necessitated. Those with four legs were often fitted with a draw-leaf to extend at each end (Fig. 2). Supports continued to be bulbous, with gadrooning and acanthus and topped with Ionic capitals, but gradually they assumed a simpler baluster form. Decoration showed chequer or other inlay, or carved gadrooning or fluting, or perhaps a run of lunette motifs. The shovelboard table is similar, except for the top, which is marked at one end with transverse lines for the game. The long dining-table was superseded after the Restoration by the use of several gate-leg tables. Folding tables were not new; they occur in Tudor inventories. A number in the Arundel list have 'falling leaves' – falling or folding sides, suggesting the familiar piece with a fixed centre and a gate-support to a hinged flap on each side. Another is simply 'a little folding table'.

Other furniture includes pieces used for display or storage: dressers, cupboards and presses, chests and trunks. The dresser was of a height suitable for carving meat. Early Stuart examples are long, and fitted with a row of drawers over a range of cupboards; mouldings to drawer-fronts and door-panels are simple. Cupboards are in two categories: the court cupboard, with three tiers of open shelves, and the hall cupboard, enclosed above and below. An intermediate type was open below, with a recessed or splay-fronted cupboard above.

The court cupboard (Fig. 14) had a drawer under the top and middle shelves, with supports evolving from the bulbous vase to a simpler form. In rare examples, heraldic or grotesque beasts take their place. The hall cupboard often had two doors, variously panelled and with simple mouldings; the slightly-recessed upper cupboard again has corner supports to its frieze and cornice. Cupboards for food were made with open panels, usually filled with turned balusters and sometimes designed to hang as shelves. The press or wardrobe, fitted with pegs for clothes, sometimes had shelves for linen. Surviving examples show drawers either above or below the two panelled doors; these latter were often decorated with arcading or light strap-work.

Early Stuart chests with a name and date indicate a bridal chest

Although presses were becoming increasingly popular, the traditional chest was still in favour for clothes, household linen and even books. The panelled front continued to bear contemporary decoration, inlay or carved lunette or leafy scrolls. Early Stuart pieces with a name and year-date normally indicate a bridal chest. Chests were often fitted inside and across one end with a suspended lidded box to hold gauntlets and small objects. The hutch, with sloping top, had its front panels pierced in some decorative pattern, which suggests it was used as a bread cupboard. The coffer, or travelling trunk, with a curved top, is commonly found covered with leather and closely studded with a complex design in brass-headed nails (Fig. 9). There are records of some which were covered with coloured velvet.

Smaller objects of interest which to some extent reflect contemporary ornament include boxes, portable desks, shelves and spoon racks. Boxes were often used to hold Bibles, lace collars or gauntlet gloves. The portable desk is a box covered with a hinged sloping lid over an interior fitted to hold an ink-pot and a sand-box (Fig. 8). These were sometimes covered with crimson velvet, and open shelves, perhaps with an arcaded top, were sometimes carved on the front surfaces. Spoon racks are

12

Fig. 14 **Court cupboard,** *early seventeenth century. Bulletwood and satinwood. The court cupboard was used for display and storage and has three shelves and drawers. (Victoria and Albert Museum.)*

14

Fig. 12 **Bedstead,** c.*1610. Oak with painted shields bearing the arms of Cooper and Gilbert. This superb bed was probably made to commemorate the marriage of George Cooper and Anne Gilbert. Its height and length are both over seven feet. (Victoria and Albert Museum.)*

Fig. 13 **Armchair,** *early seventeenth century. Carved oak. This beautiful chair is unusually elaborate for the period. (Victoria and Albert Museum.)*

3

distinguished by the slotted rail or bar for these silver and pewter utensils, and incorporate a box below.

Furniture foreshadowing late Stuart standards of luxury include frames for pictures and looking-glasses; the rare small cabinet and the transitional chest-with-drawers. A very elaborate frame for a portrait of James I at Knole is carved with *putti* among running scrolls, painted and gilt. No doubt, judging from the Royal Accounts, King Charles' pictures were also fittingly framed.

Sober Commonwealth taste is represented by frames of ebonised wood, carved with ripple mouldings. Some early Stuart looking-glasses apparently had splendid frames possibly made by foreign craftsmen. Elaborate native work came in after the Restoration; but an occasional Commonwealth example may be seen, veneered with tortoise-shell. Cabinets, probably imported, are prominent in Stuart inventories, but some English examples exist. The effect presages the lacquer of Restoration days. The transitional chest-with-drawers is part-cabinet, part-chest, a mid-seventeenth century development. Examples show a deep drawer above or below, and doors enclosing smaller ones. The top may be hinged and the front may display carved architectural motifs or deeply-bevelled hexagonal or octagonal projecting panels.

A rather *décolletée* lady with a looking-glass in one hand

This brief account ends with a word on that charming conceit introduced from the Low Countries, the dummy-board figure. These were life-size, in contemporary costume dating from not earlier than *c.*1620. Cut from flat boards, and realistically painted, they were made to stand upright. In the Victoria and Albert Museum there is an elegant housemaid with her broom, and a rather *décolletée* lady with a looking-glass in one hand (Fig. 7). Single figures of children were also favourite subjects. These delightful creatures seem to have been placed about the house according to fancy, standing a few inches in front of the panelling.

MUSEUMS AND COLLECTIONS

Early Stuart and Commonwealth furniture is on view at the following museums:

Birmingham:	Aston Hall
Cardiff:	National Museum of Wales
London:	Victoria and Albert Museum
Oxford:	Ashmolean Museum

Also at the following houses that are open to the public:

Derbyshire:	Hardwick Hall
Cornwall:	Cotehele House
Gloucestershire:	Badminton House
Hertfordshire:	Hatfield House
Kent:	Knole
Lincolnshire:	Burghley House
Somerset:	Montacute House
Warwickshire:	Arbury Hall

FURTHER READING

English Furniture Styles by Ralph Fastnedge, London, reprinted 1969.

The Gentle Art of Faking Furniture by Herbert Cescinsky, London, reprinted 1969.

Furniture in England: The Age of the Joiner by S. W. Wolsey and R. W. P. Luff, London, 1968.

Stuart Furniture at Knole by Margaret Jourdain, London, 1952.

ENGLISH TILES

Dutch tiles were first imported into England early in the sixteenth century; these early examples tended to follow Italian designs and to reproduce Italian colours in a rougher, more highly coloured, version. The finest surviving example is the pavement at The Vyne, in Hampshire, which was laid in 1520. Throughout the sixteenth and seventeenth centuries, work in England adhered slavishly to the Dutch model; most of the manufacturers who set up in London were of Dutch origin, and only the growth of hostility towards the Netherlands at the end of the seventeenth century encouraged the beginnings of a recognisably English style. This style was greatly influenced by designs and motifs brought back from the East, particularly from India and the East Indies. By the middle of the eighteenth century, Lambeth, Bristol and Liverpool had emerged as the three main centres of production. In Bristol, John Bowen adhered to the traditional patterns of blue and white, while the Lambeth craftsmen specialised in the *famille verte* style. In Liverpool, Guy Green and John Sadler perfected the polychrome representation of flowers, scenes from nature and other *tableaux*. These two makers alone accounted for more than a hundred different styles of painted tile. These eighteenth-century tiles were generally called transfer tiles; the designs were transferred from an engraved copper plate on to a paper, and applied to the tile, face down. The image was then fixed by firing the tile a second time. These designs were often taken from mythological scenes, from Aesop's Fables and other popular writing. Portraits were not usual, but domestic scenes and scenes from the stage were common themes.

Collecting Hints

There are so many excellent copies made of old tiles that it is very hard to identify the genuine article. Look closely at the quality of the firing as sometimes the second firing was done hastily and the imprint not fixed properly.

Where To Buy

Antique shops quite often carry interesting examples – of framed tiles in particular. It is still worth patrolling the building sites in central London in the hope of beating one of the dealers to it.

Prices

These correspond roughly with prices asked for the porcelain of the period, and depend largely on the condition of the individual tile.

A collection of eighteenth century English tiles.

From the top: ***Adam and Eve,*** *Lambeth, from £2.50 (Private Collection).* ***Landscape,*** *one of a series in the style of John Bowen, Bristol, £5 (Tristram Jellinek).* ***'Mrs. Cibber in the Character of Monomia',*** *Susannah Maria (1714–66), wife of the actor and dramatist, Colley Cibber, and a well-known actress and singer in her own right (theatre tiles are always popular, notorious actors such as Garrick being the most expensive), Liverpool, from £20 (Private Collection).* ***Vase of flowers,*** *Lambeth, from £3 (Private Collection).* ***Cow,*** *Bristol, £5 (Tristram Jellinek).* ***Goat,*** *painted in manganese red, Bristol, £3–£4 (Private Collection).* ***Two goats,*** *Liverpool, from £5 (Tristram Jellinek).*

Over page: ***Peacock,*** *Liverpool, eighteenth century, from £15 (Private Collection).*

Private Collection: R. Todd-White

Masterpieces from Mortlake

George Wingfield Digby

1

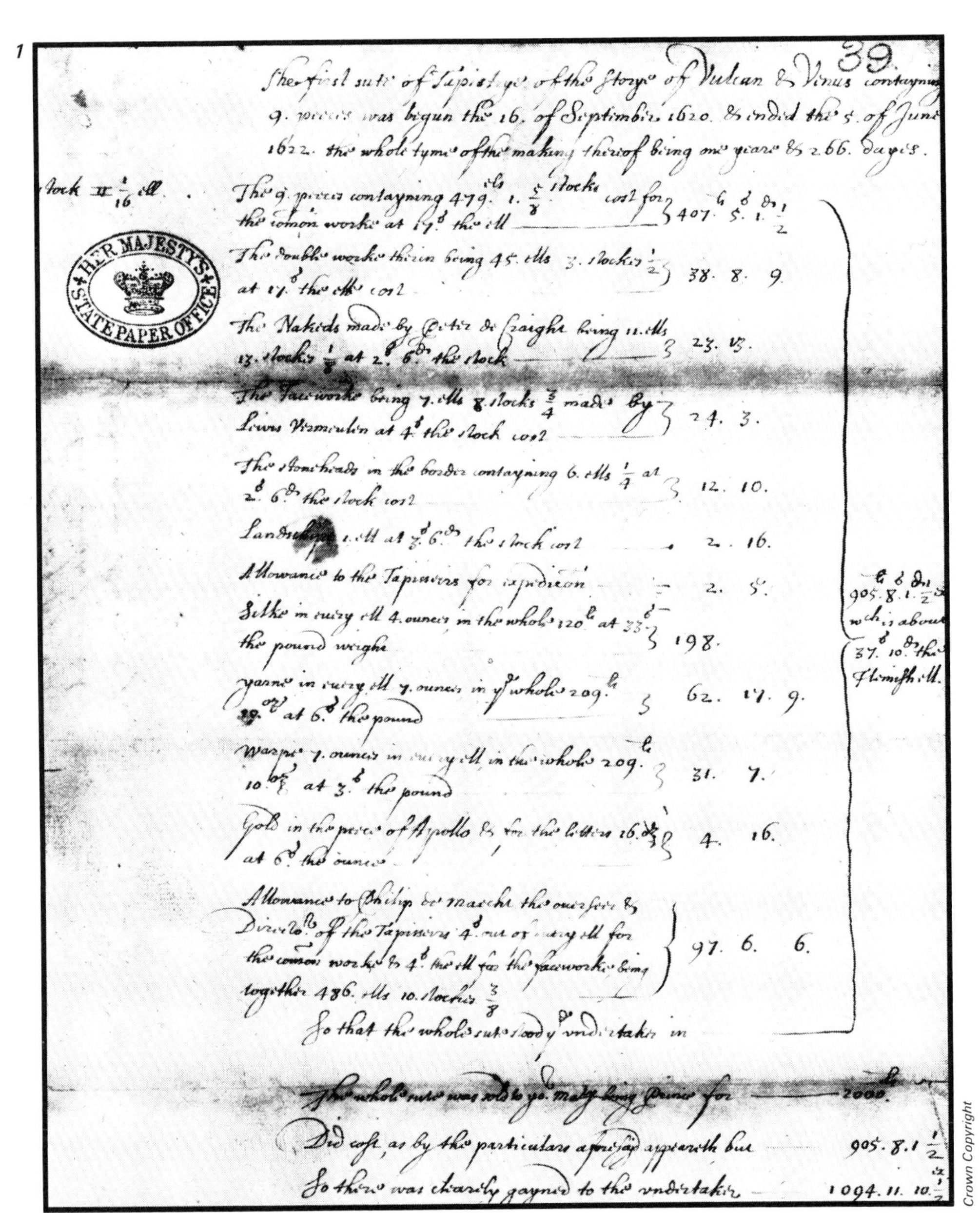

39.

The first sute of Tapistrye of the Storye of Vulcan & Venus contayning 9. peeces was begun the 16. of Septembre 1620. & ended the 5. of June 1622. the whole tyme of the making thereof being one yeare & 266. dayes.

The 9. peeces contayning 479. ells 1. 5/8 stocks the comon worke at 17s the ell cost for	407. 5. 1. 1/2
The double worke therin being 45. ells 3. stockes 1/2 at 17s the ell cost	38. 8. 9
The Nakeds made by Peter de [illegible] being 11. ells 13. stocks 1/8 at 2s. 6d the stock	23. 13.
The Faceworke being 7. ells 8. stocks 3/4 made by Lewis Vermeulen at 4s the stock cost	24. 3.
The stoneheads in the border contayning 6. ells 1/4 at 2s. 6d the stock cost	12. 10.
Landskipp 1. ell at 3s. 6d the stock cost	2. 16.
Allowance to the Tapissers for expedicon	2. 5.
Silke in every ell 4. ounces in the whole 120li at 33s the pound weight	198.
yarne in every ell 7. ounces in ye whole 209li 10oz at 6s the pound	62. 17. 9.
Warpe 7. ounces in every ell in the whole 209li 10oz at 3s the pound	31. 7.
Gold in the peece of Apollo & for the letters 16.oz at 6s the ounce	4. 16.
Allowance to Philip de Marche the overseer & Director of the Tapissers 4d out of every ell for the comon worke & 4s the ell for the faceworke being together 486. ells 10. stockes 3/8	97. 6. 6.

li s d 905. 8. 1. 1/2 wch is about 37s. 10d the Flemish ell.

So that the whole sute stood ye undertaker in

The whole sute was sold to ye Matie being Prince for — 2000li.

Did cost, as by the particulars aforesaid appeareth but — 905. 8. 1 1/2

So there was clearly gayned to the undertaker — 1094. 11. 10.

Fig. 1 *Document showing the working expenses of the first set of* ***The Story of Vulcan and Venus*** *tapestries at Mortlake, 1620–22. (Public Record Office, London.)*

Set up by James I to rival the great tapestry-works of Paris and Flanders, the Mortlake factory produced hangings of great intricacy and sumptuousness

The name Mortlake has been attached to a wide range of tapestries woven in England during the seventeenth century and varying greatly in quality. The most important period of Mortlake was from its foundation under James I in 1619 lasting until Charles I's dispute with Parliament, which led to open civil war in 1642.

The art-loving Charles, as Prince of Wales, was the chief patron of Mortlake at its inception and it was for himself, his wealthier friends and courtiers that the principal sets were woven in the 1620s and '30s. He and the Duke of Buckingham paid up to £2,000 (£40,000 by modern standards) for their best sets of tapestries of eight pieces, woven with silk and gold and silver thread as well as the basic wools, and with their arms and ciphers in the borders. In addition to the usual toll of usage and time, many of the finest works of the Mortlake weavers left England at the time of the sale of the Royal Collections under the early Commonwealth between 1649 and 1652 (although a few were bought for the Protector). The tapestries of the later Mortlake period are much more numerous but, with few exceptions, not of comparable quality.

Briefly, they divide into four main periods. The first great period of Charles I, 1619–42; secondly, the Commonwealth, 1650–60, when Mortlake work was resuscitated under the directorship of Sir Gilbert Pickering and at least one important new set was woven; thirdly, the Restoration period, first with Sir Sackville Crow (1662–1727), then the Earl of Craven and associates as proprietors; Francis Poyntz was technical director during part of this period; and, finally, the last period with changing proprietors among whom Lord (Ralph) Montagu was the most influential; he was the son of

2

Museum Photo

Fig. 2 **Abraham, Hagar and Ishmael,** *1657–58. 11 ft. 2 ins. x 9 ft. 1 in. Sarah is expelling Hagar, who carries the infant Ishmael, while Abraham looks on. The background scenes depict Hagar leaving Ishmael to die, and praying as the angel appears. (Victoria and Albert Museum, London.)*

Museum Photo

Fig. 3 *Detail from* ***The Gods Discovering the Amours of Mars and Venus*** *(see Fig. 6). This detail shows the fine quality of the Mortlake workmanship. At the top right is the monogram 'C' of Charles, Prince of Wales before his accession as Charles II in 1660. (Victoria and Albert Museum.)*

Fig. 4 *Detail of* ***Abraham, Hagar and Ishmael*** *(see Fig. 2). This charming detail illustrates the Stuart love of elaborate and grotesque borders, even on tapestries of religious subjects where they would hardly seem appropriate. Also clearly visible is the Mortlake mark, a red cross on a white shield; this mark was used again later by the London workshops, since it is also the arms of the City of London. (Victoria and Albert Museum.)*

the second Lord Montagu of Boughton, obtaining charge of the Great Wardrobe in 1670, and he had an active partner in his sister Lady Harvey, niece of the Countess of Rutland. His collections are still in part at Boughton and Bowhill, belonging to his descendant, the Duke of Buccleuch. Mortlake was finally wound up in 1703. But from as early as 1670 several of the best weavers had left Mortlake and started workshops of their own in Lambeth and other parts of London. One of them at least, Francis Poyntz, was attached to the Great Wardrobe which was responsible for supplying the Crown with furnishings and repair-work.

In founding tapestry-workshops at Mortlake on the Thames, James I's advisers were thinking in terms of the mercantile system; rather than buy expensive hangings from Brabant it was better to foster the manufacture at home, particularly as England was strong in the chief raw material, wool. There was also the incentive of creating something fine and artistically individual for the Court of St. James; to foster this the young Charles, who had studied in Italy, was keen to lend his energies and his discriminating eye for the Italian masters.

Every prince in Europe thought in this way, and nothing was more showy in the *décor* of that age than fine suites of tapestry. The precedent afforded by Henri IV of France, who had set up extensive new tapestry-workshops some ten years earlier in Paris manned entirely by Flemish weavers, was studied and fairly closely followed. Sir Francis Crane, a secretary of Charles who had recently been knighted and was a Member for Cornwall, was put in charge. Money was raised by the creation of four baronetcies (for which the recipients had to pay heavily), and further grants and mortgages of land raised the necessary capital. Fifty weavers from the Low Countries – the main recruiting grounds being Brussels, Bruges and Oudenarde – were spirited over despite the stringent laws that existed there against emigration; Crane had the necessary buildings ready for them on their arrival early in 1620. They were given full citizenship, free lodging, and exemption from taxes, with wages and all materials found; rights of worship (very necessary at that time) were also provided for. They undertook to produce a certain quantity of tapestry per year and to train apprentices. The weavers included Philip de Maecht as head of workshops, originally from Middleburg and before that

Museum Photo

Brussels (his cipher appears on several of the best extant tapestries), who had somehow been wrested from the Paris workshops. His sons married English girls and many of the other names, such as Louis Vermoulen, Van den Steen, Peter Schrijuer, Hollenberch, Benood and De May crop up again two or three generations later.

But the most important and exciting prerequisite for a successful manufacture was first-class models for the cartoons, backed by an able designer. The latter was Francis Cleyn from Mettlenburg, who had been recommended to Charles when studying in Italy. The cartoons were either developed from the best sixteenth-century tapestries in the Royal Collections (*Vulcan and Venus*), or were designed by Cleyn (*Hero and Leander*) or especially commissioned. Unfortunately Van Dyck's project was so ambitious and expensive that it never got off the ground. But Prince Charles made a coup in Genoa in 1623 (he was in Madrid at the time), by buying seven of Raphael's original cartoons for the Sistine Chapel, *The Acts of the Apostles*. Much of Mortlake's prestige in the early years undoubtedly rested on these cartoons, copied for the looms by Francis Cleyn and two of his three sons.

The first set on the looms was *The Story of Vulcan and Venus* in nine hangings, begun in September 1620 and delivered to the King in June 1622. (Fig. 1.) Two more sets of the same series were ready by May 1625, which indicates something of the speed of work. Although the Mortlake charter allowed for high and low-warp looms, it seems most unlikely that anything but low-warp was used (except possibly for portraits) despite the fact that Mazarin's inventory of 1652 gives three *Vulcan* pieces as high-warp, and Louis XIV's inventory does the same for the leading royal *Acts* set (with two others given as low-warp).

Mazarin's was presumably the second set woven for Buckingham with gold and silver; it was presented in 1657 to Charles X of Sweden by Louis XIV and part of it is still in the Swedish Royal Collections. It was possibly the third set which now hangs at St. James's Palace; it has the Prince

5

Museum Photo

6

Museum Photo

Fig. 5 Autumn, *one of a series of* **The Months and Seasons,** *1699–1719, 9 ft. 1 in. x 6 ft. 9 ins. This lively scene depicts all the different steps of the vintage with remarkable accuracy, surrounded by a simple border of fruits and flowers. The tapestry is dated to the last period of Mortlake by the arms of Lord Shelburne. (Ham House, Surrey.)*

Fig. 6 *Large detail from* **The Gods Discovering the Amours of Mars and Venus,** *c.1630–40. Overall size of the tapestry 15 x 18 ft. Probably woven for Charles II when he was Prince of Wales, it bears his motto 'Ich Dien', his monogram 'C' and his symbolic plumes at the top left. (Victoria and Albert Museum.)*

of Wales' feathers in the borders. The fine piece in the Victoria and Albert Museum showing *The Gods Discovering the Amours of Mars and Venus* (Figs. 3 and 6), may have been woven a little later for Charles II when Prince of Wales; it also has the feathers, 'Ich Dien' and the monogram 'C'. The adaptation of the cartoons from Henry VIII's sixteenth century Brussels set was accredited by Crow to Rivière, possibly Giacomo della Riviera who did work for the Barberini workshops in Rome.

In 1623 Francis Cleyn arrived as principal designer, and was given his own house at Mortlake; *The Months and Seasons* in eight pieces were begun; they were another adaptation of an earlier tapestry with new borders and generally arranged in double panels. James I wrote to Charles in Madrid: 'Sir Francis Crane desires to know if my baby will have him to hasten the making of that suite of tapestry that he commended him'. In December 1623 Charles ordered £500 to be paid against them. One of these, with gold and silver and the insignia of the Prince of Wales, can be seen hanging at Windsor. Others of the set are in store and at Holyrood Palace. There are pieces from another early set at Clandon (Surrey) and in Genoa, all with similar attractive borders.

When Raphael's cartoons for *The Acts of the Apostles*, bought for £300 in 1623, arrived in London, Francis Cleyn had to make careful copies to be cut in strips for the looms. He also designed fitting borders. Charles I succeeded his father early in 1625 and made a great financial effort for Mortlake. His set of *The Acts* with magnificent borders, the royal arms, a Latin inscription and the attribution '*Cav: Re: Reg: Mortl:*' is now in the French Mobilier National; one piece from the set, *The Sacrifice at Lystra*, may be seen in the Louvre. The quality of the work with its varied threads of wool, silk, gold and silver is magnificent and it is in such splendid condition that one may judge what a standard the best Mortlake tapestry reached in the early days of Charles I's reign.

But before we try to assess the claims made for Mortlake, we must continue the list of tapestries woven under Charles I and Sir Francis Crane which can still be seen in reasonable condition. *The Five Senses* were in the contemporary manner of grotesques with pictorial cartouches and matching borders. A set survives at Haddon Hall (Fig. 7) bearing Crane's and Philip de Maecht's ciphers, but unfortunately in poor condition. The *Story of Hero and Leander* was a happy choice in view of Christopher Marlowe's poem; it was a new subject for tapestry. The finest example, probably the first King's set, is now in the Swedish Royal Collections and it has been there certainly since 1656. At Lyme Hall (Cheshire) are four pieces with Crane's and De Maecht's initials; the fifth piece,

Fig. 7 Smelling, *one of five tapestries of* ***The Five Senses****, early seventeenth century. This beautiful series was probably made for Charles I at the time when Sir Francis Crane was director of the Mortlake works. The Senses was a popular seventeenth-century subject for both painting and tapestry. This example depicts a young lady smelling a flower, in a central cartouche surrounded by grotesques typical of the period and an elaborate border which matches those of the other four tapestries in the set. (Haddon Hall, Rutland. By courtesy of His Grace the Duke of Rutland.)*

7

Hero mourning over the drowned Leander, is in the Victoria and Albert Museum and the sixth piece was burnt at Brussels in 1903.

One survivor from the *Royal Horses* set, another of Cleyn's inventions, is almost certainly the beautiful *St. George slaying the Dragon* at Ingatestone Hall (Essex). Then there is a fine chapel tapestry, *The Supper at Emmaus*, which copies Titian's painting owned by Charles I and is now in the Louvre. Three versions are known, one in St. John's College, Oxford, woven entirely in wool and silk, another in St. George's Chapel, Windsor, and one in the chapel at Hardwick Hall (Derbyshire), in very poor condition. Lastly, we come to portraits in tapestry: the *Sir Francis Crane* after Van Dyck belonging to Lord Petre is very fine as is the double portrait of Van Dyck and Sir Endymion Porter (after the Madrid picture, Fig. 3, p. 147) at Knole.

A reputation for variety and excellence

Bearing these tapestries in mind, it is not difficult to understand Mortlake's high reputation. When King Charles visited the workshops in March 1629, he might well have felt the palaces of London would soon rival even those of Paris when it came to fine hangings. But the perspective of history has a sobering effect. The De la Planche and Comans workshops of Paris had a designer of genius in Simon Vouet and in the 1620s Rubens had sketched *The Story of Constantine* for their looms, which were quite as ably manned as Mortlake's; the output also was much greater and lasted longer. In Brussels much of the vast production was only of commercial quality, but one has only to think of Rubens' *Apotheosis of the Eucharist* (1625–30), still in the Monastery of the Descalzas Reales in Madrid, and Jordaen's *Country Life*, *Proverbs* and *Ménagerie* (or *Riding Lessons*) to realise what the competition was in that quarter century; the Habsburg tapestries in Vienna show what quality the best Brussels workshops could produce.

8

Fig. 8 *Detail from* May, *one of a series of* **The Months and Seasons**, *1699–1719. Overall size of the tapestry 9 ft. 1 in. x 10 ft. 1½ ins. Like many of the later Mortlake tapestries, this was designed not for a royal palace but for an ordinary large house. It is therefore on a smaller scale than earlier ones, and has a simpler, narrower border which matches those of the other tapestries in the series (see Fig. 5). (Ham House, Surrey.)*

Mortlake's reputation was nonetheless high, as Cardinal Mazarin's purchases prove. Francis Cleyn's fame as a painter and designer was widespread at the time and Sandy's edition of Ovid's *Metamorphoses*, with his illustrations, was printed in Paris five years after the London edition; his books of engraved ornaments and illustrations to Ogilby's Classics came out rather later, in the 1640s and '50s. His designs of elaborate borders for the tapestries were very accomplished but in the same style as was favoured in Paris. The Louvre *Sacrifice at Lystra* proves that at its best Mortlake was irreproachable, but the great period was short-lived and no great Flemish artist was commissioned for designs; the misconception that Rubens' *Story of Achilles* was woven at Mortlake probably rests on the fact that Charles I presented a set to his daughter Henrietta for her wedding; it was woven by Van der Strecken and Van Liefdael in Brussels.

Returning now to the later years of Mortlake, there was one notable new subject woven under the Commonwealth, the *Triumph of Caesar* after Mantegna's ten murals which Charles had bought from the Duke of Mantua in 1628. Among the few recorded pieces there is a set at Bowhill House, Selkirk, in three pieces. Those beautiful paintings perhaps demanded too much of the weavers.

At the time of the Stuart restoration, Mortlake still depended on its old cartoons for five or six subjects with a few new ones added, for the weaving establishment had been greatly reduced. Sir Sackville Crow as proprietor, with Verrio replacing Cleyn as designer, made a brave start and some of the best later sets of *Vulcan and Venus*, *The Acts* and *Hero and Leander* probably came from this period. The *Hunters' Chase*, a derivative set first recorded as woven for the Dutch Church in London in 1645–46, was once found in many great English houses. *Horses* was an idea of Cleyn's, taking episodes from mythology with a central equestrian figure.

More interesting and very much in demand were the various *Playing Boys* suites, referred to as *Bacchanalia*, *Naked Boys*, and *Pollidore*. The latter name confirms the view that Francis Cleyn took as his model two pictures by Polidoro Caldara. Cleyn used these designs for mural decoration at Ham House. In tapestry, the subject of children at play goes back to the early sixteenth century and beyond, but Cleyn's designs have a gaiety of their own. The known pieces are many and varied; those at Boughton, Hardwick Hall and Cotehele may be mentioned. The first recorded set was delivered by Francis Poyntz to Charles II in 1668. Since Poyntz styled himself His Majesty's chief arras worker and was in charge of the Great Wardrobe in the 1670s, tapestries associated with his name, such as the *Naval Battle of Sole Bay* (at Hampton Court and Greenwich), must doubtfully be termed Mortlake. The work of the distinguished John Vanderbank can certainly not be so named. But ex-Mortlake weavers, such as William Benood, who set up independent workshops in London taking with them copies of the old cartoons, continued to use the mark of a red cross on a white shield, since it is the arms of the City of London.

The later Mortlake tapestries were no longer chiefly woven for royal palaces, but for rooms in London and country houses. The scale of the design therefore tends to be reduced, and simple borders are definitely preferred. *The Months and Seasons* Figs. 5 and 8) at Ham House are good examples of the later style. At this time, the Wauters workshops in Antwerp were also competing in the English market with their own versions of favourite English subjects. They can be recognised because many pieces bear the Wauters cipher, and both the designs and the scale and style of the work are somewhat different.

Early Mortlake work is virtually unobtainable except for fragments and borders. Though varied in quality and condition, however, the later tapestries are still plentiful. Old restoration and the possibility and cost of new restoration are key factors in determining a reasonable acquisition. The study of known designs and sets will usually make an attribution possible.

FURTHER READING

'Tapestries by the Wauters Family of Antwerp for the English Market' by George Wingfield Digby in **La Tapisserie Flamande aux XVII et XVIII siècle**, Brussels, 1960.

English Tapestries of the Eighteenth Century by H. C. Marillier, London, 1930.

Tapestry Weaving in England by W. G. Thomson, London, 1914.

1

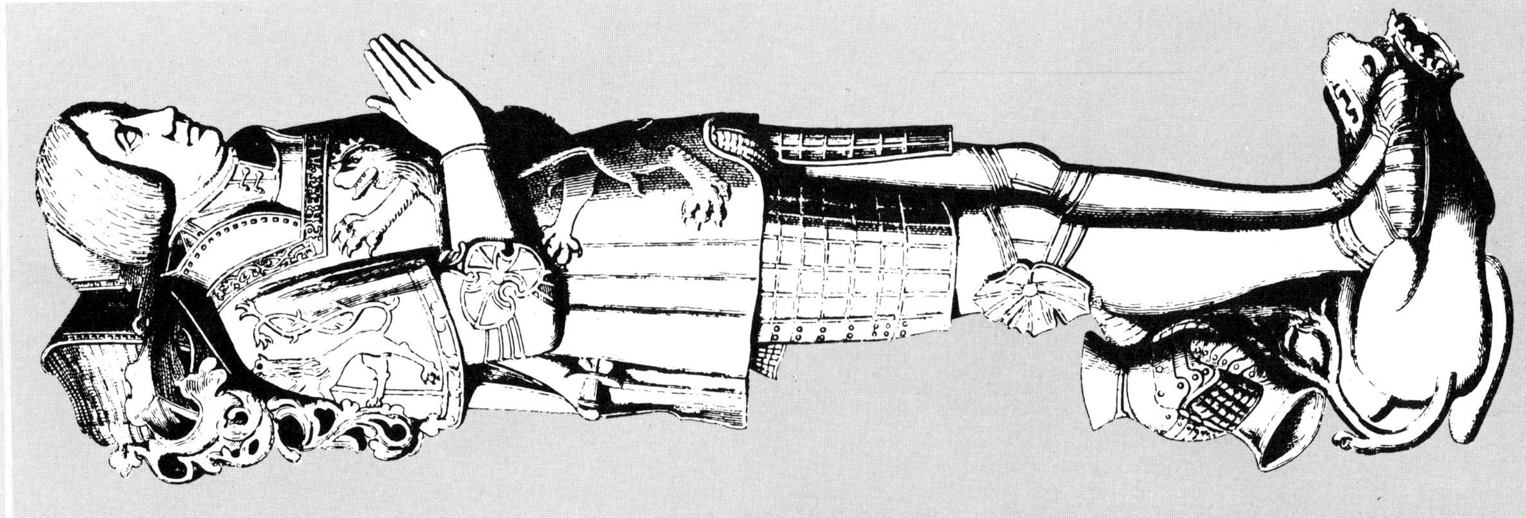

The Cuirass and the Garniture

Claude Blair

Beautifully decorated with gold, silver and elaborate engravings, armour became progressively less useful against newly-introduced firearms, and finally died out in the Civil War.

The history of English armour in the sixteenth century is dominated by the figure of Henry VIII who, when he came to the throne in 1509, was equipped by both education and natural inclination to be a renaissance monarch in the grand manner. An excellent scholar and musician, he was also tall, handsome and a great athlete with a special love of the tournament and all the military arts. The cultural and artistic resources of the country, which were still largely medieval, were not sufficient to meet his needs and he soon turned to the Continent to seek artists and craftsmen willing to come and work for him in England.

Where armour was concerned, Henry appears to have found that the native industry was not even capable of producing the large quantities of cheap harnesses he required for re-equipping his army, and the records of his reign contain many references to their importation. This was nothing new, for the English armourers, who were never apparently of more than local importance, had always had to face heavy competition from the Continent; and not only where cheap armour was concerned, for there is ample evidence to show that those who could afford to do so ordered their personal equipment from Italy, Germany or the Netherlands. It is probably for this reason that the armour shown on the effigies, brasses and portraits which, apart from the products of the Tudor royal workshop, provide our main source of information about English fashions, is virtually indistinguishable from that found on the Continent (Fig. 1).

Covered with silver, gilt, and engraved with roses and pomegranates

Henry VIII was not content merely to buy his personal armour on the Continent; he wanted his own workshop capable of producing harness equal to that obtainable abroad. So, in 1511, he invited two groups of foreign armourers to come and work for him in England. One group came from Milan and the other from Brussels, to be set up in their own workshops at Greenwich Palace. Nothing made by the Belgians is known to survive, but the Milanese were certainly responsible for at least one magnificent harness preserved, with the remnants of the old royal armoury, in the Tower of London Armouries. Made for the King, probably in 1515, its surface is entirely covered with silver – originally gilt – and engraved with roses and pomegranates involving the badges of Henry and Catherine of Aragon and framing figures of

Fig. 1 ***Monument to Sir John Peche*** *in Lullingstone Churc[h], Kent, 1552. Engraving. Like most armour on effigie[s] this suit differs little from continental models.*

Fig. 2 ***Armour of Charles I,*** *traditionally made in Londo[n] and presented to Charles by either the City Corporation o[r] Armourers' Company, c.16[...] Gilt and decorated with punched scroll-work. (Tower of London Armourie[s])*

Fig. 3 ***Armour of Henry VI[II]*** *Greenwich, dated 1540. Decorated with etched an[d] bands, apparently based on designs by Hans Holbein th[e] Younger. This is the foot-co[mbat] suit from a garniture for war [and] tournament. (Tower of London Armourie[s])*

Fig. 4 ***Armour of Henry VI[II]*** *Greenwich, c.1520. Undecorated. This armour was intended f[or] use by the young King in foot combat. (Tower of London Armourie[s])*

Crown Copyright: Ministry of Public Building and Works

3

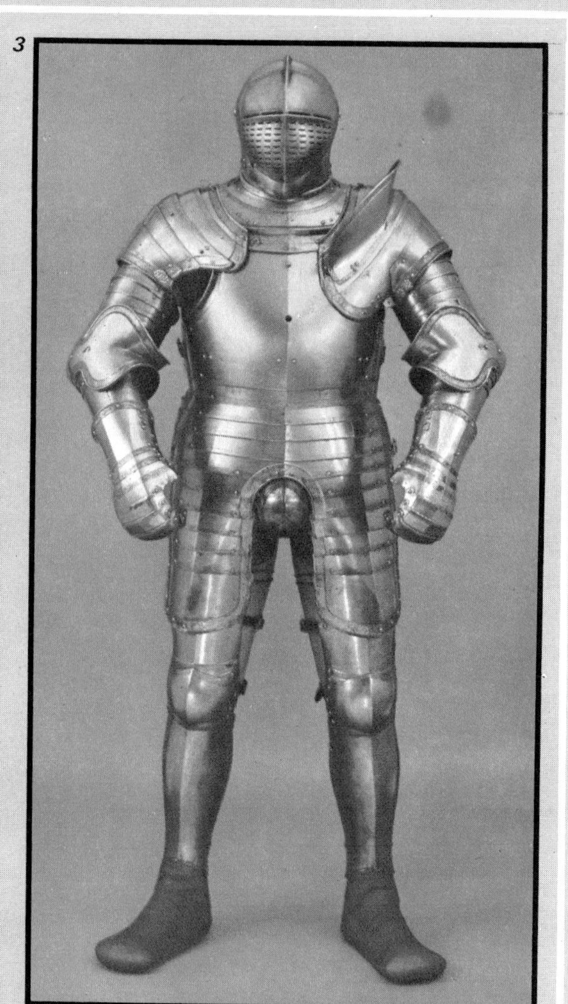

Crown Copyright: Ministry of Public Building and Works

4

Crown Copyright: Ministry of Public Building and Works

16th and early 17th century English Armour

Fig. 5 ***Jack,*** *English, c.1585–99.*
Canvas and iron.
Jacks were tunics worn by foot soldiers and their construction was simple. Overlapping plates of iron were laced between two layers of canvas; the collar and skirt were sometimes reinforced with mail.
(Tower of London Armouries.)

5

6

Fig. 6 **Harquebus armour of James II** *by Richard Hoden of London, 1686. Decorated with fine engraving and with its face defence pierced with the royal coat of arms and monogram. Armour of this kind was worn by harquebusiers, who were cavalry armed with carbines, like Cromwell's famous Ironsides.*
(Tower of London Armouries.)

7

Museum Photo

Fig. 7 ***Armour of George Clifford, 3rd Earl of Cumberland,*** *Greenwich c.1585. Clifford became Elizabeth I's Champion in 1590. (The Metropolitan Museum of Art, New York, Munsey Fund.)*

8

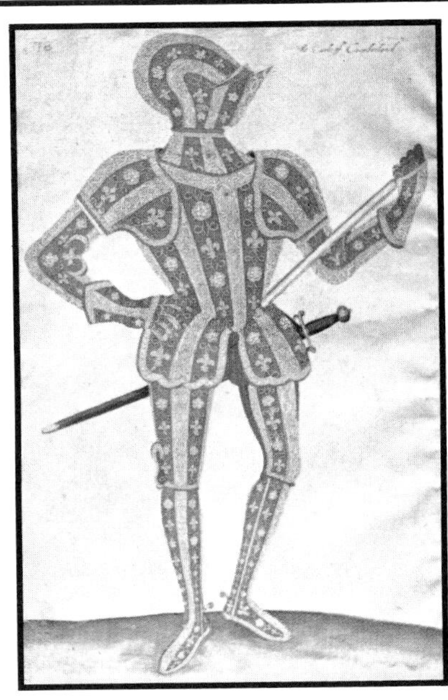

Fig. 8 ***Drawing*** *of the armour of George Clifford, 3rd Earl of Cumberland (Fig. 7), from the so-called* Jacobe Album, *Greenwich, 1556–87.*
The Jacobe Album *is a key document in the study of armour, thought to have been produced under the direction of the German master workman at Greenwich, Jacob Halder. It contains drawings for thirty armours made in the shop at that period.*
(Victoria and Albert Museum, London.)

Fig. 9 ***Drawing*** *of the extra pieces for the armour of George Clifford, 3rd Earl of Cumberland, from the* Jacobe Album *(Fig. 8), Greenwich 1556–87.*
An important continental innovation at the Greenwich workshop was the use of garnitures; these consisted of exchange and reinforcing pieces which allowed the basic suit to be used for different forms of tournament or field service.
(Victoria and Albert Museum.)

9

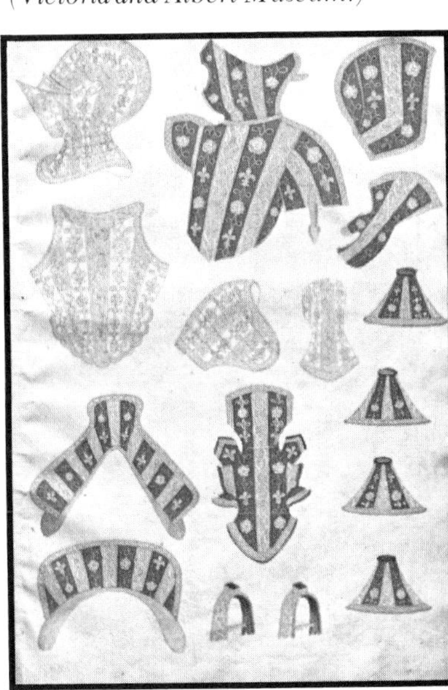

St. Barbara and St. George.

In 1515, Henry decided that his armoury should be extended, and in May of that year he set up a much bigger workshop at Greenwich. Staffed at first by eleven German and Flemish armourers – described in the records as 'Almains' – it was to remain active until the outbreak of the Civil War. For almost the whole of this period it was concerned exclusively with the manufacture of armour for the monarch's own person or for those people who were given permission to patronise it, a privilege for which they had to pay handsomely. The result was that for most of its existence the workshop was never required to make cheap, purely military, armour and a very high standard of production was maintained almost to the end.

A striking picture of Henry's development from an athletic youth to a gross old man

The earliest surviving Greenwich armours were nearly all made for Henry himself and they provide a striking picture of his development from the athletic young man, described by the first chroniclers of his reign (Fig. 4), to the gross figure that is the popular modern image of the King. All show features that derive from continental sources, but these are accompanied by details – notably in the form and construction of the helmets and shoulder-defences – that appear to be unique to the Greenwich workshop and which continued to appear in all its products.

One important continental innovation that the workshop was probably responsible for introducing into this country was the multiple armour, or garniture, as it is now usually called. This comprised a set of exchange and reinforcing pieces from which the different types of armour required for different forms of tournament or field service – heavy cavalry, light cavalry or infantry – could be constructed. These obviated the need for an entirely separate suit for each. From the 1520s onwards many of the Greenwich armours were simplified garnitures, a characteristic example being the one in the Tower Armouries, which was made for Henry in 1540 (Fig. 3). It is of particular interest in that the etched and gilt bands with which it is decorated appear to be based on designs by Hans Holbein the Younger.

The tournament became an elaborate theatrical performance

Despite the fact that from 1553 to 1603 the English throne was occupied by women, the Greenwich workshop continued to flourish, though it now worked exclusively for the aristocracy. Under Elizabeth I the tournament became, as never before, a courtly game forming part of the elaborate theatrical performances in which the aristocracy participated. There was thus a demand for finely made and finely decorated armour.

It is to this period that the key document for the study of the armoury belongs, the so-called *Jacobe Album* (Figs. 8 and 9). Now in the Victoria and Albert Museum, it is a volume of coloured line-drawings representing thirty armours with their extra pieces, both for the field and the tilt, made in the Greenwich workshop between 1556 and 1587. Each drawing is inscribed with the name of the person for whom the armour was made, the names, with one exception, all being those of Queen Elizabeth's courtiers. Two drawings also bear the name *Jacobe*, undoubtedly that of the German master workman at Greenwich, Jacob Halder, who held office from 1576 to 1608.

A number of armours illustrated in the Album survive, mostly in the Tower Armouries and the Metropolitan Museum, New York, while a few others are known from portraits. They include the armours of the Queen's Champions, Sir Henry Lee and George Clifford, Earl of Cumberland, of her favourites Robert Dudley, Earl of Leicester (Fig. 10), and Sir Christopher Hatton, and of such great noblemen as the earls of Worcester and Pembroke. The best preserved is the armour made for George Clifford in about 1585 (Fig. 7). In the Metropolitan Museum, it is a small garniture comprising a basic suit and a series of extra pieces for use in both the field and the tournament. The surfaces, which are in almost original condition, are blued except where they are crossed by recessed gilt bands etched with strap-work and foliage involving the Queen's initials. No other surviving armour evokes so clearly the colourful and splendid sight that a major Elizabethan tournament must have presented to the spectator.

The harnesses illustrated in the Album represent the best of the Greenwich workshop's production during the period that it covers. The greater part of its staff's time was, however, taken up with the manufacture of plain armours for the less wealthy members of the aristocracy.

The workshop continued to produce both decorated and plain armours of the same type during the remainder of the century but, in the absence of the second volume of the Album that almost certainly existed, we know rather less about them.

The advent of James I, a monarch notoriously opposed to warlike pursuits, marked the beginning of the decline of the Greenwich workshop. Under him, and more especially under his successor Charles I, the purely theatrical masque gradually supplanted the tournament as the popular form of entertainment at Court, and the demand for the workshop's services was reduced. A few finely decorated suits were still produced, notably one made in 1610 for Henry, Prince of Wales, now at Windsor Castle, which is of particular interest in that we know that the then master workman at Greenwich, William Pickering, was paid £340 for making it. The majority of surviving armours from this period are, however, quite plain. In 1630, as a result of complaints about abuses, the armoury was reorganised and apparently set to work making armour for the royal forces. It survived until the early years of the Civil War, but its glory had departed.

From the early seventeenth century onwards rather more information is available about the London armourers. This is chiefly because in 1599 the Armourers' Company began to mark its members' products with an A under a crown – replaced by a helmet during the Interregnum – so that for the first time they can be readily identified. All that are known to survive are of sound serviceable quality but, apart from a few half-suits made for commanders of pikemen, they

16th and early 17th century English Armour

are completely plain and functional.

There is, however, one elaborate suit of *c.*1630 in the Tower Armouries which, though unmarked, has some claim to a London manufacture; according to an old tradition, it was presented to Charles I by either the City Corporation or the Armourers' Company (Fig. 2). Well made, but clumsy in outline, its whole surface is gilded and covered with fine punched scroll-work.

By the outbreak of the Civil War in 1642 the use of full armour was everywhere on the decline. It could only be made effective against the improved firearms of the period by increasing its weight almost unbearably. Most cavalrymen followed the already well-established fashion of confining defensive equipment to a cuirass, an open helmet usually with a peak and a barred face-guard, and an elbow-length gauntlet for the bridle-arm. This was worn over a long skirted coat of buff leather that was thick enough to turn a sword-cut. The pikeman continued to wear half-armour, without arm-defences, accompanied by an open helmet with a brim. Functionalism was more than ever the keynote and the many armours of this kind that survive are mostly serviceable but rather rough.

After the Restoration the use of armour of all kinds declined rapidly, and with it the armourers' craft. Nevertheless, at least one English armourer was still capable of producing very good work as late as 1686. This is demonstrated by an armour made in that year for James II by Richard Hoden, of London, now in the Tower Armouries (Fig. 6). Though basically a simple horseman's armour of the kind described above, it is of much finer quality than was usual; the face-guard is formed of a plate elaborately pierced and gilt with the King's arms and monogram in place of the usual bars, while it is elsewhere decorated with bands of engraved trophies, all originally gilt.

10

Fig. 10 ***Henry Hastings, K.G., 3rd Earl of Huntingdon*** *(1535–95), in a Greenwich armour, anonymous, 1588. Oil on canvas. This magnificent armour is shown in the* Jacobe Album *as the property of Hastings' brother-in-law and Queen Elizabeth's favourite, Robert Dudley, Earl of Leicester (d.1588). It is decorated with elaborately etched and gilt bands and the bear and ragged staff device of the Dudley family. (Tower of London Armouries.)*

HINTS TO COLLECTORS

The best that most collectors in the field of English armour can aspire to is one of the late sixteenth-century close-helmets of Italian form. They usually have a skull with a fairly high roped comb, a pointed two-piece visor with a stepped sight, pivoted at the same point on either side as the chin piece, deep gorget-plates and, an especially distinctive feature, locking-catches formed as pivoted hooks. Examples appear occasionally in the sale-rooms and the trade and normally sell for prices that are comparatively modest. Many have iron funerary-crest spikes (or traces thereof) and heavily patinated surfaces bearing signs of painted scroll-work, indicating that they once hung in churches. Before acquiring such a piece the collector would be very well advised to make sure that it has not appeared in the market as a result of one of the many recent thefts from churches: otherwise, he might find himself in the position of having to return it without compensation.

The vast majority of English armour that is offered for sale dates from the seventeenth century, and especially from the period of the Civil War. The commonest pieces are the rather rough Civil War cavalry-troopers' cuirasses and three-barred helmets, but pieces of better-quality pikeman's armour, including occasionally complete suits, do sometimes appear, as do also the long bridle-gauntlets of the period.

MUSEUMS AND COLLECTIONS

English armour of the sixteenth and seventeenth centuries are on view at the following:

Museums

Glasgow: Art Gallery and Museum

London: London Museum
Tower of London Armouries
Wallace Collection

York: Castle Museum

Houses open to the public

Berkshire: Littlecote, near Hungerford
Windsor Castle

Hertfordshire: Hatfield House

Warwickshire: Warwick Castle

FURTHER READING

The Silvered Armour of King Henry VIII in the Tower of London by Claude Blair, reprinted from *Archaeologia*, XCIX, Oxford, 1965.

Tower of London Armouries catalogue of **Exhibition of Armour made in the Royal Workshops at Greenwich**, London, 1951.

Fragmenta Armamentaria by F. H. Cripps-Day, privately printed by the author, Frome, 1934–52.

Dispersal and Development in Plate

Judith Banister

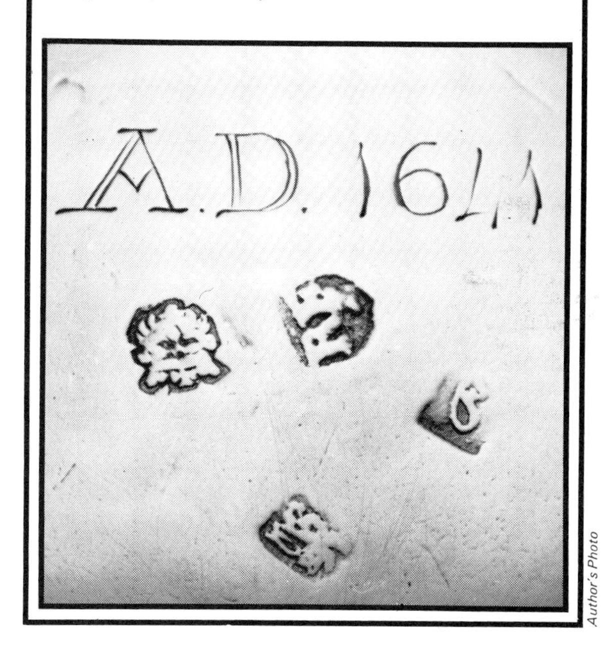

2 Fig. 2 **London hallmarks for the year 1641** *(enlarged). From the left, the marks are the lion's head for London, the maker's mark RF in a shield, the lombardic character 'd' for the year, and the assay mark, a lion rampant.*

Author's Photo

1 Fig. 1 **Leopard flagon** *(one of a pair), maker's mark a triangle intersected, London, 1600–1. Silver-gilt, height 27½ ins. This magnificent and very Germanic pair of leopards sejant would have been used as flasks. They are among the latest pieces made in England in the full renaissance style, and have survived the great meltings of heavy or outmoded plate only because they were safe in the Kremlin. (The Armoury, Kremlin, Moscow.)*

Society for Cultural Relations with the USSR

The seventeenth century saw the change-over from renaissance ceremonial silver to silver for the home, with Puritan plainness, restoration ornament and baroque formality laying the foundations for eighteenth-century greatness.

To the student of English silver, the seventeenth century is one of the most stimulating yet frustrating periods. The hiatus in production and the dispersal and destruction caused by the Civil War was followed by the Restoration; with it came the revival of display, the re-establishment of homes and the accent on domestic silver. To search for formerly lost pieces and to follow the early development of domestic silver is a rewarding study. For the collector, it is equally fascinating and, though expensive, most satisfying.

'Unserviceable, from decay, imperfection or being out of fashion'

In 1600, Queen Elizabeth I consigned large quantities of plate to the Mint for melting. Though primarily 'unserviceable, from decay, imperfection or being out of fashion', the disposal of some 900 ozs. of gold and some 14,000 ozs. of silver was also symbolic of the end of the great era of ceremonial silver. Further depredations were made in lavish presents to Spain by James I in 1604, and to Christian IV of Denmark during his visits in 1606 and 1614, though of course the Jewel House was also replenished by gifts from abroad and, in small measure, by new plate made at home. It is a curious fact that the destroyers of old plate were almost always under the impression that replacements of treasures could easily be made;

Fig. 3 **Scroll salt**, *London, 1638. Height 6½ ins. By the reign of Charles I, the age of the great salt had come to an end, and the central salt was no more than an enlarged version of the individual trencher salt. The scroll brackets supported a covering-dish or napkin. (Worshipful Company of Mercers.)*

P. Parkinson

A. C. Cooper

Fig. 4 **Winecup**, *maker's mark IB over a crescent in a kite-shaped punch, London, 1640. Height 7 ins., weight 13 ozs. 11 dwts. Plain drinking-cups of this sort were very popular throughout the seventeenth century; the Armourers' and Brasiers' Company has a set of six of the same maker and date, and the Leathersellers' Company has a set of four. (Christie's, London.)*

A. C. Cooper

Fig. 5 **Tankard**, *maker's mark HG, London, 1661. Height 8 ins., weight 62 ozs., capacity 4¾ pts. This historic tankard was given to St. Michael's Church, Lambourn, Berkshire, in 1701. Many tankards of around this date are decorated with a broad band of matting, which helped to overcome finger-marking as well as giving an interesting texture to the surface of the piece. (Christie's.)*

James I, for instance, ordered considerable quantities of new plate to be made, to the consternation of his goldsmiths who were unable to repeat such work.

Fortunately, and by chance, the Stuart generosity to European monarchs and ambassadors salvaged for posterity many fine pieces of English silver that might otherwise have been melted during the Civil Wars or under the Commonwealth. The silver now in the Kremlin in Moscow, for instance, links early Stuart silver with that of the last of the Tudors. These were the years of the renaissance style proper, and among them in this manner are a very Germanic pair of leopards (Fig. 1). In these essentially courtly pieces, the rather heavy Flemish and German styles persisted, with the accent on embossed and chased strap-work, swags of fruit, foliage, shells and cherub heads.

Besides the water-pot and the flagon, the standing cup was perhaps the most notable survival from the previous century (Fig. 6). The foot was usually circular, rising to a slender baluster stem, sometimes applied with small scrolling cast bracket. The bell-shaped, or sometimes octagonal, bowl was in the finest examples richly chased and matted, the usual subjects being strap-work enclosing formal flower and foliate motifs. Other, more serviceable winecups, were, however, left quite plain (Fig. 4), engraved with no more than the owner's arms or initials; this style, that persisted throughout the period until Ravenscroft's flint glass at the end of the century, ousted the silver winecup.

A curious and relatively short-lived style of cup made from 1599 until 1646 was the steeple cup (Fig. 8), of which one hundred and forty-nine have been recorded. The ornament of the cup might vary from foliage and strap-work to shells, lilies of the valley, a fox, hounds and hare, or a series of acanthus and fruit motifs around the base.

The age of the great standing salt was virtually over

By the time Charles I came to the throne, the great salt was a thing of the past; for banquets the central salt was no more than an enlarged version of the individual trencher salt, a spool or capstan shape to which were added scroll brackets on the broad rim to support a covering dish or napkin (Fig. 3).

At Court, however, even the money-pressed years after his accession in 1625 saw some of the most sophisticated silver ever made in seventeenth-century England in the work of his court goldsmith, Christian van Vianen, who arrived from Utrecht in 1633. Van Vianen's beautifully executed chargers and standing dishes, bowls and ewers, put art before function, interpreting classical and grotesque ornaments in the swirling fluid style that became unmistakably his own. Many of his grand commissions must have gone into the melting-pot during the war and the subsequent interregnum, but a few survive.

Van Vianen himself probably made, or at least designed and supervised, the beautiful and unique inkstand of 1639 bearing the mark AI, probably for Alexander Jackson, which was sold at Christie's for a record £78,000 in July 1970 (Fig. 7). The entire surface is enriched with repoussé-chased scroll-work in the 'auricular' style of Van Vianen. The fame and influence of such pieces lingered even during the Puritanism of the Commonwealth.

Taste was veering towards simplicity with the rare extravaganza

Such treasures tantalise the student of English silver with surmises about how much must have been lost, leaving him with, as a rule, only the less extravagant and simpler examples of early Stuart craftsmanship, or those which, because of their limited value as bullion, were scarcely worth the melting. Besides those pieces which found refuge abroad, others were well hidden in the collections of the Oxford and Cambridge colleges and the City Livery Companies by householders who took no part in politics, and by the churches; it is obvious that, despite the rare extravaganza for courtly patrons, taste was veering towards simplicity.

The 1620s saw the last of the great tankards and flagons with their overall chased or engraved motifs and, by the early years of Charles I's reign, the plain tapering cylindrical tankard, with either a skirt foot or no foot at all, was fully established. The only concession to ornament was the thumb-piece, still cast and fairly intricate in design, and perhaps a plumed mantling for the owner's arms. In about 1636, a broad band of matting might help to overcome finger-marking (Fig. 5), though the smaller covered globular mugs of the period were still frequently decorated with formal foliate

Fig. 6 ***Grace Cup,*** *maker's mark RP, London, 1619. Gilt, height 7 ins. (Worshipful Company of Goldsmiths.)*

Fig. 7 ***Inkstand in the style of Van Vianen,*** *maker's mark AI, London, 1639. Weight 172 ozs. (Christie's.)*

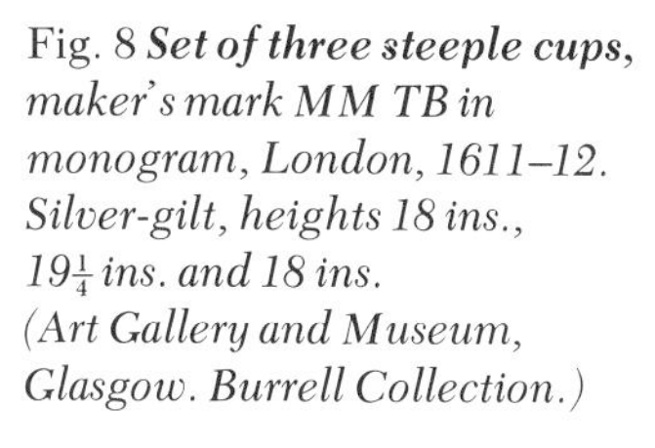

P. Parkinson

Christie's Photo

Museum Photo

Museum Photo

P. Parkinson

Fig. 8 ***Set of three steeple cups,*** *maker's mark MM TB in monogram, London, 1611–12. Silver-gilt, heights 18 ins., $19\frac{1}{4}$ ins. and 18 ins. (Art Gallery and Museum, Glasgow. Burrell Collection.)*

Fig. 9 ***Spice box,*** *maker's mark II or TI with mullet below, London, 1620. Length 6 ins. (Ashmolean Museum, Oxford. Carter Bequest.)*

Fig. 10 ***Cagework cup and cover,*** *maker's mark TI with two escallops, c.1675. The pierced and chased 'sleeve'. is of silver, the plain base silver-gilt. Height $7\frac{5}{8}$ ins., weight 52 ozs. 9 dwts. (Worshipful Company of Goldsmiths.)*

A. C. Cooper

Fig. 11 ***Hoof spoon,*** *English c.1627. (Christie's.)*

chasing and strap-work.

There was domestic silver throughout England, even in the politically troubled 1620s. Elizabethan merchant adventuring had brought to England not only new ideas but new products; sugar and spices, for example, were now more plentiful, and the shell-shaped spice-box became fashionable (Fig. 9).

From the time of Charles I's accession come a series of small saucer-like dishes, used perhaps for sweetmeats, sauces or even, it has been suggested, dry mustard. Perhaps because most were relatively small and light, they have survived in fairly large numbers. Many are by a maker identified as William Maundy (Fig. 15) dating between about 1629 and 1634, when Thomas Maundy seems to have taken over the workshop.

They did not wish to emulate the exiled Court in their expenditure

The growth of a merchant class market for silver maintained, to some small extent, the craft of silversmithing during the lean years of the Commonwealth. Few, indeed, had much money to spare for luxuries such as silver, although when pottery was porous and unrefined, and the only metal alternatives for spoons were brass (or latten) and pewter, silver was hardly a luxury. Those who esteemed the government did not wish to emulate the exiled Court in their expenditure on such frivolities as plate, but there were still people able to support a small band of silversmiths.

The two-handled cup, with or without a cover, was perhaps the most typical of all mid-seventeenth-century silverwares. In about 1655, the acanthus leaf in a rather stylised form or freer floral motifs were coming into favour for the bases, becoming more and more naturalistic by the end of the 1650s. These drinking-cups, which vary in size from about three to as much as six inches in height, are variously described as posset, or caudle cups (for use in taking spiced hot drinks), porringers, pottagers and loving-cups. No doubt those with covers, some of which have disc finials so that the cover could be placed flat on the table like a footed salver, were used for hot foods and drinks, the smaller ones perhaps for spirits and stronger beverages, or even for custards and other foods. At all events, the two-handled porringer was firmly established as part of the silversmith's main stock-in-trade by the 1650s and continued, in either the straight-sided or the bulbous-bodied style at least until 1690, though each new design fashion saw changes in the style of decoration.

The earlier style of spoon, with fig-shaped bowl and hexagonal stem topped with a decorative finial – by the seventeenth century usually an apostle or saint, a baluster seal (Fig. 12), lion sejant or other ornament – gradually gave way to the spoon with oval bowl, and flattened stem without any terminal; a sliced top is usually termed a slip-top, a straight or notched end a Puritan (Fig. 13).

When the Court and Charles II finally returned in

Fig. 14 ***Chinoiserie casket*** *from a toilet set, maker's mark WE, knot of ribbon above, London, 1683. Width 10 ins. The cover chased. (Christie's.)*

Fig. 15 ***Saucer*** *by William Maundy, London, 1633. Diameter including the handles 7½ ins., weight 3 ozs. 1 dwt. Used for sweetmeats, sauces or mustard. (Worshipful Company of Goldsmiths.)*

Fig. 16 ***Porringer and cover,*** *maker's mark GS, a crozier between, London, 1658. Height 4 ins., weight 8 ozs. 10 dwts. Used for hot foods and drinks. (Worshipful Company of Goldsmiths.)*

12

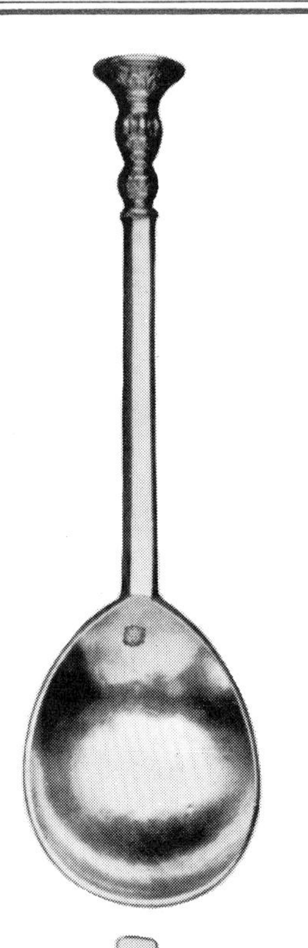

Author's Photo

15

P. Parkinson

14

A. C. Cooper

16

P. Parkinson

13

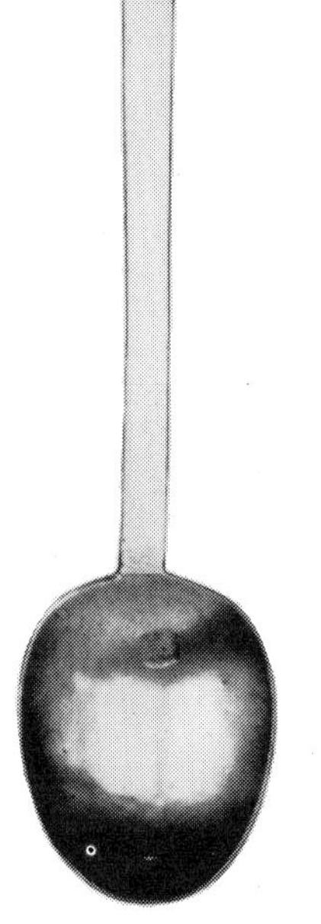

Author's Photo

Fig. 12 ***Baluster seal-top spoon,*** *maker's mark D enclosing C, London, 1634. Although this type of spoon with a decorative finial was still quite common in the early seventeenth century, it was gradually being supplanted by a completely new concept in spoons, as seen in Fig. 13. (Private Collection.)*

Fig. 13 ***Puritan spoon,*** *probably by Stephen Venables, London, 1663. The Puritan spoon was a direct ancestor of the modern spoon. For the first time, the bowl became oval, and the stem was flattened out. (Private Collection.)*

1660 there was a tremendous upsurge in spending and refurnishing. At first, the silversmiths depended on the old patterns, especially when faced with making more sumptuous plate for display at Court and in the palaces and great houses of nobility. The Court had, however, learned to appreciate continental silver during their years of exile. The plainness of much native English design was now overlaid with ideas from France and Germany and, most of all, the Low Countries. Flower motifs and the acanthus leaf were both exceptionally popular in Holland, and now were used around the bases of porringers and tankards, tumbler cups and beakers, and along the bases and on the knopped stems of candlesticks. The skill with which they were chased varied very much – some were sketchy and poorly executed, others were meticulously and finely chased with attention to detail and the depth of the embossing.

In their search for new decorative motifs, the English silversmiths of the later seventeenth century found inspiration in the tales brought back by sailors and merchants from the Orient, and developed the naïve, but charming, style known as *Chinoiserie*. Sometimes flat-chased, sometimes engraved, the theme was the exotic and the curious: there were long-robed mandarins and strange temples, furious warriors on horse-back and long-beaked birds, palm trees and marigolds and orange-trees. The fashion was relatively short-lived, lasting from about 1670 to 1685, but during its heyday it appeared extensively on tankards, porringers and, above all, on toilet services. Toilet services with an array of caskets (Fig. 14), brushes, trays, candlesticks, pincushion and mirror, were a standard wedding gift from groom to bride, and must have seemed in keeping with the silver 'garnitures' of vases, jars and so on.

Besides *chinoiseries*, which seem to have been entirely English in concept, there was another rare style of ornament – the pierced and chased 'sleeve' of silver overlaying a plain, usually gilt, base. Here the foliate patterns of the chaser, with cherubs and peacocks, flowers and other naturalistic motifs intricately interwoven, were pierced out with great effect for sumptuous cups and covers (Fig. 10).

If *chinoiseries* or rich chasing cloyed, then by the 1680s the silversmith could also offer a new formal style, the baroque, with its gold gadrooned borders and its fluting, its bold lion masks and formalised acanthus foliage. The style swept England, and in with it swept the refugees from France, the craftsmen who, in spite of opposition from English silversmiths, gave England the style we call Huguenot, and set the seal of greatness on eighteenth-century English silver.

MUSEUMS AND COLLECTIONS

English silver of the early Stuart period may be seen at the following:

Cardiff:	The National Museum of Wales
London:	Victoria and Albert Museum City Livery Companies, all of which have annual open days
Oxford:	The Ashmolean Museum

FURTHER READING

Old English Silver by Judith Banister, London, 1965.
The English Silver in the Kremlin, 1557–1663 by Charles Oman, London, 1961.
Old English Plate by W. J. Cripps, London, 1911.
Restoration Silver by Charles Oman, London, 1970.

The Flamboyant Years

Museum Photo

Maurice Ashley

2

Museum Photo

Fig. 1 (Frontispiece) ***Portrait of Charles II*** *(1660–85) from the studio of Michael Wright. Oil on canvas, 49¾ x 39¾ ins.*
Wright was Court Painter to Charles II. He was not universally considered to be a great artist and Pepys compared him to Lely with the words: 'Lord! the difference'. The other great diarist of the period, Evelyn, did however note that most of his portraits were 'very like the persons they represent' (National Portrait Gallery, London.)

Fig. 2 ***The Fire of London, 1666,*** *Dutch School. Oil on canvas, 35⅞ x 60⅛ ins.*
The Great Fire which started in Pudding Lane on 2 September, 1666, raged for four days, devastating a great area of the City of London. It was finally halted when the King ordered that the houses in the direct path of the fire be blown up by gunpowder.
(London Museum.)

Charles II, the Merry Monarch, returned to England in 1660, bringing with him the gaiety and light-heartedness of the continental courts. Freed from the restraint of Puritanism, the English enthusiastically followed their King in his taste for opulence

Charles II was not as great a patron of the arts as his father, Charles I, but he was a lover of beauty and beautiful women. In this he was unlike his brother James II, whose mistresses were said to be conferred on him by his confessors as penances. But if Charles had a major interest outside politics – besides walking, fishing and playing tennis – it was in the progress of science which, in his time, was called 'natural philosophy'. From the days of William Gilbert and Francis Bacon at the beginning of the century the practice of experimenting in every kind of science, from anatomy to astronomy, had blossomed. Groups of academicians and amateurs had held meetings in Oxford and London during the Protectorate of Oliver Cromwell and had formed the nucleus of the Royal Society of which Charles II became patron soon after his restoration to the throne in 1660.

Nevertheless, in those days there were no watertight compartments between the sciences and the arts: no 'two cultures'. Charles II's first Surveyor was the poet, Sir John Denham; his second, Sir Christopher Wren, was the brilliant architect who had been Professor of Astronomy

3

A. F. Kersting

4

Museum Photo

Charles II
Born 1630
Crown restored 1660
Died 1685
James II
Born 1633
Acceded 1685
Deposed 1688
Died 1701

Fig. 3 ***Belton House,*** *Lincolnshire, by an anonymous architect, perhaps William Winde; foundation stone laid 1685.*
Belton House is a typical country house of the period. It is in what is erroneously called the 'Wren' style, but was in fact based on the style of Sir Roger Pratt, a pupil of Inigo Jones.

Fig. 4 ***Portrait of Sir Christopher Wren*** *by Sir Godfrey Kneller (1646 or 49–1723), 1711. Oil on canvas, 49 x 39½ ins.*
Sir Christopher Wren (1632–1723) was unquestionably the greatest Restoration architect. He began life as a mathematician and was Professor of Astronomy in London and in Oxford. He began his career in architecture in 1663 with the Sheldonian Theatre, Oxford, and Pembroke College Chapel, Cambridge. His most important work was the designing of the City churches after the Great Fire and his masterpiece, the rebuilding of St. Paul's (1675–1709). His originality and versatility can best be seen in the spires of the City churches and his mathematical genius in the intellectual refinement of the dome of St. Paul's. (National Portrait Gallery.)

Fig. 5 ***The Monument*** *by W. A. Toms. Engraving. 202 ft. in height, the Monument was designed by Wren to commemorate the Great Fire of London, 1666. It is situated near Pudding Lane where the fire started.*

both at Oxford and at Gresham's College, London. Of Wren, Robert Hooke, his friend and assistant, once wrote: 'I must affirm that since the time of Archimedes there scarce ever has met in one man in so great perfection such a mechanical hand and so philosophical a mind'. John Evelyn, the diarist and a prominent member of the Royal Society, was also an expert on gardens and an amateur architect. Samuel Pepys, like his king a lover of women and practical science, was also a regular theatre-goer and a musician. Men of artistic taste and men of scientific skill were equally welcome at Court. While, on the one hand Charles had his own private laboratory, on the other he prided himself on his Raphaels, Titians and Holbeins and tried to retrieve some of the paintings from his father's collection, which had been dispersed.

Sir Arthur Bryant has written that Charles 'made his Court a home for artists: Streater of "land skip" fame whom he created Serjeant Painter and loved; Cooper, "the rare limner"; Dankaerts from The Hague who painted his ships and palaces; Verelst, "king of flowers" by whose leafy dewdrops Pepys was impressed; and the fashionable Lely'. But the truth is that there were few good English painters and no native school of painting. Consequently, Charles and his successors looked abroad to find artists to undertake court portraits; Lely was a Dutchman, Kneller a German and Michael Dahl a Swede.

Similarly, in music Charles turned to France and Italy (although towards the end of the reign Henry Purcell emerged as a native genius), and even in the domestic arts foreign influences tended to predominate.

Silversmiths were often French and towards the end of the century news about Far Eastern fashions arrived; a book on japanning, or lacquering, was published.

'The riches and splendour of this world, purchased with vice and dishonour'

Doubtless Charles II's favourite sister, married to the brother of the French King, and his French mistress, whom he met through his sister and whom he was to create Duchess of Portsmouth, stimulated his French tastes. In 1683 John Evelyn visited the Duchess of Portsmouth's dressing-room in the company of the King, where his curiosity was aroused by 'the rich and splendid furniture of this woman's apartment, now twice or thrice pulled down and rebuilt to satisfy her prodigal and expensive pleasures'. There he saw 'the new fabric of French tapestry, for design, tenderness of work and incomparable imitation of the best paintings beyond anything I had ever beheld . . . then for Japan cabinets, screens, pendulum clocks, huge vases of wrought plate, tables, stands, chimney furniture, sconces, *braseros* . . . all of massive silver without number'. Afterwards, he contentedly returned home to his quiet villa, wondering what joy there could be 'in the riches and splendour of this world, purchased with vice and dishonour'.

One reason for the dominating foreign influences on English artists and craftsmen was that little progress had been achieved during the Interregnum. It is true that Cromwell was fond of organ music and that the first English opera, *The Siege of Rhodes*, written by Sir William Davenant,

5

supposedly the illegitimate son of William Shakespeare, was performed privately in London during the Protectorate. But the Puritans closed the theatres, sold the royal pictures, destroyed stained glass in churches and patronised the second-rate Robert Walker as their principal portraitist. Meanwhile, Charles II and his exiled Court had moved about Europe in France, Germany, the Low Countries and Spain, and brought back with them artistic ideas from abroad. It was only in architecture and to a lesser extent in furniture that original native genius was to be detected.

On the whole, the classical spirit was supreme, as it had been in the first half of the century. It has been described as a world in which all the arts and sciences were united in their dependence on ancient Greece and Rome. The writings of Vitruvius were widely read and studied and John Evelyn was outspoken in his condemnation of gothic buildings and gothic styles. Most admired were geometrical design in buildings, town-planning and furniture. The first building commissioned from Christopher Wren (when he was just over thirty years old) by the Bishop of London, was the Sheldonian Theatre at Oxford, in which (as Sir John Summerson has written) 'grandeur of mass' was 'sacrificed', while 'the architectural treatment as a whole is mechanical'. A model was shown to the Royal Society as an experiment in natural science.

Christopher Wren's career was a remarkable one. He seems first to have impressed himself on Charles II by making for him a relief map of the moon. Then he was invited to go to Tangier to survey the works and fortifications there – Tangier had been acquired by England as part of the dowry of Charles' wife, Catherine of Braganza. It was indicated to Wren that, if he accepted this offer, which was made to him as 'one of the best geometricians in Europe', he would be considered next in the succession for the post of Surveyor of the King's Works, a position held by Inigo Jones until his death in 1652. But Wren refused the offer and instead went to study architecture in Paris, where he met the great Italian architect and sculptor, Bernini, who had been invited there to submit new designs for the Louvre. But it was not until after the Great Fire of London in 1666 that Wren achieved architectural fame.

The fire, which began at a baker's shop in Pudding Lane in the early hours of the morning of Sunday, 2 September, was spread by winds right across the square mile that constituted the City of London, and destroyed churches, company halls and over thirteen thousand houses, most of which were built of wood. Only the firm orders given by the King to blow up buildings by gunpowder prevented the fire from reaching Whitehall. The fire was finally halted on 5 September, and by 11 September Wren had submitted to the King an elaborate plan for rebuilding London. Other plans were put forward by John Evelyn and Robert Hooke, another geometrician. None of these plans was put into effect; they were too complicated and costly. Wren's plan would have provided for vast open vistas, a road system converging on a new royal exchange and a broad public quay along the river from the Temple to the Tower. But for practical reasons the City had to be rebuilt largely along the old lines and an historian of the Great Fire gives the credit for the speed with which the work was carried out largely to the King himself. By 1685, London was mainly a city of brown and red brick instead of wood.

Eighty-seven parish churches were destroyed in the fire and they were replaced by fifty-one new ones. Obviously Wren did not do the detailed work on all these new churches but he designed many of them and supervised the rest. The designs were of many kinds and in the furnishings much latitude was allowed to the craftsmen. Some of the churches were burnt during the last war, but in St. Stephen's

6

Country Life

7

Mansell Collection

8

Crown Copyright: National Building Records

9

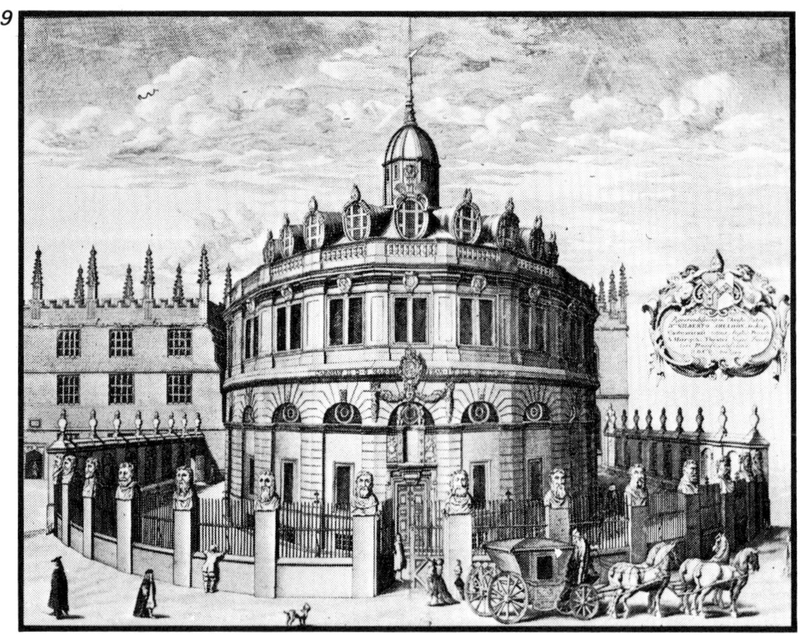

Photo-Hachette

Walbrook there has survived a fine example of Wren's genius with the dome, anticipating that on St. Paul's Cathedral, which was to be Wren's masterpiece. In the towers and spires of the churches, Wren was at his most ingenious, for he neither copied the Gothic nor had he classical precedents to follow. In addition to supplying drawings of all these new churches, Wren was responsible for a new customs house and contributed to the design of the Royal Exchange and the Monument which commemorates the fire.

The West End of London came into being and Piccadilly was built

By 1670 Wren had become the King's Surveyor. John Webb, a pupil of Inigo Jones and an able architect chiefly famed for the houses he built and for the Palace of Greenwich, was passed over. Sir Roger Pratt was another disciple of Inigo Jones whose few buildings had an important influence on English domestic architecture – on Belton House at Grantham, for example, a perfect example of a country gentleman's home in the reign of Charles II. Wren himself built few houses. As Surveyor he was responsible for the royal palaces and had under him a body of artisans. Sir John Summerson observes that 'it was a "school" of building of the highest importance and wherever it led, in design or in craftsmanship, the nation followed'.

Independently of this post, the Royal Commissioner put Wren in charge of the rebuilding of St. Paul's, to which he devoted much of his long life. Inigo Jones had started converting the old gothic church by giving it a classical front. Wren, though following the cruciform pattern of medieval cathedrals, made St. Paul's more compact and added a dome, based on that of Michelangelo at St. Peter's, Rome, and a giant portico at the west end. Outside the City, Wren's achievements include the library of Trinity College, Cambridge, Tom Tower at Christ Church, Oxford, and Chelsea and Greenwich Hospitals.

10

A. F. Kersting

Fig. 6 ***Font** by Grinling Gibbons (1648–1721). Marble. This is one of the rare Gibbons pieces not carved in wood. (St. James's, Piccadilly.)*

Fig. 7 ***View of St. James's Square** by T. Bowles, c.1760. Engraving. St. James's Square was one of the first parts of the West End to be built.*

Fig. 8 ***The Saloon** at Belton House, Lincolnshire, c.1685. This is a perfect example of a late Charles II interior.*

Fig. 9 ***The Sheldonian Theatre**, Oxford, by David Loggan, 1663. Engraving. This was Wren's first building and already the trussed roof indicates the structural ingenuity for which he was later acclaimed.*

Fig. 10 ***Tom Tower**, Oxford, by Wren, 1681–82. Tom Tower shows the full extent of Wren's originality in the intermingling of unusual motifs.*

Titled rogues filled their houses with fine furniture, paintings and silver

During the reign of Charles II, what is now called the West End of London came into being. Henry Jermyn, Earl of St. Albans, was responsible for building St. James's Square and the surrounding streets. Piccadilly was built and Wren was commissioned to design St. James's Church, which, though damaged seriously during the last war, can still be seen according to Wren's plan with a row of six piers on each side holding up the gallery; from the gallery rise Corinthian columns supporting an entablature from which spring the vaults arching the windows and the vault which spans the church. Here, too, may be seen typical work by Grinling Gibbons, including the reredos (the ornamental screen behind the altar) and the rare marble font representing the Tree of Life. (Gibbons seldom carved except in marble.)

Not only in Charles II's London, which comprised the West End and the new City rebuilt after the fire, but throughout England a fresh and rich character of life was reflected. Furniture became gayer; chairs were taller and often elaborately carved; book-cases were rectangular; cabinets, chests and clock-cases exuberant in design, with coloured marquetry.

Walnut instead of oak came into fashion in about 1660 and various methods of polishing were used. The titled rogues of Charles II's reign, such as Lord Montagu and the second Earl of Sunderland, who were bribed with French money, filled their houses not only with Italian paintings and French silver, but also with the finest products of English furniture-makers who retained their own individuality. Thus the antiques of this period reflect wealth well spent, ingenuity and good taste.

RESTORATION ARCHITECTURE

by Sir Christopher Wren:

Cambridge: Trinity College Library

London: Chelsea Hospital
Greenwich Hospital
St. James's, Piccadilly
St. Paul's
St. Stephen's Walbrook
The Monument, Pudding Lane

Oxford: Sheldonian Theatre
Tom Tower, Christ Church

Also:
Belton House, Grantham, Lincolnshire, open daily, except Friday, from 3rd May to 4th October, 12 noon to 6 p.m.
St. James's Square, London, and the surrounding streets, and many parts of the City and the West End.

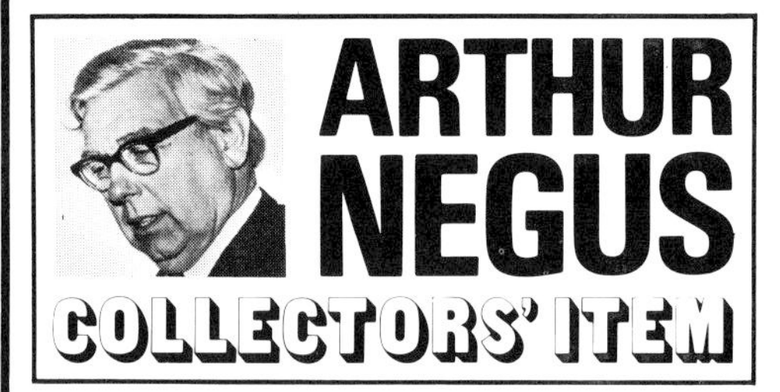

LACE BOBBINS

English lace bobbins were mostly made in north Buckinghamshire, west Bedfordshire and the south of Northamptonshire. The ones which interest the collector were made over a period of roughly three centuries, from 1550 to 1850. Lace bobbins are made chiefly of close-grained wood, or bone; but silver, pewter, brass, glass and ivory have been used. It is thought that the earliest were made of boxwood and were small with a bulbous shaft and no beads at the end, because the laces then woven were made with very fine thread which would have broken with the weight. The earliest decoration was made by wrapping onion skin around the bobbin and then boiling it. Another very beautiful decoration was made by the inlay of boxwood in fruitwood, or vice versa. Among many different varieties were the very plain, slim, straight bobbins in either wood or bone known as 'Old Maids'. Others were inlaid with pewter; some had bands of pewter around the shaft and were known as 'Bedfordshire Tigers'; others had dots of pewter let in and were called 'Bedfordshire Leopards'. A beautiful variant added coloured beads to the wires to form intricate patterns. Bone bobbins lent themselves naturally to decoration, the pattern being either incised, or drilled and coloured powders mixed with gum arabic being applied to the holes. The colours were mostly red, blue, black, yellow and green; the different colour combinations being used by the different bobbin-makers. Many bobbins had births, deaths and weddings recorded on them. It is possible to collect whole families, all dated. Others have the place as well, and a few had the occupation of the owner. There are bobbins that record famous people such as politicians, divines, and murderers. Others bear political slogans or popular songs. Every bobbin had coloured beads at the bottom to prevent the bobbin rolling off the pillow and to provide sufficient tension. The correct number of beads in the early light bobbins was five. Some of the bottom beads had one brown spot and one blue and were called after the popular actress of the late eighteenth century, Kitty Fisher, who had eyes of different colours. The large bobbins had nine beads. The large decorated bottom bead is sometimes of Venetian or Bristol glass, and many are very lovely.

Prices

Starting at as little as 20p, bobbins may cost as much as £7-£8. The more expensive include commemorative bobbins, particularly those commemorating notorious murderers.

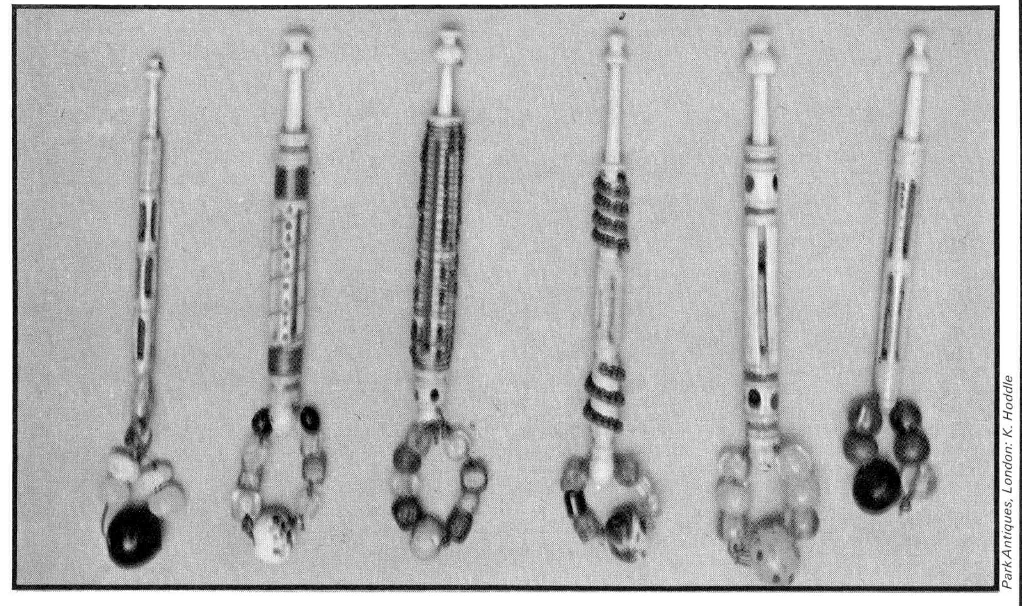
Park Antiques, London: K. Hoddle

Above: ***Six 'church window' or 'mother in babe' lace bobbins,*** *so-called because they are carved through in the centre; bone with various bead and other decorations. Around £1.50 each.*

Below left: ***A collection of beaded bobbins,*** *mid-nineteenth century; carved wood or bone. Around £1.50 each.*

Below right: ***A collection of coloured bone bobbins,*** *mid-nineteenth century; decorated with beads such as the 'birdcage' bead in the centre and at the corners. About £1.50 each.*

Opposite: ***Four beaded bobbins,*** *mid-nineteenth century; three are carved bone decorated with beads, costing about £1.50 each; one is carved with hearts and the date 1860, commemorating the second birthday of a child, and costs £2.50.*

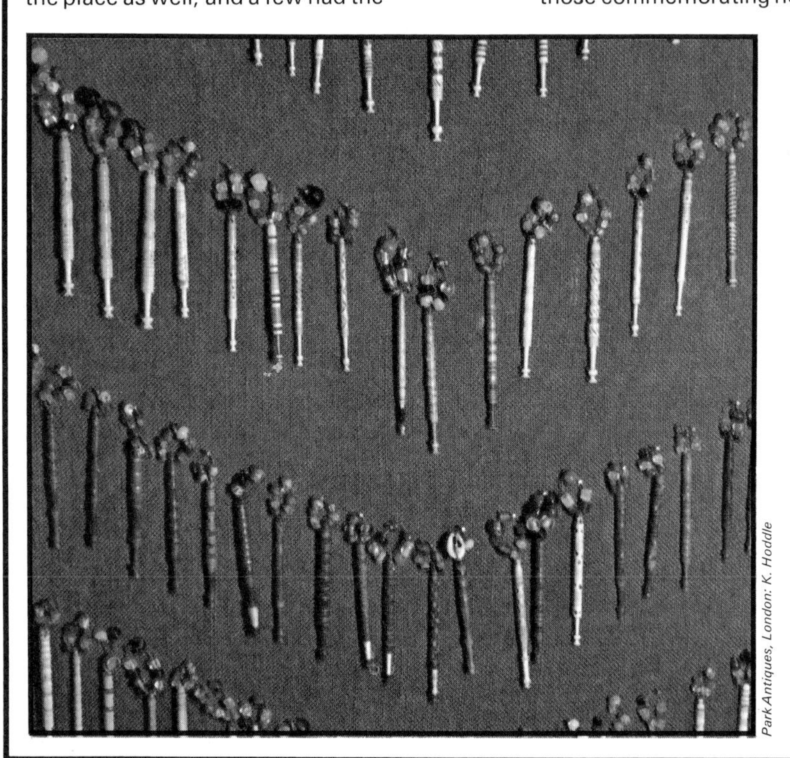
Park Antiques, London: K. Hoddle

Park Antiques, London: K. Hoddle

Park Antiques, London: K. Hoddle

Edward T. Joy

The Age of Walnut

1

A. C. Cooper

2

A. C. Cooper

With the revived optimism of the restoration of Charles II and the extensive rebuilding in London after the Great Fire, oak furniture fell from favour. Walnut became the fashionable wood and continental veneering and marquetry gave elegance and lightness to the pieces

Sixteen hundred and sixty, the year of Charles II's restoration to the English throne after eleven years of exile abroad, was an important landmark in the history of English furniture. For almost a quarter of a century progress in the arts and crafts in England had been seriously hampered, first by the quarrel between Charles I and Parliament, which had led to the Civil War and the King's execution in 1649, and secondly by the eleven years of Puritan rule imposed by Cromwell.

During his exile, Charles II had become fully acquainted with the high standards of furniture design and craftsmanship in France and Holland and on his return he was determined to introduce these standards into England. His example, and that of his luxury-loving Court, was eagerly followed by the aristocracy, landed gentry and merchants, encouraged both by the inevitable reaction to Puritan austerity and by the rising national prosperity brought about by trade and colonisation. The spirit of the age was aptly summed up by the famous diarist, John Evelyn, when he wrote in 1685, on the occasion of Charles II's death, that the King had 'brought in a politer way of living which passed to luxury and intolerable expense'.

The furniture industry received an unexpected stimulus when the Great Fire of London in 1666 destroyed a large number of houses and their contents. To speed the rebuilding of the capital, and with the lessons of the recent catastrophe clearly in mind, the authorities adopted a standard scheme for new houses, dividing them into four main types, and ordered them to be made of brick and stone instead of timber framing. Houses had an entrance hall and staircase, two or three rooms on each floor and two to four storeys with a garret, depending on the size of the building.

The desire was for elegant and compact pieces

Inside, walls were covered with painted pine panelling, and ceilings with moulded plaster. Large sash windows replaced the old casements, making the interiors much brighter than before. In this new setting the traditional oak furniture was altogether too bulky and clumsy; the desire was for more elegant and compact pieces. The answer lay in veneered furniture made with all the most up-to-date processes from the Continent, and in the use of more varied and more convenient types of furniture.

Veneers were thin sheets of wood especially selected for the beauty of their pattern, or figure, which were sawn from blocks and glued to the carefully prepared flush surfaces of the carcase or frame. Saw-cut veneers varied from about one-sixteenth to one-eighth of an inch in thickness (and were therefore thicker than modern machine-produced veneers) and, as they repeated the pattern of the block from which they were sawn, they could be laid on to the carcase in a number of attractive ways to match or reverse the pattern. Among particularly interesting figures were oval 'oyster' pieces cut transversely from small branches of trees, crotches cut from the intersection of branch and trunk, and burrs – taken from the malformation of tree trunks which produced a tangled mass and not a regular figure and were difficult to use as they tended to curl.

The wood most often associated with this period is walnut, so much so that the late Stuart era is usually referred to as 'the Age of Walnut'. But although walnut, especially the continental variety which was imported because of its fine figure, was well favoured, there were other timbers which were constantly in demand, including yew, maple, elm, mulberry, ash and kingwood. For oyster pieces, the favourites were olive and laburnum.

Even more woods were required for marquetry, a form of veneering in which intricate patterns were cut in a series of veneers and then fitted on to the prepared surface very much in the manner of a jigsaw puzzle (Fig. 1). For this technique a great variety of colours was called for, and veneers were

Fig. 1 **Detail of a marquetry box**, *English, c.1670. Various woods. Marquetry was the most fashionable form of furniture veneer of this period. Many different woods were used, dyed, stained or scorched to the right colour. Sycamore was dyed green to form 'harewood' which made up the foliage of the ever-popular floral marquetry. (Victoria and Albert Museum, London.)*

Fig. 2 **Companion figure**, *English, c.1690. Painted wood. Painted realistically in contemporary dress, these dummy figures were a charming Stuart conceit. (Victoria and Albert Museum.)*

3

Fig. 3 **Gate-legged table**, *English, third quarter of the seventeenth century. Oak. Folding tables were used for dining, card-playing and many other purposes in small Stuart houses. (Victoria and Albert Museum.)*

Museum Photo

4

Fig. 4 **Sleeping-chair**, *one of a pair, English, c.1675. Gilt wood with contemporary upholstery. The winged back of this chair, designed to keep out draughts, can be adjusted by ratchets. (Ham House, Surrey.)*

Museum Photo

Museum Photo

Fig. 5 **Armchair,** *English, c.1675.*
Carved, gilt and painted wood with dolphin motifs; original satin brocade upholstery. (Ham House.)

Fig. 6 **Table,** *English, c.1675*
Carved and gilt walnut and softwood with silver mounts. (Ham House.)

Museum Photo

Fig. 7 **Bookcase of the Samuel Pepys type,** *c.1665–70. Oak. (Victoria and Albert Museum.)*

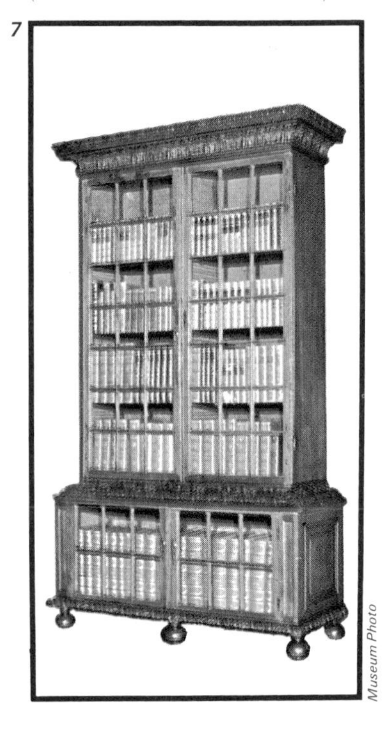

Museum Photo

dyed, stained or scorched to get the right shade. For most of Charles II's reign floral marquetry was fashionable, and to get the green colour for leaves, sycamore was stained and given the name of harewood. Parquetry was a form of marquetry which employed geometrical patterns and, for these, oyster pieces were used, set in thin lines of light coloured woods such as box, holly or sycamore.

These new techniques reached England from the Continent and were taught to English craftsmen by immigrants from Holland and France. The old joiner's technique of panel-and-frame was now outmoded, for it could not provide the flush surface for veneers, and the joiner had to give way to the cabinet-maker. Oak, so long the traditional woodworker's material, went out of fashion for the best furniture. Joinery, however, continued to flourish in country areas where old methods were largely untouched by the dictates of fashion.

Flowers and foliage and occasionally birds were set in oval panels

Mention of the cabinet-maker takes us naturally to the cabinet, the great prestige piece of the Restoration. Cabinets made with expensive materials such as precious woods, ivory and tortoise-shell, and enriched with metal mounts, sometimes of silver, had been made on the Continent since about 1650. Foreign cabinets of this date can be seen today in England but these have almost invariably been imported by dealers in fairly recent times. In general, the English cabinet of the post-1660 era copied contemporary Dutch and French models (Fig. 13). Its interior was enclosed by two large doors and consisted of many drawers of different sizes arranged around a central cupboard also containing drawers. The cabinet was supported on a stand – another continental innovation – with four or six legs united by waved stretchers. It was used as a receptacle for documents and the valuable collections of small curiosities, such as coins and medals, in which rich men invested a great deal of their money. In the days before banks could offer any real security it was very useful in case of an emergency to have family papers and valuables in one place for easy removal. These early English cabinets were usually decorated with parquetry of oyster pieces of olive, laburnum or walnut, or with floral marquetry. Flowers and foliage and occasionally birds were set in oval panels and surrounded by borders of oyster pieces of walnut veneer. This attractive display of colour, even though there is often some fading after three centuries, makes these cabinets the most brilliantly decorated pieces of furniture ever produced in England. One peculiarly English feature emerging from this foreign influence is the drawer with convex front which is often found in the frieze of the cabinet below the moulded cornice.

Another type was the 'Indian' cabinet imported from Japan and China by the East India Company. Decorated with lacquer on the front door and sides and on the drawer fronts, it had elaborate gilt copper hinges and lock-plates. The Chinese were fond of decorating cabinets with figures set in landscapes, while the Japanese concentrated on animals, flowers and birds. It was Chinese decoration which was mostly imitated by English

Museum Photo

Museum Photo

Museum Photo

Fig. 8 **Scriptor on stand,** *English, c.1675. Kingwood oyster veneer with silver mounts.*
Made from deep brown king- or princewood, a wood closely allied to rosewood, this scriptor or writing-desk contains fourteen pigeon-holes and six veneered drawers.
(Ham House.)

Fig. 9 **Day-bed,** *English, c.1670–80. Walnut and cane.*
Copied from the French lits de repos, *day-beds became popular after about 1660.*
(Victoria and Albert Museum.)

Fig. 10 **Cabinet on stand,** *English, c.1670–80. The cabinet japanned, the stand silvered wood; the cabinet mounts of gilt copper.*
Japanning, a process using coloured varnishes, was widely used in imitation of oriental lacquer-work during the seventeenth century.
(Victoria and Albert Museum.)

craftsmen whose substitute for lacquer, varnish mixed with paint colours, became known as japanning. They preferred bright grounds of reds, greens and tortoise-shell, while genuine lacquered cabinets almost always had a black ground. English japan, however, is a poor substitute for lacquer. It cracks and fades in strong sunlight and most japanned furniture of this time has disappeared. Even when it has survived it has usually been heavily restored. Oriental cabinets required a stand for use in England and they were often given an elaborately carved and gilt (or silvered) support (Fig. 10).

The chest of drawers developed into its modern form by the end of Charles II's reign. For some time after 1660 it was usual for the upper section to have a deep drawer which, because of its weight, moved in and out on bearers attached to the inside of the carcase, the sides of the drawer being grooved to slide on them. By 1685 the present familiar arrangement was achieved in the pattern of two short, shallow drawers at the top and three long, deeper ones beneath, now moving in and out on runners. For decoration, chests of drawers often had floral marquetry or matched walnut veneers. Various decorative devices were used to mask the gap between drawer and carcase. The earliest was the half-round or double half-round moulding attached to the framework. Later the moulding or beading was attached to the edge of the drawer as an ovolo or 'quarter-round' lip moulding. All these developments meant, of course, that the chest was at last beginning to lose its long-established popularity.

simplicity when they began to be adopted in large households. Their height was increased and the framework of the cane panel in the back, set in spiral-turned uprights, was elaborately carved as also were the deep cresting and the front stretcher (which often matched each other). The arm supports and front legs were formed of elongated scrolls, and the arms themselves, of round or oval section, scrolled boldly over their supports. Made of walnut, or of beech stained to imitate walnut, these chairs perhaps typify better than any other piece of furniture the flamboyant spirit of Charles II's England (Figs. 11 and 12). Many had a patriotic motif in the cresting in the form of a crown supported by *amorini* – 'boyes and crowne'.

The simpler form of cane chairs remained popular in smaller houses. This was indeed the age of cane chairs, so much so that upholsterers petitioned Parliament for protection against the importing of canes. Their petition was unsuccessful and cane chairs continued to be made in large quantities until well into the eighteenth century. Very similar in style and decoration to the more elaborate chairs were day-beds which, after 1660, copied the *lits de repos* then fashionable in France. Now they began to resemble couches, and one end had a back which in some cases was adjustable. The seat and back were made of cane set in frames of walnut which were carved and turned in the prevailing mode (Fig. 9).

11

Fig. 11 **Detail of an armchair,** *English, c.1675. Walnut and cane.*
Chairs in the reign of Charles II are known above all for the elaborate ornamentation of their carving, as this detail of a chair-back amply illustrates. The pascal lamb forming the crest, is lost in a profusion of angels, cherubs and swirling foliage. The caning is typical of the period.
(Victoria and Albert Museum.)

12

Museum Photo

Fig. 12 **Set of chairs,** *English, 1685. Walnut and cane.*
This set of one armchair and six matching straight chairs is typical of everyday furniture in the late seventeenth century. Twisted supports and caned seats and backs are frequently found, while the matching cresting and front stretcher are more fanciful but still commonplace features.
(Victoria and Albert Museum.)

Chairs typify the flamboyant spirit of Charles II's England

Chairs of Charles II's reign are a byword for their elaborate ornamentation, but in fact the first new type to appear in the decade after 1660 was a light and simple cane chair with its back and seat composed of a mesh of split rattans derived from a kind of oriental palm imported by the East India Company. This kind of chair, which was already known in France and Holland, was unusual in that it was found in ordinary houses before it became fashionable in higher society. It used the cheap method of spiral turning on all its structural members. There seems little doubt that many of these chairs were supplied in sets to the new houses built in London after the Great Fire, and that they began to replace stools, which had for so long been the common type of seat.

It was not until about the middle of Charles' reign that chairs of this kind lost their earlier

But in spite of the complaints of upholsterers against cane chairs, upholstered chairs employing rich materials, which were often fringed, remained a prominent feature of late Stuart furniture (Fig. 5). Among such chairs appeared, about 1670, the famous large winged armchair, then known as an 'easie' chair. The wings were no doubt added to keep draughts out. Ham House, Surrey, has a pair of interesting upholstered winged armchairs with adjustable backs worked by ratchets (Fig. 4). They were made about 1675 when Ham house was being refurnished and are entered as 'sleeping chayres' in the inventory of the contents of the house which was drawn up in 1679.

New types of writing furniture also appeared at this time. The much improved postal services in London after the Great Fire, and in the country generally, led to a great increase in letter-writing. The earliest writing-cabinets, called variously scriptors, scriptoires and scrutores, were, like so many other new pieces, taken directly from continental models (French: *escritoire*). They were box-like structures, mounted at first on stands, and had a large fall-front which let down on chains or stays to provide a flat writing surface, disclosing numerous small drawers and pigeon-holes for letters. Later, in Charles' reign, a chest of drawers was used to form a steadier support for the heavy superstructure. These writing-cabinets made a fine field for decoration in parquetry, marquetry or beautifully figured walnut and other woods. The large fall-front, however, was awkward in one respect – all papers had to be cleared off the desk before it could be shut up. By 1700 the bureau was being introduced. This was more convenient because its sloping fall-front left space at the back on which to clear papers when the hinged front part was folded.

Two well-known and attractive scriptors at Ham House which are also in the 1679 inventory, are of smaller dimensions than the usual kinds. One, described as a 'Scriptoire of Prince Wood, garnished with silver', is veneered with oyster pieces of kingwood (a deep brown wood allied to rosewood and also known as princewood) and is supported on a kingwood stand with a drawer in the frieze and spiral-turned legs with carved volute feet joined by waved stretchers (Fig. 8). The interior has fourteen pigeon-holes and six veneered drawers. This splendid piece of Carolean furniture has embossed silver key-plates and handle escutcheons and silver ring handles on the interior drawers. The other scriptor at Ham House, which also has silver mounts, is decorated with veneers of burr walnut. Scriptors were luxury pieces found only in rich households; elsewhere the small writing-desks of traditional form continued in use.

Another new piece of furniture was the domestic bookcase (Fig. 7). Samuel Pepys made, on 23 July, 1666, what must be the earliest reference to this type of furniture: 'Comes Simpson the joiner; and he and I with great pains contriving presses to put my books up in: they now growing numerous, and lying one upon another on my chairs'. Pepys had a number of these bookcases made and twelve are preserved in the Pepys Library. Magdalene College, Cambridge. From this time, bookcases were to be an established part of the rapidly growing libraries of large houses.

As separate eating rooms evolved, the old draw table went out of fashion and its place was taken by oval or circular gate-legged tables with two flaps, which could be conveniently set up for meals, then folded and removed (Fig. 3). Plenty of useful small tables stood about the house, often with spiral-turned legs, flat-waved stretchers, and decoration of parquetry or marquetry. They served a number of purposes, including card-playing, but tables made especially for cards did not appear until William and Mary's reign, in spite of the great passion of the time for all kinds of card games and gambling. On the other hand, tables designed for the toilet emerged quite clearly after 1660. It was fashionable to make up a set called 'table, glass and stands', composed of a dressing-table beneath a mirror flanked by a pair of candlestands. Most dressing-tables were small unless their owner was rich enough to afford one of the elaborate silver toilet sets for which a larger surface was essential. Knole, Kent, has a silver dressing-table, but walnut, ebony or olive were the woods usually employed.

Rich men still spent lavishly on beds, particularly those in the state bedrooms reserved for important visitors. New houses had higher ceilings and consequently the height of beds increased, often to exaggerated proportions when ostrich plumes were added to the four corners of the testers. The framework was no longer left exposed but was entirely covered with expensive materials. One of the most extravagant sets of hangings – curtains, valances, tester and bases – is of gold cloth lined with faded coral taffeta, all embroidered with silver, gold and coloured silks. This bed can be dated to 1670–80 and was said to have cost some £7,000.

Fig. 13 **Cabinet on stand,** *English, late seventeenth century. Walnut and marquetry. Based on continental models, cabinets of this sort were the prestige pieces of the Restoration era, and were used for the storage of valuable documents and small curiosities. (Victoria and Albert Museum.)*

13

Museum Photo

MUSEUMS AND COLLECTIONS

Restoration furniture can be seen in its original setting at the following:

Ham House, Surrey: administered by the Victoria and Albert Museum, London.

Knole, Kent.

Examples may also be seen at the following:

Victoria and Albert Museum, London.

FURTHER READING

'Walnut Furniture' by Edward T. Joy in **The Connoisseur's Guide to Antique Furniture,** edit. by L. G. G. Ramsey and Helen Comstock, London, 1969.

'Furniture' by R. Fastnedge in **The Connoisseur's Complete Period Guides,** *The Stuart Period,* edit. by R. Edwards and L. G. G. Ramsey, London, 1968.

Furniture Making in Seventeenth and Eighteenth Century England by R. W. Symonds, London, 1965.

Delights for Eye and Ear

Graham Wells

Fig. 1 **Harpsichord** *by Jan Ruckers, Antwerp, 1634. Ruckers made the finest harpsichords in Europe in the early seventeenth century. (Ham House, Surrey.)*

A. C. Cooper

For these finely-made and often beautifully decorated instruments the great renaissance and baroque music of Praetorius, Monteverdi, Bach and Vivaldi was created

One of the great joys of early musical instruments is that they encompass two forms of art, being pleasing to both ear and eye. Sometimes their visual beauty lies in exquisite inlays or carving and sometimes in the lack of it, giving pleasure only in the grace of their lines. In fact, the instruments of serious or professional musicians were more often than not without added ornament, everything being secondary to the tone.

The sixteenth century and the first half of the seventeenth belong to the renaissance period, and the last half of the seventeenth to the early baroque. The influence of these periods was as much apparent in music as in all other fields of artistic endeavour. Directly related to changes in musical style, the type and design of instruments underwent considerable change and development in the mid seventeenth century.

The musical renaissance distinguished itself in the immense variety of instruments that it produced yet, despite the rich palette of sound available, the composer seldom specified the instrumentation of a piece, performance varying with the availability of suitably pitched instruments. With the advent of the Baroque and its accent on structural clarity, there was at least some tightening up on this freedom as the beginnings of modern orchestration began to take effect.

It is convenient to consider musical instruments under three main headings – keyboard; stringed, both plucked and bowed; and wind.

KEYBOARD

The most important domestic keyboard instruments maintained through both centuries were those of the harpsichord family. All such instruments are sounded by a plectrum held in a strip of wood, the jack. When a key is depressed the jack rises and the plectrum plucks the string.

To play at least one musical instrument was considered an essential part of education

In English sources of the period, harpsichords, virginals and spinets are all referred to indiscriminately as virginals. The most common keyboard instrument for the household of moderate means was the virginal (used here in the particular rather than the general sense). Initially these were polygonal in shape with a projecting keyboard. Italy was a centre for makers of this type of instrument, the fine example in Fig. 2 being of Italian origin, despite its strong connections with the English Court. Such instruments were usually designed to stand on a table, having no legs of their own, and were often enclosed in a fitted outer case decorated in matching style.

From the Low Countries came the rather more

2

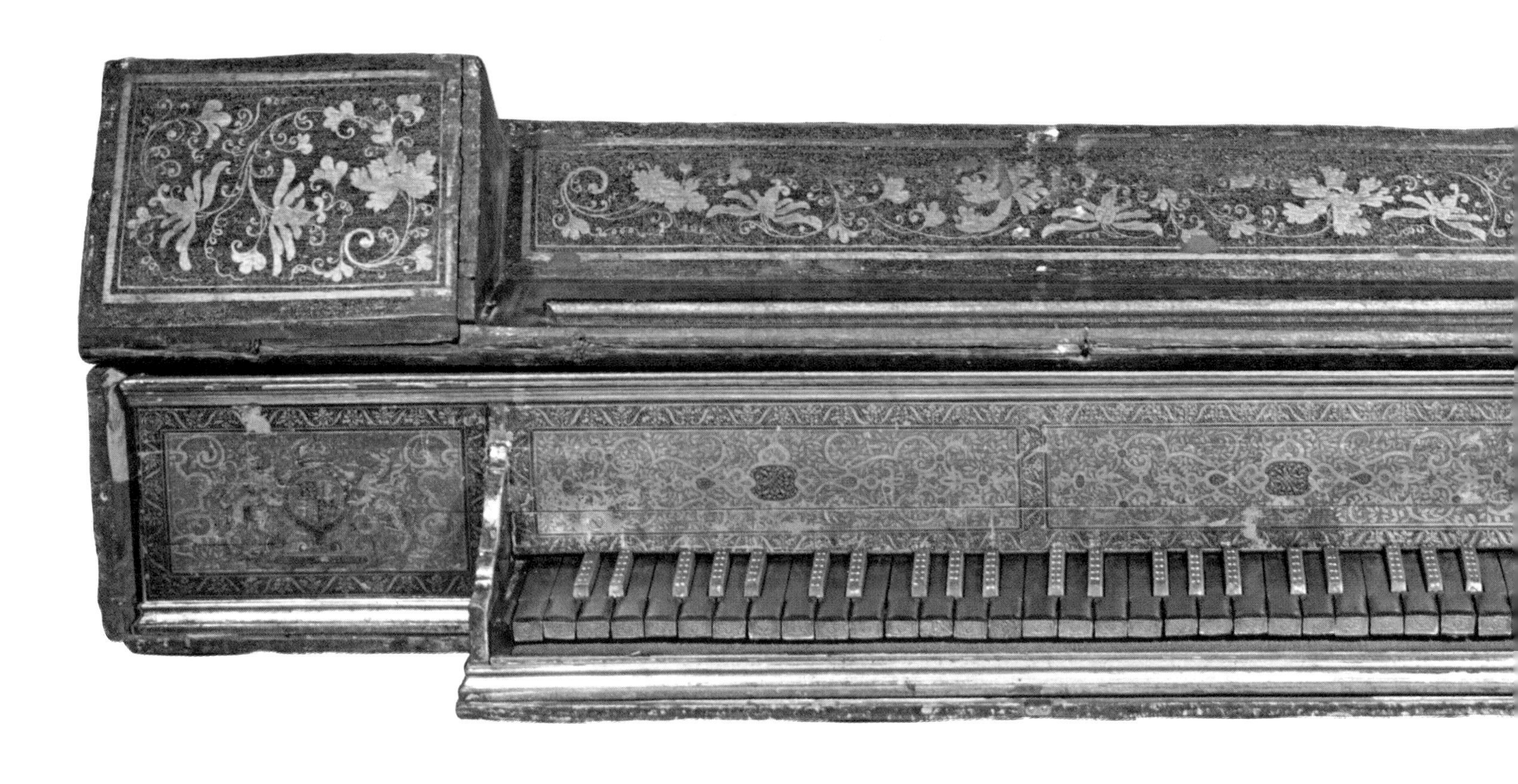

3

Fig. 2 ***Queen Elizabeth's Virginal,*** *Italian, sixteenth century.*
Queen Elizabeth is reputed to have played 'excellently well'. This virginal may have been used by her for it is inscribed with her arms and bears the Boleyn badge. Although made in Italy, it may have been decorated in England.
(Victoria and Albert Museum, London.)

Fig. 3 *Illustration from* ***The Division Violist,*** *by Christopher Simpson, published 1659.*
This illustration shows the bass viol in its classical form. It continued in use until it was superseded by the 'cello during the eighteenth century.

Fig. 5 ***The Music Master*** *by Jan Steen (1626–79). Oil on canvas. The decoration on the harpsichord suggests that it may have been made by one of the Ruckers family, but the artist has inserted his own name on the name board in place of the maker's. The background figure carries a theorbo.*
(National Gallery, London.)

bulky rectangular virginals with recessed keyboard. Instruments of this design were made in England during the mid seventeenth century.

The wing-shaped spinet which first appeared in about 1650 was to thrive right through the eighteenth century. Samuel Pepys owned just such an instrument, as the following entry in his diary bears out:
'15 July, 1668 . . . At noon home to dinner, where is brought home the espinnete I bought the other day of Haward; costs me £5'. His entry on the occasion of the Great Fire of London is interesting in that it bears witness to the number of instruments to be found in London homes at the time and to the value placed on them.
'2nd September, 1666 . . . The River full of lighters and boats taking in goods, and good goods swimming in the water, and only I observed that hardly one lighter in three that had the goods of a house in, but there was a pair of Virginalls in it'. It is worth noting that the ability to play at least one musical instrument was considered an essential part of education.

The harpsichord is basically of the 'grand' piano shape. Initially the instrument had only one keyboard, or manual, and the earliest known authentically dated example has only one set of strings. This is by Jerome of Bologna, dated 1521, and is at present in the Victoria and Albert Museum. Long before 1700 the fully-equipped harpsichord had two manuals and three sets of strings, one of them tuned an octave above the other two.

The finest harpsichords of the late sixteenth and early seventeenth centuries were made by the

Hamlyn Group

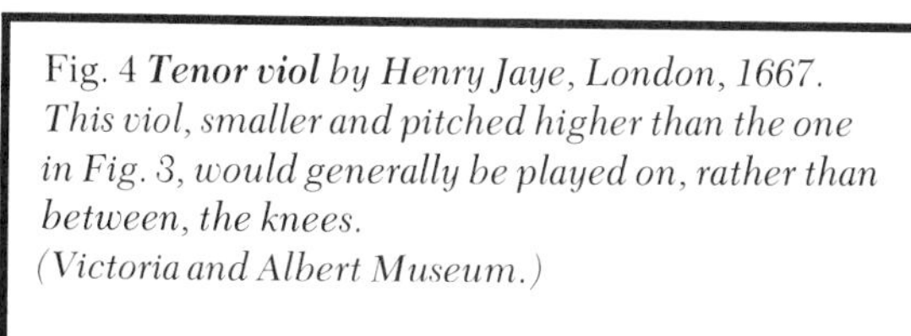

Fig. 4 ***Tenor viol*** *by Henry Jaye, London, 1667. This viol, smaller and pitched higher than the one in Fig. 3, would generally be played on, rather than between, the knees.*
(Victoria and Albert Museum.)

A. C. Cooper

Museum Photo

Ruckers family of Antwerp (Fig. 1), and indeed the esteem in which they were held and the security of their position can be judged from the following incident. In 1637, Sir Francis Windebank, Secretary of State to Charles I, ordered a harpsichord for the King from Jan Ruckers. When it arrived it proved to have the upper keyboard tuned to a different key from the lower, a common practice on the Continent at the time and intended to facilitate accompanying. When the mistake (which could have been rectified without difficulty) was queried, Ruckers retorted: 'This virginall cannot be altered, and none else made on sale', and this was how the matter rested.

The bellows were pumped with one hand and the keyboard played with the other

The clavichord strings are not plucked but struck by a small metal blade, the tangent. The resultant note makes up in delicacy of sound for much of what it lacks in volume. In appearance clavichords are rectangular with inset keyboards. They epitomise the general trend in renaissance music towards a low sound level.

The organ is still fairly closely associated in the minds of many with religious music, but in the renaissance period it found extensive use in secular music. In addition to permanently positioned church organs there existed the smaller so-called positive organ, with several ranks of pipes; and the portative organ, which carried one rank of 'flue' pipes and which often had a compass of little more than two octaves. The bellows were pumped with one hand and the keyboard played with the other. A third variety, the regal, consisted only of 'reed' pipes. The term 'Bible Regal' originates from the practice of making organs so that they would fold in half and give the outward appearance of a book.

STRINGED INSTRUMENTS

Foremost among stringed instruments that are sounded with a bow was the viol family. The classical viol bears a resemblance to the violin, but detailed inspection reveals six strings instead of four, the back flat instead of arched and the neck partially fretted. According to size, the viols are played either on or between the knees and bowed with the palm of the hand uppermost. The definitive outline of the viol did not emerge until the mid seventeenth century. The illustration from Simpson's *The Division Violist* (Fig. 3) shows the final classic form of the bass viol *(viola da gamba)* which was to last well into the eighteenth century until it was finally supplanted by the 'cello as *basso continuo* in chamber music. The beautifully decorated bass viol of 'festoon' outline by John Rose from the Hill Collection in the Ashmolean Museum, Oxford, shows one of the many possible variations in shape.

For some five centuries before the advent of the violin, the 'fiddle' had held a prominent position in European music. The violin originated in Italy in about 1520. It gradually gained respectability and finally ousted the much-loved viols (except for the bass) during the second half of the seventeenth century. This period also saw the first half of the working life of Antonio Stradivari, whose name is nowadays revered above that of any other maker of musical instruments.

If it were necessary to pick out the one musical instrument which was beloved above all others in the sixteenth century, it would probably be the lute. Of Arabic origin, it was brought back to Europe with the returning Crusaders. It developed steadily until the second half of the seventeenth century when, except for a short eighteenth century revival in Germany, it fell into decline.

The lute, with its distinctive reflex peg-box, usually has eleven strings made up into five double 'courses' and one, the top treble string, single. Like the viol, the lute has tied gut frets on the neck. The ornate 'roses' pierced into the belly are generally carved out of the belly-wood itself.

As the sixteenth century progressed, additional bass strings were added to the lute to extend the compass of the instrument downward. To accommodate these necessarily longer strings, the main peg-box was brought to an upright position and a secondary one mounted on top of it. In this form the instrument is known as a theorbo (Fig. 6). The term theorbo-lute applies to yet another variety in which the reflex head is maintained and the secondary peg-box projects upwards from the side of the neck. The theorbo principle was taken to yet further extremes in the chitarrone where the secondary peg-box was mounted on a long neck above the main head, the whole instrument thus measuring some six feet in length with anything up to and around twenty-six strings. Lute strings were of gut which is very susceptible to changes in humidity, hence the saying that 'if a lutenist lived to eighty, he spent forty years of his life tuning his instrument'.

Unfortunately, of the early lutes that still survive most have a history of theorbic conversions behind them and some are merely nineteenth-century collectors' pieces, made up by unscrupulous dealers from oddments.

Another plucked string instrument which enjoyed popularity up to the mid seventeenth

Fig. 6 **Theorbo** *by Matteo Sallas, Venice, 1637.*
The body of this beautifully-made instrument is of ivory, and the decoration on the neck and head is of ivory and ebony inlay. (Victoria and Albert Museum.)

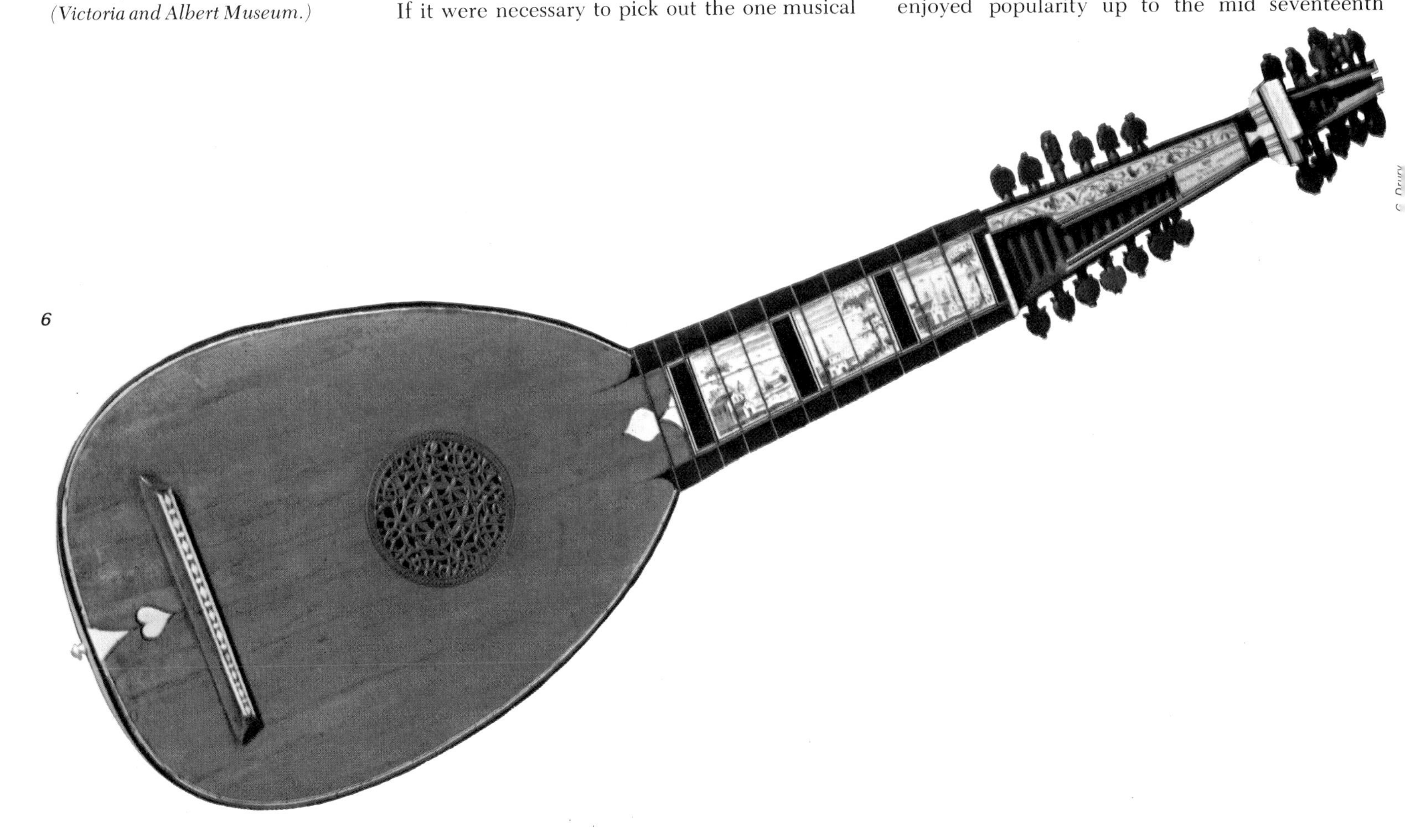

6

7

Fig. 7 ***Bassoon** by J. C. Denner, Berlin, late seventeenth century. The instrument has three keys, although only one is visible in the illustration. (Institut für Musikforschung, Berlin.)*

century was the cittern. It was, broadly speaking, of pear-shaped outline, with a flat back and sides that tapered towards the base giving the body the appearance of a wedge. Its main advantage was the metal strings which held their tuning well. In addition to holding a recognised place in serious music, the cittern was hung up in such places as barbers' shops so that customers could amuse themselves while awaiting their turn.

WIND INSTRUMENTS

It is among the renaissance wind instruments that the really bewildering array of varieties occurs. Each basic type was usually to be found in 'families' corresponding to the pitches of the human voice – soprano, alto, tenor and bass – with extra instruments to explore the extremes of pitch at each end. In his treatise *Syntagma Musicum*, published 1619, the composer Michael Praetorius lists eight sizes of recorder but recommends that the higher sounding ones should not be used in a mixed consort – 'for they do shriek so'.

Loud instruments were suitable for outdoor use

Renaissance wind instruments are arbitrarily divided into two classes, soft and loud. Among the soft instruments the most common was the recorder, which at this time was made in one piece. The larger members of the family had a key for the bottom note. The modern convention of using the left hand uppermost was not in force, and keys were made with a fish-tailed touch-piece to accommodate left-handed players. The key was protected by a wooden barrel pierced with rosettes of holes called a fontinella. The advent of the baroque period was to see only one member of the recorder family, the treble, left in common use. From about 1650 onwards it was made in three jointed sections, the narrow bore giving a more refined sound and greater range.

The transverse flute, which was eventually to supplant the recorder during the eighteenth century, was very much the 'poor relation' in the sixteenth century. It was a cylindrical pipe with no keys and no ornamentation. The late seventeenth century brought some refinement to the flute: the bore became conical and one key was added. (In the mid nineteenth century, Theobald Boehm was to return to the cylindrical flute to produce the instrument which is now the modern concert flute.)

To twentieth-century eyes, the crumhorn appears a somewhat extraordinary instrument as the bore is bent in the manner of an umbrella handle. The sound is produced by a double reed (as in the oboe) but this reed is enclosed in a wooden cap so that it is not touched by the player's lips. The tone is somewhat similar to the buzz of a kazoo and is most pleasing to the ear when the whole family is playing together in consort. The crumhorn was almost as popular as the recorder, but its restricted range and lack of dynamic variations made it unsuitable for baroqúe music.

The dulcian, forerunner of the bassoon, was also made on the double reed principle. The bore doubled back on itself, making the sounding length double the outward measurement. This concept was taken to its extreme in an instrument called, not too appropriately, the rackett. To all outward appearances the instrument is a canister, some eight inches high, with holes issuing at apparently random spots, and surmounted by a bell and a bassoon-like crook. Inside, the bore doubles back on itself some ten times and the resultant notes are rich and dark.

The sackbut corresponds to the modern trombone

Outstanding among the loud instruments was the shawm, another double-reed instrument and the direct ancestor of the oboe. The loud, raucous tone of the shawm bands must have been stirring, to say the least. There still exist examples of great bass shawms of up to nine feet long. It must be left to the imagination as to how the giants were played. These latter instruments are a far cry indeed from the refined oboe which was developed in France, around 1660, and which was to be the leading wind instrument for another hundred years.

The natural trumpets of the day were ceremonial instruments, and the cornett (not to be confused with the modern cornet), which used a similar but smaller mouthpiece, also enjoyed popularity. The cornett was usually made of leather-bound wood and its slightly curved conical tube was pierced with finger-holes – thus it was, in part, a woodwind instrument.

More familiar to the modern eye would be the sackbut which, but for a narrower bore and less-flared bell, corresponds in all other respects to the modern trombone. It was frequently employed as the bass instrument in a consort of loud instruments.

In recent years there has been a healthy trend towards the performance of early music not only on reproductions of early instruments but on the originals themselves, thus allowing contemporary audiences the delight of an aural excursion into the past.

MUSEUMS AND COLLECTIONS

Musical instruments of the sixteenth and seventeenth centuries may be seen at the following:

GREAT BRITAIN

Cambridge:	Fitzwilliam Museum
London:	Fenton House
	Horniman Museum
	Victoria and Albert Museum
Oxford:	Ashmolean Museum
York:	Castle Museum

U.S.A.

Boston:	Boston Museum of Fine Arts
New York:	Metropolitan Museum of Art
Washington:	Smithsonian Institution
	Washington Library of Congress

FURTHER READING

European and American Musical Instruments by Antony Baines, London, 1966.
Old English Instruments of Music by F. W. Galpin, London, 3rd ed., 1965.
The Harpsichord and the Clavichord by Raymond Russell, London, 1959.
The History of Musical Instruments by C. Sachs, London, 1942.

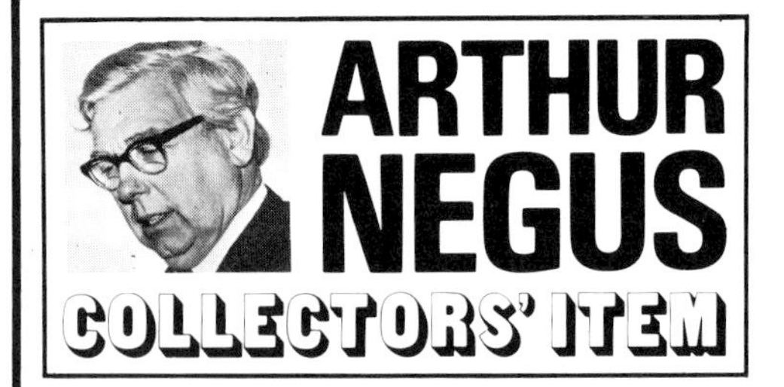

PAPIER MÂCHÉ

Despite its first appearance in the seventeenth century, papier mâché is usually associated with the Victorian era.
In the eighteenth century it was widely used for making tobacco or snuff containers, since it was light, dry and airtight. In 1772, Henry Clay developed a new form of japanned, heat-resistant paperware that was much harder and more durable than anything produced previously. When his Birmingham factory was taken over by Jennens and Bettridge in 1816 they began the large-scale manufacture of household furnishings, making innumerable articles from chairs to inkpots, card-cases to cruet-stands. They had large show-rooms in Belgrave Square, London. The heyday of papier mâché was the period between 1830 and 1860. Letter-racks, match-holders, portfolios and pen-boxes, elaborately decorated and inlaid, were to be seen in many libraries and studies, while fire-guards, fans and work-boxes were placed in drawing-rooms and bedrooms; tea-caddies and snuff-boxes were also made. In the early nineteenth century the latter tended to be plain, often with mottoes, although, as the century progressed, they were more heavily decorated.
As the centre of the trade shifted from Birmingham to London, so the quality of the work declined. In 1864, Jennens and Bettridge closed down, and although cheap papier mâché continued to be made, it became thinner, more brittle and coarser in decoration.

Hints To Collectors

It is unusual to find an identifying mark on any of the smaller pieces of papier mâché. The value of each item depends on its condition, shape and quality of decoration. These factors also help to give a date to a piece. Earlier pieces, particularly if signed, can cost double the price of a later imitation. The later and cheaper examples can be recognised by their lightness and fragility; the surface has a gloss markedly different from the deep shine of earlier work, and any imperfections are plainly visible. Don't use soap, still less detergent, in cleaning a piece; a very small quantity of liquid furniture cream is best.

Opposite: ***Pair of papier mâché fans*** *of a type that were very popular in the 1850s. £9.50 the pair.*

Stall F.2. Antiquarius: A. C. Cooper

Above: ***Letter-rack*** *(£11),* ***pencil-box*** *(£6) and* ***blotter*** *(£7.15), typical of the papier mâché work made on a large scale in the 1840s and '50s.*

Esmé Gambier – Parry, Antiquarius

Right: ***Crumb-tray and brush,*** *typical of the many domestic items of declining quality produced after 1860. Price £9.50.*

Below: ***Inkstand and pen-tray,*** *signed Jennens and Bettridge. c. 1850.*

Philippa Lewis Collection: A. C. Cooper

Stall F.2. Antiquarius, London S.W.2: A. C. Cooper

Hulton Picture Library

Hulton Picture Library

Figs. 1, 2 and 3 ***Three views of Stuart Women*** *by Wenceslans Hollar (1607–77), 1644. Engraving.*
Hollar, born in Prague, was one of the finest illustrators of the time. He came to England in the service of the Earl of Arundel, whom he had met in Cologne; his work consists of etchings and water-colour drawings dealing with every aspect of English life. These women show the characteristic elements in female dress of the period; the fullness of the dress falling from the waist, the very wide and decorative collar and the predilection for pearls which were not only worn as jewellery in necklaces and brooches but also to decorate collars and bodices.

Hulton Picture Library

Fig. 4 ***An English Noblewoman*** *by Hollar, 1644. Engraving. When Elizabethan costume, with its ruff and farthingale, finally disappeared, this type of dress, with its wide collar and cuffs, became fashionable for noblewomen.*

STUART COSTUME AND JEWELLERY

James Laver

During the era of the Stuart monarchs, fashion in dress altered radically – from costumes akin to the Elizabethan mode, through the flamboyant Cavalier and simple Puritan styles, to the innovations of Charles II

'We live in an age of transition', as Adam and Eve might have said, walking out of the Garden of Eden. All ages are ages of transition, but some periods more obviously than others. This is particularly true of the seventeenth century. In the opening years of the century – until the death of King James I – costume was still, in its general outline, Elizabethan. The farthingale and ruff of Anne of Denmark were hardly distinguishable from those of Elizabeth herself. Then came the change, under Charles I, into what is convenient to call Cavalier costume, the falling collar, the long hair, the wide-topped boots (Fig. 11). This lasted (although we must not forget that there was a Puritan as well as a Cavalier costume) until the last quarter of the century, when there was a dramatic change, to the breeches, the many-buttoned coat and the 'vest' underneath it; the neck-cloth instead of the falling collar; the full-bottomed wig instead of natural hair and to what was already assuming the form of the three-cornered hat.

Women's dress (Figs. 1, 2, 3, 4, 9 and 10) was less drastically modified during the century. The farthingale disappeared, the ruff likewise and, for a brief period under Charles II, female costume had a certain loose and even lascivious look, characterising the morals of Whitehall during the reign of the 'Merry Monarch'. But women made one advance during the period. The jewels which had adorned the doublets of their husbands were now scattered over their own clothes (Fig. 5).

When we look at those admirable engravings by Abraham Bosse depicting French nobility of about 1620, the costume, although fantastic enough to satisfy the taste of the Three Musketeers, seems to be decorated with very little jewellery.

The corsages of the ladies of that period were sometimes adorned but jewellery, even for them,

Lauros-Giraudon

Museum Photo

Fig. 5 ***Queen Henrietta Maria*** *by Pierre Mignard (1610–95). Wife of Charles I, she is portrayed in a richly jewelled dress with fine lace cuffs. (Musée Condé, Chantilly.)*

Fig. 6 ***Elizabeth of Bohemia*** *by M. J. van Mierevelt (1567–1641). Daughter of James I, her 'ropes of pearls' were renowned. (National Portrait Gallery, London.)*

Fig. 8 ***Shoes,*** *mid seventeenth century. Kid with braid. The narrow-toed shape is typical of the period. (London Museum.)*

Museum Photo

Fig. 7 ***James I,*** *attributed to John de Critz the Elder (c.1554–1642), 1610. James came from Scotland in 1603, bringing with him very expensive tastes. He is seen here in a jewelled and embroidered costume. (National Maritime Museum, London.)*

K. Hoddle

now began to consist of necklaces, often of large pearls. There was a passion for lockets set with miniature portraits, like the two of about 1610 in the Fitzwilliam Museum, Cambridge, enamelled in tawny red and set with diamonds. One of them contains a miniature of Anne of Denmark by Nicholas Hilliard. Even when jewellery took the form of pendants, it no longer formed part of the dress but was pinned on to it. The same was true of the jewelled and enamelled watches which began to be worn at this period.

A curious feature of the time was the fashion for mourning jewellery (Fig. 14). This could take the form of a necklace of jet beads interspersed with enamelled skulls. Sometimes the emphasis was even more extreme, with pendants in the shape of miniature coffins each containing an exquisitely worked skeleton in white enamel.

Pearls – for those who could afford them – were a popular form of jewellery. An engraving of the period of Louis XIV shows every lady present, from the Queen downwards, wearing a little choker collar of large pearls. Sometimes the 'ropes of pearls' were unusually long, like those possessed by Elizabeth of Bohemia, daughter of James I (Fig. 6). These are

9

Hulton Picture Library

10

Hulton Picture Library

Fig. 9 ***Stuart Woman** by Hollar, 1638. Engraving. Fur muffs and bonnet-like caps were fashionable for outdoor dress.*

Fig. 10 ***The Wife of a Mayor or a Lord Mayor of London** by Hollar, 1649. Engraving. The mayoress is wearing what is basically a Stuart costume although it shows traces of Elizabethan fashions – particularly in the ruff. She holds a fan of the type used before the folding fan in Fig. 2.*

still in the possession of the Royal Family.

The Commonwealth in England had a depressing effect on jewellery as on so much else. The Puritans were naturally averse to such a manifestation of human pride. In France, however, it was very different and Louis XIV is reputed to have worn at the *fêtes* at Fontainebleau held in 1667 a coat of gold tissue and over it a great baldric (shoulder-to-hip belt) consisting entirely of precious stones. In the whole field of jewellery design at this period the French undoubtedly held the lead. The French jewellers engraved their designs on copper plates and prints from these were sent all over Europe for the use of working jewellers. Their influence was especially marked in England after the restoration of Charles II, when the famous Gilles Legaré may be said to have dictated jewellery styles for a whole generation.

The ladies were *en négligé* – as the amorous monarch preferred to think of them

There was not much change in women's dress during the greater part of Charles' reign. The long pointed waists continued and gradually became tighter. The tucked-up skirts became more formal in appearance and the general outline of the figure became stiffer and narrower. In this respect, the paintings of court beauties by Lely are apt to be misleading. They are shown in somewhat loose and apparently careless clothes – as it were, *en négligé* – which is presumably how the amorous monarch preferred to think of them; but this was just as much a studio convention as the fashion for painting kings and soldiers in armour which they never wore in battle or at any other time.

But while women's clothes remained comparatively static, those worn by men underwent a real revolution. Samuel Pepys in his *Diary* for 8 October, 1666, notes: 'The King hath yesterday in Council declared his resolution of setting a fashion of clothes which he will never alter'. On 15 October he comments: 'This day the King begins to put on his vest, and I did see several persons of the House of Lords and Commons too, great courtiers who are in it, being a long cassock close to the body of black cloth, and pinked with white silk under it and a coat over it, and the legs ruffled with black riband like a pigeon's leg'.

The other famous diarist of the period, John Evelyn, described the new garment as a 'dress after the Persian mode', and one has to admit that it did bear a certain resemblance to the Persian coat, except that the latter had long sleeves whereas the sleeves of Charles' 'vest' were extremely short. In the end the overcoat became the coat, and the vest became what was later, when it had grown much shorter, to be called a waistcoat.

The English King's action was looked upon as a deliberate attempt to break away from French fashions, but scholars have pointed out that a very similar garment was introduced at the French Court as early as 1662. It was at first worn by a few privileged courtiers but by 1670 its use had become universal. The later portraits of Louis XIV show him wearing it.

The general effect was plain and sober. There was no attempt to decorate the coat with jewels or even with embroidery. Jewellery was now almost

11

Museum Photo

12

Museum Photo

13

Museum Photo

Fig. 11 **English Costume,** c.1630. Silk, with modern collar and cuffs added to give the impression of the complete costume.
This is the style which may be described as Cavalier. It was the fashionable male dress in the reign of Charles I and the main features are the waisted jacket, the cloak, the breeches terminating below the knee, the wide-topped boots, and the falling collar.
(Victoria and Albert Museum, London.)

Fig. 12 **Pair of Breeches,** c.1680. Silk damask, length 19 ins., waist 32 ins.
(Victoria and Albert Museum.)

Fig. 13 **An Unknown Lady** by Isaac Oliver, c.1605. Miniature.
The feminine appeal of a billowing lawn shawl is captured in the words of the poet Robert Herrick: 'A sweet disorder in the dress Kindles in clothes a wantonness: A lawn about the shoulders thrown Into a fine distraction'.
(Fitzwilliam Museum, Cambridge.)

Fig. 14 **Design for an IHS pendant** by Arnold Lulls, seventeenth century. Water-colour.
Mourning jewellery was extremely popular. The IHS motif was often executed in sombre black jet set in gold.
(Victoria and Albert Museum.)

Fig. 15 **Part of a shirt,** early seventeenth century.
Linen with insertions of needlepoint lace.
Originally much longer, this shirt has, at some stage, been cut down, making the body now look strangely disproportionate.
(Victoria and Albert Museum.)

Fig. 16 **Two designs for aigrettes** by Arnold Lulls, seventeenth century. Water-colour.
Richly ornamented with precious stones, aigrettes – jewellery imitating plumage – were worn in the hair.
(Victoria and Albert Museum.)

14

K. Hoddle

15

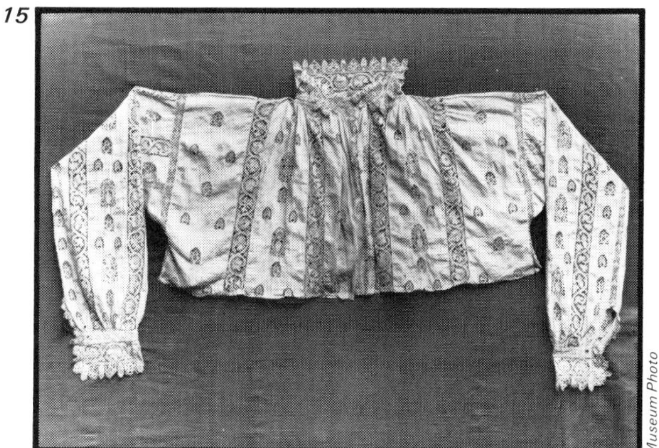

Museum Photo

16

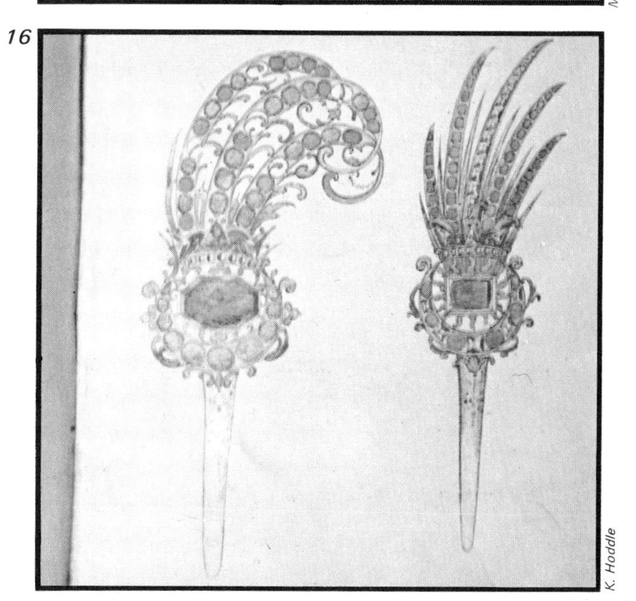

K. Hoddle

entirely confined to the many buttons on both coat and vest. Naturally enough the French King had the most splendid specimens. We learn from an inventory of 1691 that he owned two complete *parures* of diamonds. One consisted of one hundred and twenty-three buttons for the *justaucorps*, or coat, and forty-eight buttons for the *veste*. The other comprised one hundred and sixty-eight buttons for the coat and forty-eight for the waist-coat. Both *parures* included a diamond ornament for cocking the hat, garters, the cross of the Order of the Saint Esprit and a diamond-hilted sword. No English king could afford such splendour, and it is a fascinating comment on the cost of such things that James II, when in exile, was able to obtain £3,000 (a very large sum in those days) for a pair of diamond shoe-buckles.

His daughter, Queen Mary, wife of William III, found some difficulty in settling her debts. At the time of her death in 1696, she owned – but had not paid for – a whole collection of diamond buckles, sleeve clasps and other ornaments. Her picture in the National Portrait Gallery shows her wearing a large diamond brooch with an oblong centre stone surrounded by six pearls. Her waxen effigy in Westminster Abbey is dressed in clothes decorated with matching brooches, but the jewels have been replaced by 'paste' as it is called in England. The French name is *stras*, after that of the Paris jeweller who invented a method of backing crystals with foil to make them shine like diamonds. Both countries towards the end of the century began to produce imitation jewels in large numbers for those who could not afford the real thing, for the great days of jewellery as goldsmiths' work were over. The invention of improved methods of cutting diamonds made the jewel itself all-important – the setting was often reduced to a mere claw.

MUSEUMS AND COLLECTIONS

London: London Museum
Victoria and Albert Museum

PORTRAITS OF THE PERIOD SHOWING COSTUME AND JEWELLERY

Bedfordshire: Woburn Abbey

London: Hampton Court Palace
London Museum
National Gallery
National Portrait Gallery
Wallace Collection

Wiltshire: Longleat

FURTHER READING

A History of Costume in the West by François Boucher, London, 1967.
A History of Jewellery, 1100–1870 by Joan Evans, London, 1963.
The Cheapside Hoard of Elizabethan and Jacobean Jewellery, London Museum Catalogue, No. 2, London, 1928.
English Jewellery from the Fifth Century A.D. to 1800 by Joan Evans, London, 1921.
Jewellery by H. Clifford Smith, London, 1908.

1

Museum Photo

2

Museum Photo

3

Museum Photo

4

English Delftware

Oliver Van Oss

Museum Photo

Fig. 1 ***Winebottle**, London, c.1670. Height 5¾ ins. Of characteristic globular shape, this attractive winebottle was made for the off-licence before glass became readily available. The decorative portrait of Charles II is unusual; normally only a description of the contents is shown. (Victoria and Albert Museum, London.)*

Fig. 2 ***Drug jar**, London (?), c.1660–1700. Height 6¾ ins. Drug jars of this type were made from the Commonwealth onwards. Unspouted examples such as this one were intended for dry drugs: in this case 'Rosar Rubr'. (Victoria and Albert Museum.)*

Fig. 3 ***Mug**, Lambeth, 1642. Height 5 ins. Made for Ann Chapman, whose name appears on it, this mug is characteristic of early shapes, showing a strong Flemish influence. (Victoria and Albert Museum.)*

Fig. 4 ***Posset-pot**, Lambeth (?), 1696. Height 6 ins. This charming pot was intended for hot spiced and herbed drinks, which were sucked through the strainer-spout. The blue decoration is derived from Wan-Li porcelain designs, seen on the popular imported wares from China. (Victoria and Albert Museum.)*

Fig. 5 ***Ornamental shoe**, Lambeth, 1707. Height 4⅛ ins. The idea of imitating natural objects in pottery was popular in Holland at this time, and it was probably imported from there. (Ashmolean Museum, Oxford. Warren Collection.)*

Fig. 6 ***Posset-pot**, Lambeth, 1687. Height 5¼ ins., width 10⅛ ins. Like the posset-pot in Fig. 4, this rather crude piece has a sucking spout. The rope twist handles are an unusual detail. (Ashmolean Museum. Warren Collection.)*

5

6

Museum Photo

Museum Photo

Firmly baroque in character, and inspired by the designs of the Orient and the Netherlands, English Delftware was nonetheless a distinctively national art form of great charm and beauty

The earliest tin-enamelled pottery known to have been made in England is the group of globular jugs called the Malling jugs, after a specimen originally preserved in a church in Kent. They are handsome objects, sometimes with contemporary silver mounts of between 1550 and 1580, and they are exceedingly rare. The glaze is mostly a dark blue and blackish purple, occasionally flecked with orange, and a clear turquoise is also found. In shape they seem to derive from the much imported stoneware of the Rhineland, and the mottling may well be an attempt to reproduce the variety known as tiger-ware.

True delftware, made some years before such pottery was made in Delft itself, was introduced late in the sixteenth century by a succession of Dutch and Flemish immigrants. The pioneers were Jasper Andriesz, a descendant of the Guido di Savino who had moved from Castel Durante to Antwerp early in the century, and Jacob Janson. These two started up at Norwich in 1567, but moved to London and founded a pottery there by 1571. The earliest wares, of which considerable quantities have been dug up in London, were mainly short globular jugs, drug jars (Fig. 16) and ointment pots. The decoration consists chiefly of thin encircling bands of blue, occasionally enlivened by green, yellow and manganese hatching. Sometimes simple patterns of flowers and branches were attempted.

It is extremely difficult to distinguish these early wares from the Flemish and Dutch pieces imported in great numbers, but as a general rule it may be said that the English designs are less sophisticated and the colours paler. A delightful two-handled jug found in King William Street and now in the London Museum, where all these early wares may best be studied, shows a long-tailed bird in a reserve of dark blue and orange, of a type familiar in Faenza *albarelli* of about 1480, and here again one must forget one's patriotism and suspect a Netherlandish origin. The earliest dated piece with an English inscription is a large dish, meant for display, showing a city water-gate – possibly the Tower of London – surrounded by a border of renaissance grotesques. It is painted in the full range of maiolica colours, is dated 1600, and bears the proud inscription: 'The Rose is Red The Leaves are Grene God Save Elizabeth Our Queene'. There is nothing to compare with it, except possibly a unique dish with a Dutch inscription and the date 1570, now in the Boymans Museum in Rotterdam. Each is a masterpiece and neither ties up with any other object that has survived.

By the first quarter of the seventeenth century the London potteries at Lambeth and Southwark were fully established and were producing delftware in shapes and with types of decoration peculiar to England. These included drinking-mugs, at first barrel-shaped and, gradually, as the century progressed, growing a more pronounced upright neck; winebottles and, most characteristic of all, straight-sided posset-pots, the English equivalent of the posset-bowls made at Frankfurt. These were intended for hot spiced and herbed drinks, which were sucked out through a spout at the front, with strainer holes at its base on the inside (Figs. 4 and 6).

'Whit', 'Sack' or 'Claret' over a date and a diminishing flourish of whirligigs

Blue decoration, crudely imitating that on Wan-Li porcelain, is considered typical of Southwark and consists almost invariably of birds perched on rocks and surrounded by highly stylised flowers made of an oval of dots radiating from a centre. Some of the mugs are just sponged over with manganese, leaving a band on which is inscribed in black or blue the owner's name. This was a favourite embellishment, and the bold clear capitals spelling out: 'Elizabeth Brocklehurst 1628', 'John Potten and Susanna', and the like, are highly decorative, quite apart from their period charm (Fig. 3). In all this early London delftware the white enamel is milky and brilliant and the blue, bright and fresh. Christian Wilhelm, who opened a pottery at Pickleherring Stairs in Southwark in 1612, had started as a cobalt manufacturer, and it is possibly to his expertise that the excellence of the pigment is due. The white is at its best on the small globular winebottles made for the off-licence trade before glass became readily available (Fig. 1). These are some of the most attractive objects in the whole history of English pottery, and are free from any foreign influence. The decoration, except for an occasional name or coat of arms, is in plain blue, simply describing the contents – 'Whit', 'Sack', 'Claret', etc., over a date and a diminishing flourish of whirligigs.

Gradually the shapes of the posset-pots became more ambitious and the decoration closer to the Chinese originals. The sides developed a rounder belly and a more marked waist, the handles sprang from serpentine coils, the foot splayed out and the lid grew into a grandiose royal crown, often topped with a Maltese cross and flanked by fleurs-de-lis, the whole being fragile, elaborate and baroque: magnificent and faintly absurd.

A special group is formed by the small caudle cups, either straight-sided or incurved, showing Charles II in his full regalia, sometimes between pillars and beneath a rounded arch (Fig. 18). These derive from an earlier type, yet they are something quite distinctive and apart. Charles in his ermine robes is found more rarely on flat bottles and oval dishes, some of which may well have been faked. The genuine articles have notably clear, firm colouring and are boldly drawn.

It is the dishes and chargers which have survived in greatest quantity and are most familiar to collectors. In the earliest days these still show strong foreign influence and include crude versions of the Netherlandish pomegranates and oranges, and plain geometrical designs of bright colour. Most were show pieces, not intended for use as tableware.

Biblical subjects, sparsely coloured within a border of Wan-Li motifs, often in the Southwark idiom, were popular from the 1630s until about 1665. The earliest survivor – and in many ways the most remarkable of these – is a plate of the Magdalen in front of a very English-looking church. It is dated 1637, and the bordér has that pattern of crosses and raised knobs already familiar in Holland.

A famous charger at Chequers shows Charles I and his children beneath a pillared arch, echoed in the Charles II mugs referred to above. Oddly enough, it bears a Commonwealth date – 1653. It is copied from a print of that date, an early example of what was to become a common practice with more elaborate designs, which were often 'pounced' – or traced by rubbing pumice or charcoal through pinholes made in the design and thus reproduced on to the object. It is also one of the earliest of the long series of portraits of royalty and popular heroes, such as the Duke of Marlborough or Doctor Sacheverel, which was to extend right down to the days of John Wilkes.

More immediately these took the form of the 'blue-dash chargers', so called from the sloping slashes of blue around the edges, simulating the rope-like indentations on metal dishes (Fig. 11). All sovereigns until George II are represented (Fig. 9). Another popular subject was that of Adam and Eve beneath the apple tree, around

7

Museum Photo

8

Museum Photo

9

Museum Photo

10

Museum Photo

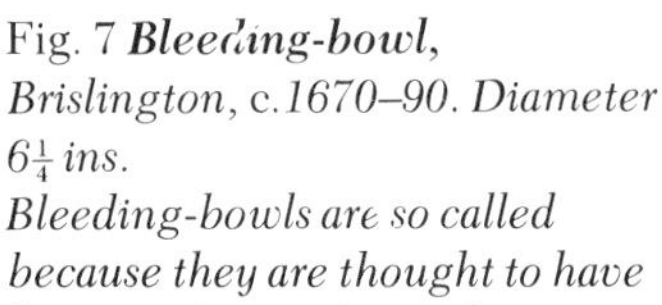

Fig. 7 **Bleeding-bowl,** *Brislington, c.1670–90. Diameter $6\frac{1}{4}$ ins.*
Bleeding-bowls are so called because they are thought to have been used in medicine, but another theory is that they were used for hot soups and porridges. (Ashmolean Museum. Warren Collection.)

Fig. 8 **Coffee-pot,** *Lambeth, 1705. Height $7\frac{1}{2}$ ins.*
This early coffee-pot with its attractive polychrome decoration is a unique survival, but it is missing the silver chain which would have joined lid and handle. (Ashmolean Museum. Warren Collection.)

Fig. 9 **William and Mary Plate,** *London (?), 1687–1694. Diameter $13\frac{3}{4}$ ins.*
Called a blue-dash charger because of the borders. (Ashmolean Museum. Warren Collection.)

Fig. 10 **Teapot,** *Lambeth, 1700–10. Height $4\frac{5}{8}$ ins.*
This rare teapot is an early example of the K'ang Hsi patterns which were later to become so popular. (Ashmolean Museum. Warren Collection.)

which is coiled the serpent (Fig. 12). It is always difficult to be certain which of these chargers were made in London and which in Bristol and Brislington, where delftware was certainly being made from early in the 1640s. It is often claimed that the Bristol versions have a thin line of manganese within the border, which London has not. The foliage in the Bristol versions tends to be heavily sponged rather than drawn, and one may suspect that the cruder Adam and Eve plates, showing less familiarity with engraved sources, were not made in London.

Impressive pieces – some of the finest peasant pottery ever made anywhere

A sub-section of this group is that of the Tulip chargers (Fig. 15). Originally derived from sixteenth-century Isnik dishes, possibly by way of Padua, these bold designs develop from a fairly naturalistic representation early in the century into something highly stylised, a pattern of broad leaves, coloured a pale green, and deep orange flowers, alternating on occasion with seed pods or carnations, the whole enlivened with touches of blue within a clear yellow border. For the most part they are tin-enamelled on the front only, the back being covered with a lead glaze which shows the rich ochre body of the material. These tulip dishes are impressive pieces, some of the finest peasant pottery ever made anywhere.

Museum Photo

Museum Photo

Museum Photo

Museum Photo

Museum Photo

Fig. 11 ***Blue-dash charger,*** *English, 1637. Diameter 14¾ ins. Chargers of this sort represented not only sovereigns of the period, but popular heroes as well. The name blue-dash derives from the border, which is slashed to imitate the rope-like indentations found on metal dishes. (Fitzwilliam Museum, Cambridge. Glaisher Collection.)*

Fig. 12 ***Adam and Eve plate,*** *English, 1640. Diameter 14 ins. (Fitzwilliam Museum. Glaisher Collection.)*

Fig. 13 **Charger,** *English, 1620. Diameter 17 ins. The unusual decoration is painted in the style of maiolica. (Fitzwilliam Museum. Glaisher Collection.)*

Fig. 14 ***Jug,*** *English, second half of the seventeenth century. Height 3 ins. Decorated in the manner of late Ming porcelain. (Fitzwilliam Museum. Glaisher Collection.)*

Fig. 15 ***Tulip charger,*** *London, late seventeenth century. Diameter 13½ ins. The decoration is Turkish in style. (Victoria and Albert Museum.)*

16th and 17th century English Delftware

Fig. 16 **Drug jar**, *London, early seventeenth century. Height $3\frac{7}{8}$ ins. This drug jar is one of the earliest types of wares made in England. These are similar to Flemish pieces of the period – the art was introduced into England by Dutch and Flemish artisans – but in general the colours are paler and the designs less sophisticated. (Victoria and Albert Museum.)*

16

Museum Photo

17

Museum Photo

18

Museum Photo

Fig. 17 ***Fécondité* dish,** *London, c.1635. $19\frac{1}{2}$ x $16\frac{1}{4}$ ins. Intended as show pieces, these curious dishes, with their combined renaissance and Ming borders, were copied from those made by Bernard Palissy in France a hundred years earlier. (Victoria and Albert Museum.)*

Fig. 18 **Caudle cup**, *Lambeth, c.1665. Height $2\frac{3}{4}$ ins., diameter $3\frac{1}{4}$ ins. A large number of these attractive mugs were made at this period, all showing Charles II in full regalia. (Victoria and Albert Museum.)*

Fig. 19 **Wine jug**, *English, 1660. Height 7 ins. Dutch influence is shown in the cartouche. (Fitzwilliam Museum. Glaisher Collection.)*

Two types from the middle fifty years of the century are derived from French originals. The first is that of the oval *Fécondité* dishes, copied from those made by Palissy a hundred years earlier (Fig. 17). A naked lady surrounded by naked children, within a border in which Ming artemisia leaves and renaissance masks alternate with curiously Dutch landscapes and the arms of City Livery Companies, such as the Grocers'. Figures and border are sometimes shown in relief, and the colouring is predominantly blue with a rich ochre and occasional touches of copper green and manganese. The ensemble, intended solely for ornament, is curious rather than beautiful. The other type is of useful wares painted in white slip on a very rich dark blue, in direct imitation of the *bleu Persan* made at Nevers, but without its orange touches. These were made in Lambeth between 1680 and 1710. The designs are in the

19

Museum Photo

Chinese style, simply and rather crudely executed (Fig. 14).

One final type of ware remains to be described. In the early 1670s a Dutch potter, Jan v.d.Hamme, settled in London and was, incidentally, one of the prime movers in demanding the prohibition of imports from Europe. Ironically, he is possibly responsible for the clear Dutch influence shown in a series of plates, jugs and drug pots (Fig. 19) decorated with the characteristic Dutch cartouches, with sphinxes, birds, cherubs and crowns. The glaze is still a brilliant white, the decoration crisply professional. Perhaps the most attractive are the sets of six 'Merryman' plates, often octagonal, inscribed in series:

1. What is a merry man.
2. Let him do what he can
3. To entertain his guests
4. With wine and merry jests
5. But if his wife do frown
6. All the merriment goes down.

The spelling is often shaky, but this is household stuff of admirable quality.

Many other shapes were made: pill slabs with the arms of the Apothecaries' Company; bold jugs and slender winecups, both often adorned with the arms of a City Company; cats and books, provided with stoppers, which served as hand-warmers; bleeding-cups, where the handles, pierced with heart-shaped holes or holes arranged in a cross, denote a London origin, whereas those of Bristol have a solitary round hole in a leaf-shaped handle (Fig. 7). Drug jars, spouted for wet drugs or plain, were made from the Commonwealth years onwards (Fig. 2). The name of the drug is boldly inscribed within a plain cartouche, again of Dutch origin, and the dark blue is sometimes heightened with touches of red.

The most ambitious pieces were bowls and monteiths, as the bowls with indented edges were called, which were used to cool wineglasses in water. Some are decorated in simple Chinese designs, others with highly elaborate scenes of buildings or groups of people, equal in quality to what was being produced in Delft. There are also noble vases and *cache pots*, with highly confident decoration of birds among plants, in Ming style. The colouring is predominantly dark blue, with a clear rusty red, a lemon yellow and an olive green which had superseded the earlier clear copper and is specifically English in character.

All this seventeenth-century pottery is firmly baroque in shape and decoration. The earliest is Netherlandish in inspiration, that in the mid century idiomatically English. The white is very bright, the blue smokier than on wares made in Europe. From 1680 onwards, particularly on 'useful' objects, a greenish blue glaze was introduced. The Chinese decoration ceased copying Wan-Li patterns and those of K'ang Hsi became more popular and were to prevail throughout the eighteenth century when, as throughout Europe, shapes and decoration were to become less dignified and more intimate (Figs. 5, 8 and 10).

MUSEUMS AND COLLECTIONS

English delftware may be seen at the following:

Bristol:	City Art Gallery
Cambridge:	Fitzwilliam Museum (Glaisher Collection)
London:	British Museum London Museum (especially for earliest pieces) Victoria and Albert Museum (Schreiber Collection)
Oxford:	Ashmolean Museum (R. Hall Warren Collection)

FURTHER READING

English Delftware Pottery by A. Ray, London, 1968.

English Delftware and Pottery by F. H. Garner, London, 1948.

Catalogue of the Glaisher Collection by Bernard Rackham, London, 1935.

Early English Drug Jars by G. E. Howard, London, 1931.

Catalogue of the Schreiber Collection, by Bernard Rackham, Vol II, London, 1929.

English Pottery by Bernard Rackham & Herbert Read, London, 1924.

Catalogue of English Pottery in the British Museum by R. L. Hobson, London, 1903.

William and Mary Interiors

Geoffrey Beard

Fig. 1 (Frontispiece) ***Heaven Room,*** *Burghley House, Lincolnshire, painted by Antonio Verrio (1639–1707), 1695–96.*
Executed for the 5th Earl of Exeter, who paid all Verrio's expenses as well as his fee, the Heaven Room is decorated with a riot of illusionist decoration representing tales of the Olympian gods: Mars and Venus, Neptune and his Court and Vulcan's forge. On the ceiling is depicted An Assembly of the Gods

2

A. F. Kersting

3

A. F. Kersting

4

Transglobe

5

Transglobe

6

A. F. Kersting

7

Fig. 2 **Drayton House,** *Northamptonshire. The gateway and Talman's cupolas are of the William and Mary period.*

Fig. 3 **State Drawing-room,** *Chatsworth, Derbyshire, c.1692, the ceiling painted by Louis Laguerre. The tapestries after Raphael were made at Mortlake, c.1635.*

Fig. 4 **The Balcony Room,** *Dyrham Park, Gloucestershire. Wood-carving by Robert Barker; 1693.*

Fig. 5 **Staircase,** *Treasurer's House, York.*

Fig. 6 **Dyrham Park,** *Gloucestershire, west front by Samuel Hauduroy, c.1692. The rest of the house was designed by William Talman, c.1700.*

Fig. 7 **Petworth House,** *Sussex, rebuilt from 1688.*

With a superabundance of carved wood, wrought iron, gilt stucco, rich damasks and velvets, the aristocracy adorned their homes; for social position was bought with material possession

The end of the seventeenth century saw by the elusive development of taste the appearance in England of finer plasterwork and more interesting woodwork and decorative paintings than ever before. Patrons were, for the most part, still breaking away from the restrictive pattern of Jacobean times. This pattern involved working with a builder and books of instruction, and with the advice of knowledgeable friends.

'First resolve with yourself', said Sir Roger Pratt, the architect, a pupil of Inigo Jones, in 1660, 'what house will be answerable to your purse and estate, and after you have pitched upon the number of rooms and the dimension of each, and desire in some measure to make use of whatsoever you have either observed, or heard to be excellent elsewhere, then if you are not able to handsomely

8

Photo-Hachette

Fig. 8 **King William and Queen Mary** *(1688–1702) from an engraving by R. de Hooge, after C. Allard. After the Glorious Revolution of 1688, William of Orange was invited by the English Parliament to accept the throne jointly with his wife Mary, daughter of the deposed James II. They affirmed Protestantism as the faith of the nation but tolerated Catholicism.*

contrive it yourself, get some ingenious gentleman who has seen much of that kind abroad and been somewhat versed in the best authors of architecture: Palladio, Scamozzi, Serlio, etc., to do it for you . . . .' Towards the end of the seventeenth century, this period of amateur competence had played itself in, but the splendours of interior decoration had changed little since the days of Inigo Jones.

To build a large country house a talented army of craftsmen, many of them foreign, were assembled by the patron and his advisers. Grinling Gibbons, Jonathan Maine and Edward Pearce were hard at work, wood- and stone-carving. Antonio Verrio, Louis Laguerre and Sir James Thornhill were embellishing almost every ceiling of note, and the skilled decorative smith, Jean Tijou, was creating filigree patterns in wrought iron. George London and Henry Wise were transforming or making gardens and bringing order and pattern with parterres and long vistas of fountains and canals. Leonard Knyff and Johannes Kip busied themselves with their perspective engravings, fulsome dedications and elevations of the 'great fine houses'. John Vanderbank inherited the traditions of the long-seated tapestry manufacturers, and soon his exciting and colourful Soho *Chinoiseries* were hanging over sombre wainscoting. Dufresnoy and Francis Lapierre stretched their damasks and velvets over skilfully wrought wood and papier mâché and erected the great state beds which still adorn houses like Belton and Chatsworth. Edward Goudge was the leading plasterer and, as the architect Captain William Winde told his cousin Lady Mary Bridgeman, 'is looked on as the beste master in England in his profession'. John Wilkes provided delicately wrought locks with elaborate mechanisms and Thomas Tompion's clocks stood on ornate overmantels, surmounted by portraits of patrons by Kneller, Closterman, Riley and Van Dyck.

'A thin ill-natured ghost . . . of no reputation with any party'

Craftsmen travelled extensively; from York plasterers went north to Scotland and south to London in search of work and ideas, and London craftsmen such as Edward Pearce, the carver, and Robert Bradbury and James Pettifer, the plasterers, went to Sudbury in Derbyshire in 1676. Pearce carved the staircase and 'ye carved work in ye p'lour and ye dore cases on ye top of ye great staires and the panel in ye staire head chamber'. Domination over the craftsman by a trade guild, while showing signs of decline, was yet strong in centres like London, York, Bristol and Chester. It was a process which found encouragement among new patrons advanced to royal favour when William and Mary came to the throne. Sculptors and painters were needed for portraits in marble and on canvas, and a welcome was given to the many Huguenot craftsmen fleeing to England and Holland from the religious persecution pursued in France by Louis XIV. Queen Mary herself was filling the long, echoing corridors of Hampton Court with tulip jars and vases in blue Dutch delft, and William gave as presents to his friends opulent works of art and fine pieces of walnut furniture. Hampton Court became William's favourite house and he moved there the best of the royal collection of pictures. What the King and Queen were anxious to do, their aristocratic subjects were eager to emulate. Two such were the fifth Earl of Exeter and Thomas Osborne, first Duke of Leeds.

The Duke of Leeds was one of the leading politicians of his day: Treasurer of England, Lord President of the Council and an active supporter of William, Prince of Orange. Described by contemporaries as a 'thin ill-natured ghost' and 'a gentleman of admirable natural parts, great knowledge and experience . . . but of no reputa-

William III (1650–1702) Mary II (1662–1694) Proclaimed king and queen 1689

Fig. 9 ***Design for a fireplace*** *by Daniel Marot (c.1663–1752). Marot's designs were the most powerful influence on the late Stuart style. A Huguenot, he left France for Holland in 1684 and came to England in the last decade of the century. This room is planned to include 'japanned' panels. The many vases and plates reflect the contemporary passion for Chinese porcelain. (Victoria and Albert Museum, London.)*

K. Hoddle

tion with any party', he amassed a considerable fortune and in the later years of his career spent large sums on building and decoration. His house, Kiveton in Yorkshire, was built over ten years, from 1694 to 1704, but was pulled down (regrettably, for it would have been as revered as Belton or Chatsworth) in about 1812. The example is, however, useful in tracing the decoration and cost of a large house in the late seventeenth century. All the craftsmen necessary to create gilded splendour came to Kiveton and it must have presented a lavish scene to contemporary eyes.

Kiveton contained twenty-four chimney-pieces, that in the Great Dining-Room being largely composed of rich purple marble. As at Dyrham, William Balthwayt's house near Bristol, gilt-leather panels hung in the lower vestibule. Some twelve feet high and ranging in width from a foot to four feet six inches, they would vie for attention with Jonathan Maine's superb wood-carvings in soft fruitwoods and Louis Laguerre's ceiling painting representing the history of the marriage between Psyche and Cupid. Over the many doors were fifty-six painted panels, many inspired by Dutch marine views, and scenic groupings of fantastic, exotic birds. The staircase balustrading was finished black and had gilt coats of arms wrought by Jean Tijou, the French smith who had worked at Hampton Court and whose daughter was married to Louis Laguerre, the painter, and godson of Louis XIV. The total expenditure on the house, other than on furniture, came to £15,028 18s. 6d. in the ten years of building. It was enough to indicate status to one's friends.

The owner of Burghley House was the Earl of Exeter, a relative of the Duke of Devonshire (for whom Chatsworth was rebuilt and decorated) and a traveller and lover of architecture and painting. He started to alter his house just as William came to power. The fine, fretted plaster ceilings with their rich displays of simulated fruit and flowers were the work of craftsmen who had worked for Sir Christopher Wren, the King's Surveyor. An interesting example of shared responsibility emerges in the payments to the wood-carvers and allows the comment that some form of partnership obviously existed between them. Grinling Gibbons (whose name is synonymous with such carved wonders and of whom Nahum Tate wrote in 1684 that 'Thy Artful works are by Nature scarce excell'd') was paid £100 in two sums of £50, but Jonathan Maine, the Oxford carver who had worked at Kiveton and was to work again with Gibbons at St. Paul's Cathedral, together with his partner Thomas Young, received some £402 between 1682 and 1687. A tumultuous display of carved wood was provided to a delighted owner.

All the carved work at Burghley, however, is overshadowed by the brilliant display of the grand decorative schemes of painting by Antonio Verrio (1639–1707). The painter was allowed food, clothing and schooling expenses for his children by Lord Exeter in addition to the sum paid him for his work. After the colours had been purchased and the decisions on subject and position made, a riot of Olympians and creatures of the Zodiac were painted all over the coved ceilings. The result to some eyes, while undeniably colourful, is somewhat over-powering as the rooms (other than the richly splendid Heaven Saloon) are not high. The Earl must have enjoyed it for the amount he paid to have it done. He lived to see it all finished, but died suddenly in France in the summer of 1700.

During his lifetime, the Countess of Exeter presumably took keen interest in the decoration not only of Burghley but of her family home at Chatsworth. The architect William Talman, irascible and demanding of so much attention, rebuilt the south and east fronts for her brother, the Duke of Devonshire, between 1687 and 1696. The wood-carving in the State Rooms at Chatsworth is of a high standard. Some of the London craftsmen who had worked at Burghley House came to the house. As their assistant, they had the services of Samuel Watson, a local carver who worked at the house on and off at both stone- and wood-carving until his death in 1715. For the work at Chatsworth, wood was imported from the Baltic. Cedar-wood was used in the chapel, and some of the joinery was worked by John Chaplin of London and sent by sea to Hull. Chaplin himself did not visit the house. The decorative work at Chatsworth was completed by the painters and the metal-workers. For such an important commission, both Verrio and his pupil Laguerre joined their men at the house. On the Great Stairs, Verrio painted the walls and ceiling with various scenes representing the triumphs of Ceres and Cybele and paunchy Bacchus.

Given three times in marriage before her sixteenth birthday

Another important house which summarises the late seventeenth-century achievement in embellishment is Dyrham Park, Gloucestershire. The walls of the staircase were veined to simulate marble and William Blathwayt, the owner, paying his bills as late and as little as possible, used his money to buy books, pictures, gilt-leather hangings and china and, through his colonial contacts, to order timber and garden plants from America. But it was more restrained than some: there were no Gibbons carvings (as at Petworth), and no grand swirling allegories of sprawling saints decked in a myriad of bright velvet colours.

Petworth, home of the fabled sixth Duke of Somerset, had both these as well as a duchess, Elizabeth, who was given a huge allowance to spend as she wished – solace perhaps for being given, as the Percy heiress, three times in marriage before her sixteenth birthday. The 'Proud Duke', her husband, set about the rebuilding of Petworth in 1688 – an auspicious year for William – when his wife was of age and could dispose of her fortune. The west front façade set the tone of grandeur in its three hundred and twenty feet of nervous, runaway length. Inside, the Grand Staircase is decorated with murals by Laguerre, one wall depicting in allegory the life of the Duchess of Somerset, surrounded by her family and watched over from the heights above by an Assembly of the Gods. As the vanguard of an army of painters, Verrio, Laguerre and their assistants painted in full splendour the 'Acts that claim Triumphant Laurels and Immortal Fame'. They gave to patrons, who had learned to appreciate it all, something new and rich, peopling the painted colonnades of great rooms with an assembly of brightly clothed onlookers. The flashes of rainbow paint drew eyes to ceiling and wall, detracting attention from the

10

Fig. 10 ***The Blue Room***, *Belton House, Lincolnshire, 1684–86. Belton House is an excellent example of country house architecture and interior design of the period. The bed in the Blue Room with its heavily ornate tester exemplifies the elegant decoration loved by the nobility of the period.*

sensuous carved wood and the cool precision of marbled floor.

These ostentatious houses, made so by their florid decorations, which Ben Jonson had attacked in his poem *To Penshurst* – 'those proud ambitious heaps and nothing else' – had come to stay. The Peace of Ryswyck in 1697 enabled William's principal supporters to feel free to revive their interest for a time in French paintings and architecture. With William's fall from his horse at Hampton Court in 1702 and his subsequent death, Dutch influences gradually died away. The eager respect for decoration tumbled its way into the eighteenth century and was then swept into a whirlpool of activity by at least five moods of style. Painted colonnades gave way to precise pediments and the austerities of Palladianism came, and reigned supreme.

WILLIAM AND MARY INTERIORS

Interiors of the William and Mary period may be seen at the following:

Burghley House, Stamford, Lincolnshire. Open April–September. Closed Mondays.

Chatsworth, Bakewell, Derbyshire. Open April–September. Closed Mondays and Tuesdays.

Dyrham Park, near Bristol and Bath, Gloucestershire. Open Easter Saturday–September. Daily except Monday and Tuesday. 2–6 pm and Bank Holidays 12–6 pm.

Hampton Court Palace, London. Open May–September. 9.30–6 pm (Sunday 11–6 pm).

Petworth House, Sussex. Open April–October. Wednesdays, Thursdays, Fridays and Bank Holiday Mondays 2–6 pm.

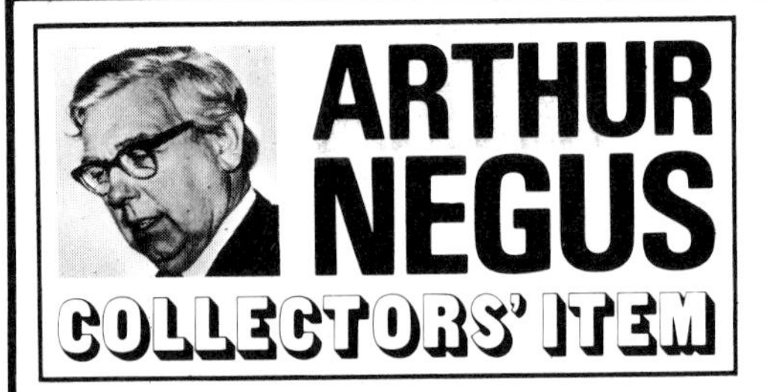

WALKING-STICKS

Walking-sticks developed from the staffs or wands carried by dignitaries of most European Courts in the fifteenth and sixteenth centuries. In England the Chancellor carried a white staff, and Henry VIII included in his wardrobe 'six walkying staves, one covered with silke and golde'. In early productions of *Twelfth Night*, Malvolio seldom appeared without his steward's staff of office, and even today Black Rod carries his staff of office before the Queen at the State Opening of Parliament.
Walking-sticks as such did not come into general use in England until the late seventeenth century, when Charles II imported the custom from France. In the eighteenth century, there was a vast increase in their number and variety.
The discovery and exploitation of the rare woods of America and the East Indies led to the use of malacca, bamboo, myrtle and kingwood for making the stick, and porcelain and ivory took the place of silver or bone in the making of handles. By the end of the eighteenth century, porcelain and precious metals were the most popular materials. Handles decorated with flowers were imported from Dresden, and handles showing pastoral scenes came from France. English makers tended to use Chinese patterns or plainer designs. Snuff-boxes, *bonbonnières*, musical boxes and watches were often incorporated in these handles.
In the nineteenth century, there were contrasting fashions. Early in the century, there was a vogue for heavy sticks, fantastically carved, and during the Victorian age, plain sticks with gold or silver heads became *de rigueur*. In the 1890s, there was a revival of porcelain crutch handles, and a brief flirtation with the use of coloured glass.

Hints to Collectors

Walking-sticks, linked as they are to the history of costume and manners, porcelain and woodwork, are an excellent subject for what Sherlock Holmes described as 'the science of deduction'. They can be dated by looking at the kind of wood used, or the porcelain from which the handle is made, quite apart from more general characteristics such as shape or decoration. It is inadvisable to keep walking-sticks near a radiator, as the heat dries out the wood.

Prices

There is no exact guide to prices. £5 is a reasonable price to pay for a Victorian walking-stick in good condition, and earlier sticks, especially if handsomely decorated, can cost £25 or more.

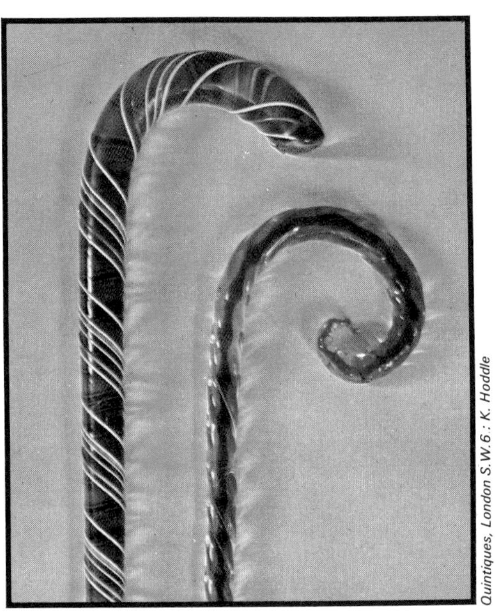

Quintiques, London S.W.6 : K. Hoddle

Left: ***Victorian glass walking-sticks,*** *probably made for indoor use, late nineteenth century.*

Below: ***Walking-sticks.*** *Left to right:* ***Russian stick*** *with tortoise-shell top;* ***Japanese cane*** *topped with an ivory figure, £30;* ***silver-topped stick,*** *c.1870, £12;* ***Art Nouveau handle,*** *£40;* ***silver-topped stick,*** *c.1880;* ***silver horse's neck handle,*** *£16.*

Opposite: ***Early nineteenth-century walking-sticks.*** *Left to right: Porcelain-topped stick, £25.50; mauve glass-topped stick with enamel band, £9.15; stick topped with amethyst and rose agate, £20; stick topped with carved ivory, £29.50.*
These sticks are representative of the many different styles which were popular throughout the nineteenth century.

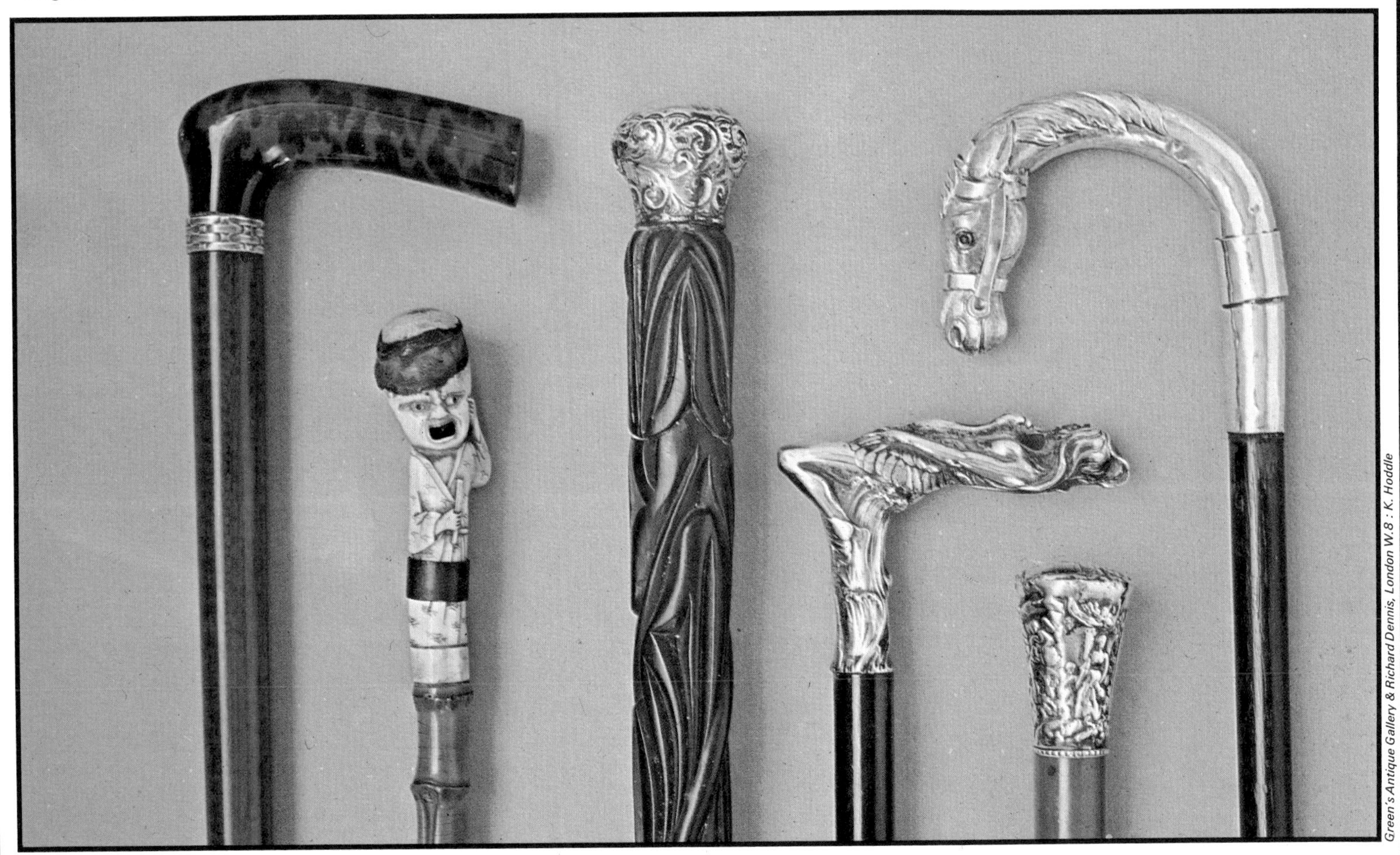

Green's Antique Gallery & Richard Dennis, London W.8 : K. Hoddle

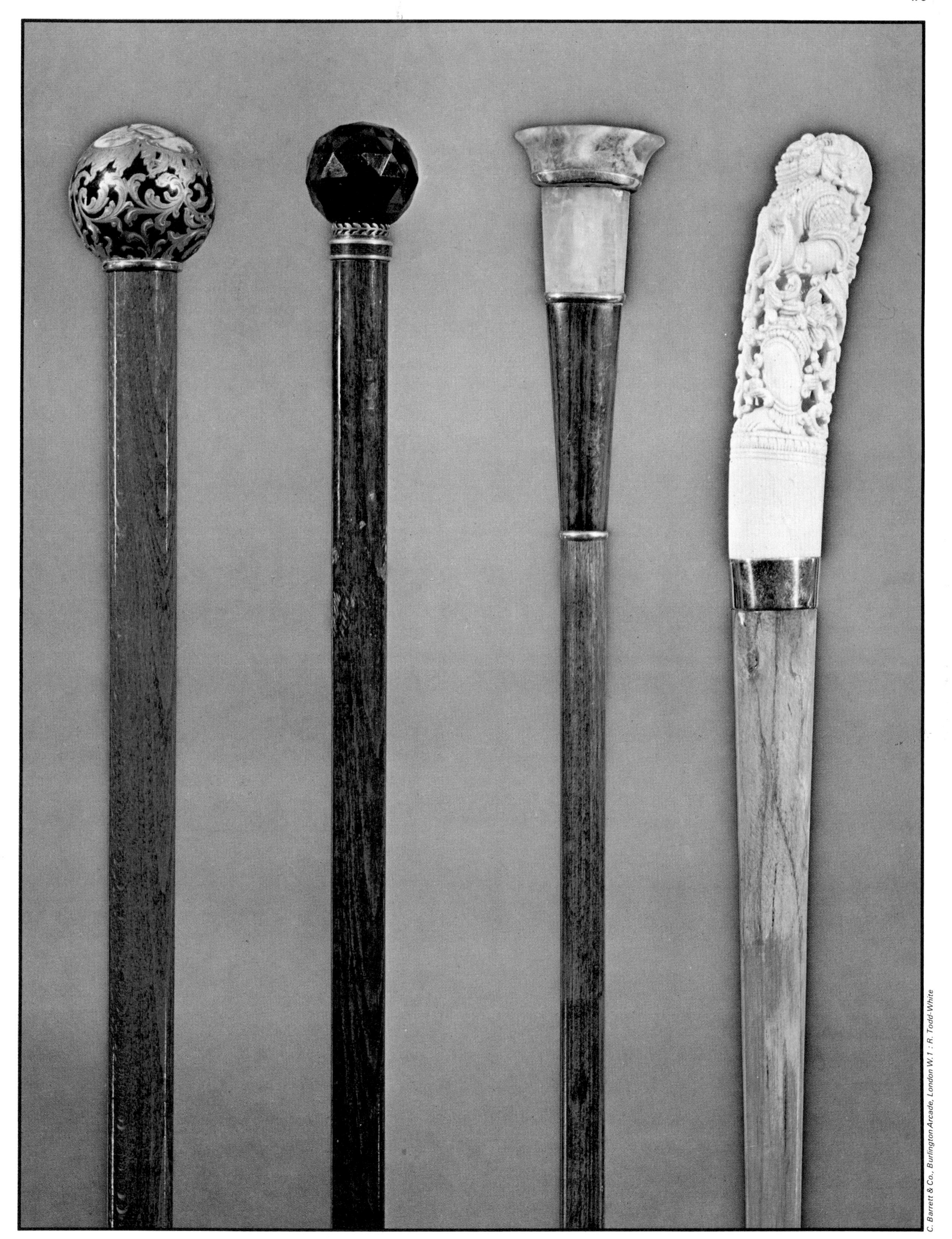

C. Barrett & Co., Burlington Arcade, London W.1 : R. Todd-White

Tijou and Flamboyant Design in Wrought Ironwork

1

Raymond Lister

Fig. 1 ***Design for a sign and bracket*** *by Jean Tijou (active 1690–1712), 1693. To be made in wrought iron. Engraving by Pieter van der Banck (1649–97) from* A New Booke of Drawings Invented and Desined by John Tijou, *1693.*
Tijou's family fled from their native France to escape religious persecution. When William and Mary acceded to the throne Tijou came to England, bringing sophistication and elegance to ironwork.
(Private Collection.)

Tijou's flamboyant designs were created in traditional blacksmithery. He breathed life into English ironwork imbuing it with a new richness and elegance.

To every art there comes at some time a figure who transforms it, after whom it is never again quite the same. Such are Chaucer, Giotto and Mozart, and, more recently, Cézanne, Fokine and Le Corbusier. The same is true of the crafts, where may be quoted Cellini, Tompion, Baskerville and Morris. Among the greatest of the creative craft-transformers was the late seventeenth-century blacksmith, Jean Tijou, under whose influence was created the finest flower of English blacksmithery.

Little is known of Tijou himself. We know that he was a Protestant Frenchman whose family had probably fled to the Netherlands to escape persecution, whence he was brought to England by William and Mary when they ascended the English throne. He is mentioned by Horace Walpole, in *Anecdotes of Painting in England*, as a 'founder of iron balustrades', and Walpole also tells us that his daughter married the mural painter Louis Laguerre (1663–1721) at the church of St. Martin-in-the-Fields. Tijou's wife was named Anne and, when he left England for the last time in 1712, she remained behind to collect, by letter of attorney,

Figs. 3 and 4 ***Panels from the Fountain Screen,*** *Hampton Court Palace, by Tijou, c.1700. Wrought iron. The motif in the central panel of Fig. 3 is based on the interlaced initials of William and Mary, and that of Fig. 4 is the heraldic rose of England. (By gracious permission of H.M. the Queen.)*

Fig. 5 ***Gates and overthrow,*** *St. Catharine's College, Cambridge, by Fuller (active 1779–81). Wrought iron, approximately 12 feet high. Illustrating a departure from the elaborate work of Tijou, these gates demonstrate the use of cast iron in the Catherine wheel in the centre of the overthrow, in conjunction with the wrought iron of the rest of the gates. (Master and Fellows of St. Catharine's College.)*

2

Thomas, Oxford

3

Crown Copyright Ministry of Public Building and Works

4

Crown Copyright Ministry of Public Building and Works

5

Author's Photo

Fig. 2 ***Gates, transom (horizontal) panel and overthrow,*** *Clarendon Building, Oxford, by Tijou or Thomas Robinson, c.1710. Wrought iron. The lower panels of the gates are interesting in that they have stylistic affinities with the work of Thomas Robinson (active 1697–1715) who worked with Tijou at St. Paul's Cathedral. (University of Oxford.)*

some money owing to him. There are also detailed records in the accounts of St. Paul's Cathedral of payments he received. In 1693 he published a book of designs called *A New Booke of Drawings Invented and Desined by John Tijou* (Figs. 1, 6, 7 and 10) which has what may be a portrait of him on its title-page. Beyond these sparse facts we know nothing about him.

Tijou's greatest contribution to architectural wrought ironwork was in the use of repoussé – that is, plates of metal with raised designs made by embossing them from the back with punches and hammers. Hitherto iron had been shaped by the techniques of blacksmithery or locksmithery. With the former the iron is hammered and punched into shape while it is red-hot; with the latter it is cut and chiselled or filed into shape while it is cold.

Locksmithery flourished during the late Middle Ages when its jewel-like finish reflected and enhanced the gothic buildings it decorated. One of the finest works executed in this technique is in St. George's Chapel, Windsor – a pair of large gates and piers by Master John Tresilian, made of hundreds of small units fitted and dovetailed together with the precision of a modern machine.

Blacksmithery is the oldest method of shaping iron and the technique has varied little over the centuries. By means of this old craft, blacksmiths have always been able to produce new variations on old themes, making – to mention only a few motifs – scrolls, volutes, leaves, twists and flame-shapes in infinite variety.

6

Author's Photo

Blacksmithery provided the bare bones of Tijou's art, affording him an armature on which to hang his repoussé swags, masks, gargoyles, cloths of estate, flowers, fruits and heraldic emblems. It was at the same time something more, for in itself it had a studied elegance so that, shorn of its repoussé decorations, it could still surpass the plain blacksmithery that was being produced in England before Tijou's arrival. How effective Tijou's basic scroll-work can be may be seen on the elegant river railings at Hampton Court Palace, one of the rare examples of his work without repoussé.

As richly conceived as the damasks of the courtiers' dresses

Until Tijou's time, repoussé had been used mainly on precious metals, which are softer and more pliable than iron and on which the raising of elaborate and lifelike shapes presents fewer problems. It was one of Tijou's brilliant successes that he made iron do the same things, albeit on a larger scale. This may be seen on his great Fountain Screen at Hampton Court Palace (Figs. 3 and 4); the masks surmounting the panels illustrate vividly his virtuosity. They are completely three-dimensional and could hardly be rendered in greater detail if they were carved in wood or stone. The acanthus leaves, too, are brilliantly conceived; if they were painted in natural colours one might even imagine them fluttering in the breeze.

The Hampton Court screen is flamboyant and ceremonious, an excuse to display the royal and heraldic appurtenances of the realm, and as richly conceived as the damasks of the dresses of the courtiers whose setting it was. Or, to look at it in another way, it is the visual counterpart of John Dryden's verse, or of the music of William Boyce. This formality made it an ideal component of the Dutch gardening popularised by Tijou's patrons, William and Mary.

The brilliance of the Hampton Court screen is unassailable. Yet for Tijou at his best we must go to St. Paul's Cathedral, where his flamboyance was controlled by the Cathedral's architect, Sir Christopher Wren. It is necessary only to compare the detailing of Tijou's Golden Gates (Fig. 9) with the coarser detailing at Hampton Court to realise this. The underlying structure of blacksmith's work is here allowed, to its advantage, to dominate the design. Repoussé is used, but not overwhelmingly, and it is, if anything, more brilliantly executed than at Hampton Court. When one considers the difficulties inherent in the hard, unresilient metal, the detail and expression is almost miraculous. The brooding thoughtfulness of the Evangelist's face is unerringly portrayed in the space of a few square inches.

8

Hawkley Studio

9

Perfecta Publications

Although Wren restrained Tijou's ebullience, it is unlikely that Wren himself would have made detailed specifications; such was not the custom at that time. Instead he would have provided a scheme of his overall requirements, expecting Tijou to work out details, subsequently criticising and modifying these proposals.

Some interpretation is always necessary between the architect's conception and the craftsman's realisation. It may be easy to draw a pattern on a piece of paper, but not always so easy to bend a bar of iron into the same shape. Many of Tijou's designs in *A New Booke of Drawings* are much more elaborate and finely detailed than would be possible to execute in iron – even for a craftsman as brilliant as Tijou.

7

Author's Photo

10

Figs. 6 and 7 ***Designs for a key handle and lock escutcheon*** *from Tijou's book of designs, 1693, to be made in wrought iron. These would not have been made by blacksmithery but by the more precise locksmith's technique, by which the metal is sawn, filed, chiselled and drilled in its cold state. It would be impossible to obtain such fine detailing on a small scale by blacksmithery. (Private Collection.)*

Fig. 8 ***Gates,*** *Burghley House, probably by Tijou, c.1710. Wrought iron. The original design appears in Tijou's* A New Booke of Drawings.

Fig. 9 ***The Golden Gates,*** *(Sanctuary Screen), St. Paul's Cathedral, by Jean Tijou, 1698. Wrought iron. Restrained yet sumptuous, these magnificent gates, though designed by Tijou, show the influence of the Cathedral's architect, Wren.*

Fig. 10 ***Design for the Fountain Screen*** *at Hampton Court by Jean Tijou, from* A New Booke of Drawings, *1693. The design, too coarse and at the same time too finely detailed was much modified in execution. (Victoria and Albert Museum, London.)*

There is ironwork in various parts of England that might be by Tijou, but documentary evidence is lacking on which one could make a definite ascription. Some smiths have personal characteristics of workmanship, and Tijou is one of them; but they also have pupils and followers who can often copy closely such characteristics, making it difficult or impossible to decide whether the work is by master or pupil. Unless some outstanding detail is present – like the masks at Hampton Court (Figs. 3 and 4) or the panels at St. Paul's Cathedral (Fig. 9) – which could only be the work of the master, a definite attribution is extremely difficult. Nevertheless, there is some reason to suspect that Tijou's skill may be seen in work on the Clarendon Building at Oxford (Fig. 2), in the hall at Castle Howard, Yorkshire, at Burghley House, Lincolnshire, and elsewhere. And we do know that one blacksmith used a design for a baluster from Tijou's *A Booke of Drawings*. This was for the staircase in Wren's library at Trinity College, Cambridge, made, according to the College accounts, in 1691–92 by 'Mr. Partridge, the London Smith'. Partridge also made the gates of the same building, which themselves show signs of Tijou's influence.

Among the smiths working for Tijou at St. Paul's Cathedral was Thomas Robinson, whose name appears in the accounts from 1697 to 1715. Indeed, it is possible that Robinson was the craftsman who made the gates on the Clarendon Building (Fig. 2), for their bottom panels closely resemble that on the gate at New College, a few hundred yards away, which were made by him in about 1711.

One of the finest extant specimens of English blacksmithery

Robinson's forge was in London at Hyde Park Corner, as we are told by John Ayliffe in *The Antient and Present State of the University of Oxford* (1714), but little else about him is known. His gate is one of the finest extant specimens of English blacksmithery. Its importance lies in the fact that repoussé work is cut to a minimum, and the effect relies mainly on the superb scroll-work. It has thus transformed Tijou's continental flamboyance into a restrained English conception. More than almost any other work, it illustrates Tijou's influence on English ironwork – a limited use of repoussé with a brilliant new treatment of scroll-work.

A blacksmith's *jeu d'esprit*, as light yet as strongly constructed as a Mozart sonata

A different continental influence was shown by Robert Davies, a Welsh blacksmith of Croes Foel. It is not known if Davies worked with Tijou. Davies' masterpiece is the white gates and screen at Leeswood Hall, Mold, Flintshire. This great work, one hundred feet long, contains many details unmistakably European in origin, but differing from the type of design usually associated with Tijou. It is more reminiscent of contemporary Spanish work, particularly in its balusters and broken pediments. At the same time, Davies used details that probably came from German or Netherlandish sources.

A west-country smith who showed unmistakably the influence of Tijou was William Edney, the maker, in 1710, of the well-known gates in the church of St. Mary Redcliffe, Bristol. Their design has many points in common with Tijou's Golden Gates at St. Paul's Cathedral, with the Clarendon Building gates at Oxford and with Robinson's gate at New College. It has been claimed that Edney worked for Tijou at St. Paul's, and these gates tempt one to agree. They have more repoussé than Robinson's gate, but this may be due to the fact that they are situated inside a building. Repoussé, being made from fairly thin sheets of iron, is more liable to rust than thick bars (although some of Tijou's repoussé on the Fountain Screen has resisted it for two and a half centuries), and Edney may have felt that the situation of these gates gave him an excuse to show what he could produce in the medium.

One of the most brilliant of English blacksmiths was Robert Bakewell of Derby, and his greatest work is the garden arbour, popularly known as the Birdcage, at Melbourne Hall, Derbyshire

11

Fig. 11 ***The Birdcage,*** *garden arbour at Melbourne Hall, Derbyshire, by Robert Bakewell (active 1708–18), completed about 1711. Wrought iron. Bakewell executed much ironwork in the Midlands. There is a reference in the parish accounts for All Saints', Derby, to 'Mr. Robert Bakewell ye Iron Man' who had received payments for maintaining the town's fire engine.*

Raymond's News Agency, Derby

(Fig. 11), which he constructed for the Rt. Hon. Thomas Coke some time between 1708 and 1711. Standing in one of England's most pleasant gardens, laid out by the Royal Gardeners, George London and Henry Wise, at the end of the seventeenth century, it is at the centre of a group of avenues and yew tunnels and stands before a D-shaped basin. It is a blacksmith's *jeu d'esprit*, as light yet as strongly constructed as a Mozart sonata, and it is unique. In our present context it is important in that it shows what could become of Tijou's conceptions when transmitted through the medium of an English blacksmith with a style almost as elaborate as his own. For although all the Tijou trappings are present – masks, swags, rosettes, acanthus, laurels and magnificent underlying scroll-work – this could not be the work of a continental smith. There is a certain almost rustic splendour about it; yet it is a restrained splendour. A continental smith would have covered the arbour with dolphins, *putti*, birds and cartouches – and it is unlikely he would have used the English oak leaves that decorate the dome.

Here was detailing of which Tijou himself would have been proud

The gates to the bridge at Clare College, Cambridge, are a splendid example of English iron-work influenced by Tijou. They were made in 1713–14 by a blacksmith named Warren. It is possible that he may be identified with a John Warren who was working in Buckinghamshire in the 1690s and whose work has details in common with that at Clare College. Simpler than Robinson's New College gate, the Clare College gates have nevertheless something in common with that work also, as they rely for their effect upon blacksmithery. There is hardly any repoussé, just one or two leaves and cloths of estate. Yet Tijou's influence is present, for one could hardly conceive such splendid scroll-work before his time.

One of the more impressive details of Warren's Clare College gates is the group of laurel branches around the shield in the overthrow. Some years ago these gates were restored and it was then possible to examine them in detail, stripped of many years' accumulation of paint. The detailing of the laurel branches came as a revelation – even the fibres were shown, where they would have been torn from the main branch. Here was detailing of which Tijou himself would have been proud.

The fading of Tijou's influence is illustrated by another, later, pair of Cambridge gates: those at St. Catharine's College, made between 1779 and 1781 by a smith named Fuller (Fig. 5). The plainer tendency in the work of such smiths as Robinson and Warren has here been taken almost to its limit. Apart from one or two minor details, Tijou, on the evidence of these gates, might never have existed. They are attractive, but they are different. It is as if the craft had changed with the times, as if a more serious, almost commercial note, in keeping with the dawning Industrial Revolution, had been sounded, ending the highly decorative courtly art of sixty or seventy years before and heralding an era of new ideas, thoughts and designs.

FURTHER READING

The Craftsman in Metal by Raymond Lister, London, 1966.

Decorative Wrought Ironwork in Great Britain by Raymond Lister, London, 1957 and 1970.

Wrought Iron and its Decorative Use by Arnold Silcock and Maxwell Ayrton, London, 1929.

English Ironwork of the XVIIth and XVIIIth Centuries by J. Starkie Gardner, London, 1911.

IRONWORK TO BE VISITED

Wrought ironwork by Tijou may be seen *in situ* at the following:

Greater London:	Hampton Court Palace
London:	St. Paul's Cathedral
Cambridge:	Clare College, by Warren Trinity College, by Partridge
Derbyshire:	Melbourne Hall, Melbourne, by Bakewell
Flintshire:	Leeswood Hall, Mold, by Davies
Gloucestershire:	St. Mary Redcliffe, Bristol, by Edney
Lincolnshire:	Burghley House, Stamford
Oxford:	Clarendon Building New College
Yorkshire:	Castle Howard, York

The gates of St. Catharine's College, Cambridge, by Fuller, illustrate the departure, towards the end of the century, from Tijou's influence.

1

Courtly Cabinet Making

Edward T. Joy

Despite the fact that there was a Dutch king on the throne, the predominant influence on English furniture during the last years of the seventeenth century was French. The Huguenots who fled to Protestant England brought with them the sophisticated designs of the Louis XIV style

The reign of William and Mary marks the baroque phase in the design of English furniture. Some of its manifestations can be seen towards the end of the century in the magnificent carving and gilding of such pieces as side-tables, mirrors, picture-frames and stands, the sumptuous upholstery on seat furniture and beds; the tall and elegant backs of chairs developing for the first time into curvilinear forms; the bold arches above cabinets and other case-furniture; the development of arabesque marquetry; and the vogue for flowing X-shaped stretchers on seats, stands and tables.

Political events played an important part in the development of English furniture at this time. In 1688, the Catholic James II, Charles II's brother and successor, lost his throne because of his attempts to gain toleration for his fellow Catholics and when, in 1689, the crown was settled jointly on William of Orange, the Dutch Stadthouder, and his English wife, Mary, James' daughter, a more formal atmosphere was evident at Court. There was a curb on the exuberant forms of decoration of furniture which were a legacy of the gay court of Charles II. John Evelyn, the celebrated diarist, described William, when he first saw him, as 'very stately, serious and reserved', words which in many ways form an apt description of the furniture which the new reign produced.

Even more decisive was the influence of the Huguenots who took refuge in England after Louis XIV's revocation in 1685 of the Edict of Nantes, by which Henry IV, in 1598, had granted toleration to Protestants in France. Even when they were tolerated, the Huguenots had still been barred by their religion from advancement in political and professional careers, and they turned their energies largely to the decorative arts. Thus, in 1685, France lost large numbers of her best craftsmen who fled to Protestant countries taking their skills with them. Those who came to England introduced the very latest French techniques and designs, the height of baroque fashion.

It was the Huguenot Daniel Marot (*c.*1663–1752), who exercised the most powerful influence on late Stuart furniture styles. He was a true all-rounder – architect, decorator, landscape gardener and designer in a variety of crafts, including metalwork and furniture. He fled from France to Holland in 1684, anticipating the revocation, and entered

Fig. 1 ***Card-Table***, c.*1700. Italian walnut. Card-tables were first made in England in the late seventeenth century. This example has gate-legs which swung out to support the top when opened.*
(Victoria and Albert Museum, London.)

2

Fratelli Fabbri

3

Museum Photo

William's service. He is known to have been in England from 1694 to 1696 and in 1698. His thorough knowledge of French baroque design, which he had already brought to Holland, now reached England, and his commanding position at Court naturally gave his work enormous influence.

Marot's decorative flair was perhaps most vividly marked in tapestries, hangings and upholstered furniture. He also designed a Chinese cabinet room which was a pioneer attempt in the adaptation of Oriental motifs to European use. His work became widely known in England after the publication of his engraved designs, first in parts, then in a collected edition in 1702, under the title of *Oeuvres du Sieur D. Marot, architecte du Guillaume III, roy de la Grande Bretagne*. He had obviously been inspired by the work of two outstanding contemporary French designers, Jean Bérain (1639–1711) and Jean Lepautre (1618–82), in whose designs can be detected the first signs of the movement from the late Baroque to the Rococo. It is clear that the resplendent beds with elaborate hangings which figure among his designs were models for executed British examples (Fig. 7). The Victoria and Albert Museum, for instance, has a state bed formerly at Melville House, Fife, which was derived from a Marot design (Fig. 3). It was made in about 1695 for the Earl of Melville, William's minister. Its pinewood frame is covered with crimson velvet and white silk and the headpiece, in typical baroque style, bears the Earl's cipher and coronet.

Another Huguenot who made a great reputation for himself in England was Jean Pelletier, carver and gilder, who appears in the royal accounts from 1690 to 1701. He supplied the royal households with carved and gilt mirror-frames, tables, screens and stands. There are at Hampton Court (which, until the Queen's death, was being rebuilt by Wren at William's order), two sets of gilt stands which

4

A. C. Cooper

5

Museum Photo

Fig. 2 ***Cabinet**, c.1700. Walnut veneer with floral marquetry of various woods and ivory. This piece, made for the marriage of George Lawson and Margaret Trotter, both members of Yorkshire families, illustrates an unusual lightness and freedom in the use of marquetry. (Victoria and Albert Museum.)*

Fig. 3 ***State bedstead**, c.1695. The frame is of pine, covered with crimson velvet and white silk, richly trimmed with red braid. The headboard bears the cipher and earl's coronet of George Melville, created first Earl of Melville in 1690 by William III. (Victoria and Albert Museum.)*

Fig. 4 ***Writing-desk,** or scriptor, English, c.1690. Walnut with arabesque, or seaweed, marquetry of various woods. The sloping front, which opens out and is supported on the two hinged legs of the stand, foreshadows the bureau. (Victoria and Albert Museum.)*

Fig. 5 ***Winged armchair** known as an 'easie chair', c.1680. Walnut upholstered with leather. The wings were probably added as draught excluders. The adjustable back is worked by ratchets. (Victoria and Albert Museum.)*

relate so closely to the entry under Pelletier's name in the royal accounts that they can confidently be attributed to his workshop. Pelletier can be credited with introducing into England the magnificent baroque gilt furniture of the kind which distinguished Louis XIV's Court. His work undoubtedly inspired the fine gilt furniture produced by the partners John Gumley and George Moore for George I, examples of which can be seen at Hampton Court.

Another foreign craftsman, this time of Flemish or Dutch extraction, was Gerreit Jensen (whose name is found anglicised as Johnson). He was furnishing royal households from *c.*1680 to 1715, and is the only man in England at that time who is known to have made furniture inlaid with metal in the manner of André-Charles Boulle, the celebrated *ébéniste* of Louis XIV's Court who specialised in the technique of brass and tortoise-shell inlay. Jensen also worked in arabesque marquetry; a writing-table (1690) and cabinet with glass doors (1693) decorated in this fashion are at Windsor Castle. This work must have been the inspiration of the arabesque, or 'seaweed', marquetry (Fig. 4) employed by English craftsmen in William's reign.

The William and Mary period is noted for some of the tallest chairs ever made in England – the backs sometimes measured two and a half times the height of the seats to the floor. Gracefulness was gained by the use of baluster forms for the uprights of the chairs instead of the spiral turning of the 1670s (Fig. 9). Front legs were still scrolled, but from about 1690 straight legs became more common, and these were either of baluster shape or square and tapered. The tops (or cappings) of the legs acquired a variety of attractive shapes, mushroom, pear, square, etc., which are a distinctive feature of this period (Fig. 8). The height of the chairs was increased by fixing the arched cresting above the uprights instead of tenoning it between them. The filling of the backs was composed of carved scroll-work and foliage or of cane (Fig. 9), which was now of much finer mesh than the kind formerly used. Although the front stretcher of many chairs was still carved to match the bold arched scroll of the cresting (Fig. 9), in other cases it was abandoned altogether and replaced by a curved X-shaped stretcher meeting beneath the seat in a central platform with a finial (Fig. 8). Walnut was still fashionable for these chairs, but less expensive examples were made of beech stained to resemble walnut.

The continued popularity of cane chairs aroused the hostility of upholsterers and woollen manufacturers who naturally regarded them as a threat to their livelihood. But Parliament refused to accede to their petition to ban or curtail the import of cane. 1690, however, may well represent the peak of the fashion for cane chairs, for in that year they were criticised by Nicholas Barbon (in his *Discourse of Trade*) as 'too cheap and common'. They nevertheless persisted well into the next century.

The ceremonial chair under a canopy, used by William, is still at Hampton Court

Rich upholstery materials were, however, used on the finest chairs of the time. The winged armchair, now a permanent feature of English homes, had thickly padded scrolled arms and deep, padded seats, upholstered in tapestry, needlework, Genoa velvet, brocatelle, brocade, embroidered silk and braid threaded with gold and silver. Some of these materials were made in England after silk-weaving had been introduced by Huguenots who settled in Spitalfields, London.

Upholstered single chairs attained a particular elegance, with their tall, narrow, rectangular backs

Fig. 6 **Day-bed,** c.1695. *Giltwood with Genoa velvet upholstery.*
Made for Hornby Castle, Leeds.
(Temple Newsam House, Leeds.)

Fig. 7 ***Design for a State bed*** *by Daniel Marot (c.1663–1752).*
(Victoria and Albert Museum.)

which were sometimes shaped at the top, probably in imitation of the arched cresting of carved and caned chairs (Fig. 9). A well-known set of walnut seat furniture from Burley-on-the-Hill, Rutland, made in about 1690, has eight single chairs shaped in this manner which still retain their original brightly-coloured needlework upholstery. This needlework is said to have been worked by the Countess of Nottingham and her daughters with coloured wools in *gros-point* on a canvas base. It was the practice of ladies in large households to work at upholstery of this kind as it was much cheaper than imported materials and extremely hard-wearing, as the Burley examples show. The Burley set includes two settees, without wings and with comparatively small padded arms; their backs are composed of two chair-backs with the same attractive shaping at the top as the single chairs.

The King's Presence Chamber at Hampton Court still contains the ceremonial chair under a canopy which William used when receiving distinguished visitors. It is flanked by a pair of stools for the use of officials – an example of the survival of the ceremonial precedence granted to the chair and of the use of stools by less important personages. Stools were made in various shapes: rectangular, square and circular (Fig. 10). Some had six or eight feet and accommodated two persons. Day-beds or couches retained their popularity in great houses and were now usually fully upholstered instead of having cane seats and backs covered with mattress and cushions. A notable gilt example of about 1695, upholstered in its original Genoa velvet, is in Temple Newsam House, Leeds (Fig. 6).

Japanned chairs, and indeed japanned furniture generally, imitating oriental lacquer, became increasingly popular. In 1688 Stalker and Parker's *A Treatise of Japaning and Varnishing* appeared as a manual of instruction. Illustrated with pseudo-Oriental scenes, figures, birds, etc., it made japanning a fashionable pastime for enthusiastic amateurs at home and greatly increased the demand for the work of professional japanners. The latter gained a notable success in 1701 when Parliament, in response to their outcry against foreign competition, raised the tariffs on Oriental lacquered goods and thus assured for home producers a near-monopoly of the domestic market. But few of these japanned pieces have survived. The varnish and paint colours which constituted the japan used by English craftsmen were poor substitutes for genuine lacquer. It cracked easily, its colours – originally bright reds, greens, yellows and blues – tended to fade rapidly, and the frameworks of deal and beech, used as the ground for japanning, were particularly liable to attack by worm.

6

Gilchrist

7

K. Hoddle

8

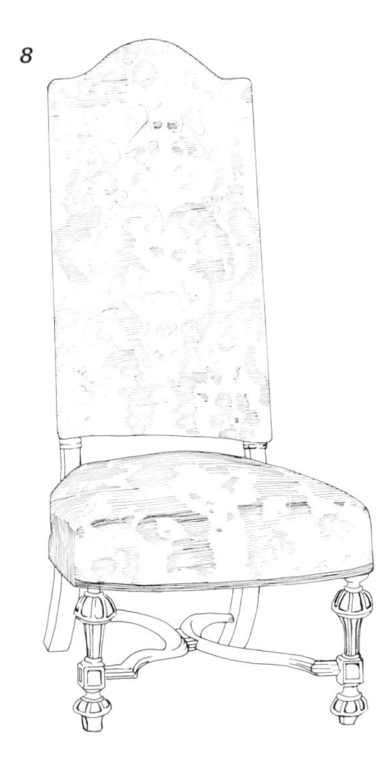

One of the most remarkable advances in chair design in the whole of English furniture history occurred in the last decade of the seventeenth century. This was the appearance of the curvilinear chair (often known as the 'Queen Anne chair' though it decidedly overlapped the limits of the Queen's reign).

A new and distinctive type of walnut chair seems also to have come from Holland at this time and is described as being 'in the style of Daniel Marot'. The back of this type had a curvilinear frame filled with pierced carved ornament. The front legs were of cabriole form joined by stretchers. It is possible, however, that the inspiration for the new design was a type of Chinese chair which was imported by the East India Company and had a yoke-shaped cresting and a simple central splat, concave at shoulder level. Whatever the origin, by about 1700 a chair of 'bended-back' type was beginning to emerge. Such chairs had a central splat, pierced and carved in early examples and later taking graceful vase or fiddle forms. For generations, chair-backs had traditionally been square or rectangular in shape as they had been developed by joiners from the 'panel backs'. Now this quite sudden break into a curved shape opened a whole new field of design for the chair-

Fig. 8 **Gilt chair,** *covered with cut Genoa velvet, c.1690. The fluted, baluster legs have mushroom cappings and the curved, X-shaped stretcher meets beneath the seat.*

Fig. 9 **Chair,** *c.1685. Carved birch with caned seat and back. The turned uprights, upon which the arched cresting rests, reflect a new sense of discipline. (Victoria and Albert Museum.)*

9

Fig. 10 **Circular stool,** *carved and gilt, c.1690. This stool still has its original brocade, embroidered in silk and silver thread. Vast sums of money were spent on fine fabrics at this period. (Boughton House, Northants.)*

0

maker. In addition the cabriole leg, as it finally evolved, was the first type of leg that did not require stretchers to support it. The line of the chair was being completely transformed and the stage was set for the great era of English chair design which was to make such an important contribution to European decorative crafts in the eighteenth century. Early cabriole legs on the Continent took the form of animals' legs, ending in hooves, and at first English chairs used narrow versions of these, still preserving stretchers and adopting either hoof or club feet. As the cabrioles became sturdier and wider at the knee, the stretchers were dispensed with.

The French-style writing-cabinet on a stand, with a large fall-front which was let down for writing, continued to be made in the last part of the seventeenth century. Its great disadvantage – that its flap had to be cleared of all papers before it could be locked – led to the appearance in the last years of the century of the bureau, which had a hinged sloping flap and interior space into which papers could be pushed. The early bureaux, which stood on stands having two gate-legs which swung forward to support the top, were narrow enough to stand conveniently against the wall between windows for maximum light. At about the end of the century, this type itself was succeeded by the bureau-cabinet – a combination of chest of drawers, desk and cabinet which, in its evolutionary stage, simply consisted of these three separate sections. The sloping top of the central desk was supported on two slides, or lopers.

The cabinets for collections of 'curiosities', which had been the prestige pieces of the post-Restoration era, were still being made but were now decorated with arabesque marquetry and surmounted by arched pediments in a variety of forms. It was more usual to support them on a chest of drawers, owing to their heavy weight, than on an open stand. Cabinets, lacquered or japanned, also remained in fashion, supported on gilt or silvered stands resembling the baroque side-tables in Marot's designs. Another, newer type of cabinet had glazed doors and an interior fitted with shelves for displaying china.

As with turning, marquetry of the William and Mary period illustrated the general tendency towards quieter forms of decoration. The former bright floral designs began to change in about 1690 into more sober shades of brown, buff and gold. This was probably a truly English version of marquetry, executed by mature craftsmen who had been trained as apprentices by immigrants. One of the most magnificent examples of this marquetry is seen on the great cabinet on chest of drawers, now in the Victoria and Albert Museum, which was made in about 1700 for the marriage of George Lawson of Harlsey Castle, Yorkshire, to Margaret Trotter of Skelton Castle, Yorkshire (Fig. 2). The decoration is floral but executed with a controlled delicacy far removed from the florid ornament of Charles II's reign. The maker is unknown but he is almost certainly also responsible for a similar cabinet at Streatham Castle, Durham, made in about 1691.

At about this time appeared the final phase of English marquetry, concentrating on arabesque patterns, the more complicated forms of which produced the version named 'seaweed' after its shape. This latter type, which no doubt owed much to Jensen's influence, used only two shades in spite of its complicated patterns – a light one (in sycamore, pear, box or holly) for the designs, and a darker one (walnut) for the background.

Grinling Gibbons (1648–1720), the greatest of all English wood-carvers, flourished at this time. He excelled in mural decoration in Wren's churches and in great houses. Only one piece of furniture by him can be positively identified on documentary grounds – a table with a walnut top set in a carved limewood frame which he presented to John Evelyn and which is now at Christ Church, Oxford. But a number of picture frames in smaller houses seem beyond doubt to be his work. His naturalistic repertory included fruits, foliage, flowers, wheat-ears and the human form, all handled with consummate skill. He was leader of a large school of carvers who made his style extensively known.

The general tendency of mirrors to become tall and upright followed the trends of the time. They had arched headings frequently filled with mirror-glass and finished off with carved crestings. On some there were glass borders set in coloured glass banding or in gilt mouldings.

It was undoubtedly French influence which inspired some of the more elaborate side-tables found in fashionable households. These marked the beginning of the great period of English gesso work. Gesso was a composition of size and whiting which was laid on the wood (usually deal) in successive layers. When hard and smooth, it was treated with clay in preparation for the application of gold leaf as either water- or oil-gilding. In rarer instances it was silvered. Less luxurious side-tables were often used, though they were attractive enough with marquetry or japan decoration; their S-scrolled legs and curved stretchers were typical of the time.

At this time, the first tables specifically designed for card-playing appeared, with oval or circular folding tops and baluster or tapered legs, two of which swung out to support the top (Fig. 1). Writing-tables were similar but had rectangular folding tops. The attractive knee-hole table, used for dressing, had a number of small drawers and baluster legs on ball or bun feet. The knee-hole was sometimes arched and had two flanking suspended finials.

MUSEUMS AND COLLECTIONS

London:	Hampton Court Palace
	Victoria and Albert Museum
Derbyshire:	Chatsworth
Sussex:	Petworth House

FURTHER READING

The Connoisseur's Guide to Antique Furniture ed. by L. G. G. Ramsey and Helen Comstock, London, 1969, 'Walnut Furniture' by Edward T. Joy.

The Connoisseur's Complete Period Guides ed. by R. Edwards and L. G. G. Ramsey, London, 1968. The Stuart Period, 1603–1714, 'Furniture' by R. Fastnedge.

World Furniture ed. by Helena Hayward, London, 1965, 'England 1660–1715' by A. Coleridge.

Furniture Making In Seventeenth And Eighteenth Century England ed. by R. W. Symonds, London, 1955.

English Huguenot Silver

David Udy

Fig. 1 *Ewer by David Willaume, London, 1700. Silver-gilt, height 8½ ins.*
This is a particularly fine example of the characteristic helmet form introduced by the Huguenots. Its comparatively small scale emphasises the exquisite quality of the cast detail, which is composed of many of the decorative enrichments used by the Huguenots throughout the period. The cast and fluted base was in use until the end of the first decade of the eighteenth century.
(Victoria and Albert Museum, London.)

Forced into exile by the suppression of French Protestantism, Huguenot silversmiths sought refuge in England. Their work was of such quality that they were finally accepted and produced the fine flower of English silver

From the Renaissance to the beginning of the eighteenth century, the evolution of the arts in England was conditioned by the mortal struggle between Protestant and Catholic which divided the whole of Europe. It was, indeed, for religious reasons that the unorthodox interpretation of the Renaissance from the Protestant North was more influential in Elizabethan England than the orthodox classical revival taking place in Italy and France. The influence of the Renaissance was disseminated not only through the printing-presses of Antwerp, but through Flemish refugee craftsmen escaping from the persecutions of the Duke of Alba from 1566 onwards.

The Huguenots were a civilised and educated community who distinguished themselves as craftsmen

Less than a century later, Dutch craftsmen, in the train of Charles II, who had become accustomed in his exile to the fashions of Holland, reasserted the artistic influence of that country for the next thirty years. Ironically, the advent of a Dutch king, William of Orange, and a further persecution of Protestants abroad, brought the eclipse of the provincial Dutch style and the precedence of the style of the Catholic Court of France. The refugees from this persecution in France were the Huguenots, many of whom fled to England, and these made a crucial impact on the art of the English silversmith.

The Huguenots had been given freedom to practise their religion and their professions by the Edict of Nantes in 1598, which brought an end to the French Wars of Religion, but after the accession of Louis XIV this freedom became increasingly circumscribed. Finally, in 1685, the Edict of Nantes was revoked and systematic State oppression became official. It has been estimated that, in that year alone, fifty thousand families left France.

The Huguenots were welcomed in England by the Government and public funds were raised to help the needy among them. The city companies, however, were traditionally jealous of their powers and privileges and the Goldsmiths' Company in particular put up a stiff resistance to the admission of Huguenots to their number. It was in a strong position to defend its members from outside competition, since silver articles might not be sold unless assayed and passed by the Goldsmiths' Hall, and only freemen of the Company might have their goods assayed. Some Huguenots were admitted before the end of the seventeenth century, largely through pressure from higher authorities. The less fortunate found work as journeymen in the workshops of English silversmiths; others appear on occasion to have persuaded freemen to take their pieces to the Hall for assay by passing them off as their own. A petition of 1697 presented to the Court of the Company by prominent silversmiths names this practice as an abuse. For these reasons, pieces made before the turn of the century may have a pronounced Huguenot character and yet be struck with an English maker's mark. Subsequently, it is evident that the English silversmith adopted the more fashionable Huguenot style himself. By the beginning of the eighteenth century, resistance had weakened to their admission to the Company and it became granted on proof of naturalisation.

Producing work of higher quality than their English competitors

The reasons for the hostility to their practising their craft are largely revealed in a petition presented by silversmiths to the Court of the Company in 1711, which states 'that by admittance of necessitous strangers, whose desperate fortunes obliged them to work at miserable rates, the representing members have been forced to bestow much more time and labour in working up their plate than hath been the practice of former times, when prices of workmanship were greater'. The objection, therefore, was not only that the Huguenots worked at lower rates. It is clearly

P. Parkinson

Fig. 2 **Wine-cistern** *by Pierre Harache, London, 1697. Silver-gilt, length 22 ins. Presented to the Barber Surgeons' Company by Queen Anne, this magnificent piece with its admirably restrained detail was intended primarily for display. (Worshipful Company of Barber Surgeons, London.)*

Greville Photography

Fig. 3 **Wine decanter** *in the form of a Pilgrim bottle, one of a pair by Pierre Harache, London, 1699. Silver, height 21 ins. These impressive pieces were made principally by Huguenots, and were also intended for display. (Eton College, Windsor.)*

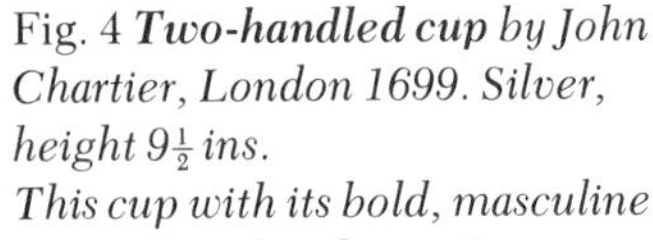

Museum Photo

Fig. 4 **Two-handled cup** *by John Chartier, London 1699. Silver, height 9½ ins. This cup with its bold, masculine proportions has decoration typical of the early Huguenot period. (Ashmolean Museum, Oxford.)*

implied that they had been producing work of higher quality than that of their English competitors and were imposing a higher standard than had been current. This was undoubtedly so. Furthermore, the Huguenot style itself involved far more advanced techniques in casting and finishing than had been employed by the English silversmiths.

The strength of the English tradition throughout the Restoration period can be seen in those pieces whose gauge was not limited by embossing and whose quality depended on good proportion alone. Surface embellishment, if used at all, was confined to cut-card work – thin metal cut into leaf or flame profiles and applied to the lower part of the body or at the juncture of handles. In the 1680s, fanciful *chinoiserie* and linear decoration was introduced, which was chased and, latterly, engraved on otherwise plain bodies.

This is among the finest English work of the period. Casting was confined principally to the thumb-pieces of tankards and the handles of porringers and was generally rough and poorly defined. Otherwise, work throughout the period was Dutch-influenced and depended principally on somewhat coarsely embossed and chased ornament of conventional flowers, *putti* and demi-beasts, the last being of classical origin but used quite unclassically. Classical motifs in the form of acanthus leaves were used at the base of tankards, beakers and porringers, and fluted Tuscan columns as the stems of candlesticks, but the allusion to their classical sources tends to be lost since the nature of embossing is contrary to the essentially sculptural character of their origin.

At its best English workmanship had a florid richness and dignity

In the 1690s, such ornament gave place to varieties of straight or spiral fluting, often combined with bands of stamped decoration and rope or gadroon borders. The gauge of metal was necessarily thin to allow the metal to be stretched by embossing which, in turn, gave it strength. The workmanship was variable; at best it had a florid richness and dignity, at worst it was mean and provincial.

By contrast, the Huguenot style was essentially

Fig. 5 ***Two-handled cup*** *by Pierre Platel, London, 1705. Silver, height 10½ ins. The treatment of the straps shows an increasing elaboration which was to continue in the next century. A comparison with the straps on the cup in Fig. 4 shows the direction in which decoration was to move. The harp-shaped handles so typical of this early period were replaced by scrolls in the eighteenth century. (Ashmolean Museum.)*

Fig. 6 ***Ice-pail,*** *one of a pair by Phillip Rollos, c.1715–20. Arms of John, 1st Earl of Bristol. Silver-gilt, height 10½ ins. This superb piece shows the development of pierced and cast decoration, enriched by surface variations of chasing and matting. The decorative themes are still based on those of the earlier designs of Daniel Marot; this suggests that the decorative elaboration may have been limited in the earlier pieces more by the conservatism of the client than by the virtuosity of the Huguenot silversmith. (National Trust, Ickworth, Suffolk.)*

aristocratic. Massiveness combined with elegance of form and a fastidious richness of detail. It is hardly surprising that these qualities gave Huguenot work an immediate appeal to the rich and noble. A heavy gauge of metal was consistently used in the bodies, and decoration took the form of applied relief details, cast with a fineness which, initially, the English silversmith was unable to approach. A characteristic form of this decoration was the strap, applied to the lower part of the body and radiating from the base. This has obvious affinities with cut-card work and in earlier examples this was also used by the Huguenots, usually reinforced by a cast spine to emphasise its sculptural character (Figs. 1, 3 and 4).

The cast strap was treated with great refinement, in the earlier examples spear-headed, and later rectangular in form, usually alternating either with the former or with a cast flute. Its surface had cast or chased decoration and, in the most highly developed examples, was pierced with interlacing patterns and surmounted by medallions or masks. The refinement of these later variations was matched by chased, matted and engraved variations of surface texture used to enhance and contrast with the sculptural nature of the applied decoration. Thus relief decoration and surface contrast were together used sensitively and with great taste, resulting in work of the highest finish and sophistication.

Compared with the unevenness of the work of the English silversmiths, Huguenot silver appears to have been of a consistently high standard, in spite of the fact that the majority of the Huguenots came from the provinces. The reason for this can be found in the reorganisation of the France of Louis XIV by Colbert, who established the Monarch's totalitarian rule as much in the arts as in industry. Under Lebrun, the Gobelins factory was organised to cover the whole field of the applied arts. Its purpose was the furnishing of Versailles, but it created a dictatorship of taste and established a high level of execution and a uniformity of style throughout France. Thus the system which rejected the Huguenots had also imposed on them a high standard of execution and design from which they rarely appear to have deviated.

This consistency of style depended on the school of French designers of ornament whose principal sources were of classical origin, and based on designs used by the Romans to decorate their ceilings. This was discovered in renaissance times in grottoes – hence the term *grotesque* for this form of decoration. The designers applied themselves also to silver designs, and there were many French pattern books from which the Huguenots were given guidance. Jean Lepautre (1618–82) was a master of the arabesque and there are two particularly fine examples of his influence in the Victoria and Albert Museum – the Calverley toilet service, hallmarked 1682, and a beautiful pair of gilt octagonal plates from Powderham Castle by Benjamin Pyne, 1698. Although both have English makers' marks, they are superior in style and quality to English work of the period.

A greater freedom and delicacy in the engraved decoration

The Huguenot Daniel Marot did much to establish the Louis XIV style in England, particularly in furniture and interiors. In the 1690s he was periodically involved in improvements at Hampton Court and, since he enjoyed royal patronage, it is hardly surprising that the lambrequin (stiff pelmet) and the tassel, the most characteristic of his design elements, appear in the silver of those employed by the King. These are to be seen in the borders of looking-glasses and sideboard dishes by Nelme, Garthorne and Willaume (Fig. 1). The lambrequin design also appears at the base of vessels in cut-card work by Pierre Harache (Figs. 2 and 3). In Marot's designs the baroque features shown in the hangings of a state bed he designed such as the scroll embellished with acanthus leaf, or the terminal classical torso, are to be found in the form of cast handles of ewers and wine coolers (Figs. 1 and 2), while the shell and mask, singly or combined, are used as cast detail throughout the period. These two, together with the geometric border patterns shown at the bed-head and the lattice, or diaper, patterns of the hangings, are also used consistently in the bands and borders of silver engraving and flat-chasing (Figs. 6 and 7).

Jean Bérain (1639–1711) also influenced the

Fig. 7 ***Detail of the cast border on a basin*** *by Paul de Lamerie, 1723.*
(Messrs. Lumley, London.)

A. C. Cooper

Museum Photo

Fig. 8 ***Hot-water jug*** *by Simon Pantin, London, 1712. Silver, height $6\frac{7}{8}$ ins.*
This is a charming example of the Huguenot ability to work in what is generally considered to be the English taste.
(City of Manchester Art Galleries. Assheton Bennett Collection.)

A. C. Cooper

Fig. 9 ***Pair of casters,*** *probably by David Willaume, London, 1731. Silver, height $7\frac{1}{2}$ ins.*
The Huguenots introduced elaborately cast and pierced covers to casters, often including engraved designs in the finest pieces.
(Messrs. S. J. Phillips, London.)

design of detail. His was of a lighter, less baroque quality, while the designs of Claude Gillot (1672–1722) showed a greater freedom and delicacy which became apparent in the engraved decoration of silver in the early 1730s and heralded the gaiety and lightness of the rococo period.

As has been suggested, the Huguenot style lends itself to display, and most of the pieces illustrated here were made principally for this purpose. The ewer (Fig. 1) shows many of the details already outlined and its helmet form is a characteristic Huguenot shape. The two-handled cup and cover, whose popularity continued throughout most of the eighteenth century, depends for its success on balance and proportion as well as on the discriminating use of embellishment. The most successful are the earlier examples on low feet with flat domed lids (Figs. 4 and 5). By the 1730s, the cup began to rise on a stem, while the cover developed a higher dome. The harp-shaped handle was a characteristic French form which soon gave place to the English scroll handle.

They excelled in those pieces which depended on simplicity of form

However, very simple, well-proportioned pieces were also made for middle-class use in France at the beginning of the period. It is not surprising, therefore, that the Huguenots were as much at home with the plain forms usually associated with the reigns of Queen Anne and George I. Indeed, they excelled in those pieces which depend on simplicity of form and good proportion alone, particularly in the octofoil salvers and the plain octagonal pieces of the second decade of the eighteenth century (Fig. 8).

As the Huguenot style became naturalised, so the Huguenots proved themselves equally adaptable to conservative English tastes. By the third decade, the style had become integrated and the resultant character unmistakably part of the English tradition and quite distinct from similar developments abroad. The new generation of Huguenots remained in the forefront of the craft, with that impeccable sense of style and fineness of execution which gave their fathers pre-eminence. The greatest of them was Paul de Lamerie, whose powers of invention were as astonishing as his technical brilliance. It is well to remember that the work that bears his mark was not that of one man but of a factory of craftsmen bred in the Huguenot tradition, whose standards reached an unrivalled excellence.

MUSEUMS AND COLLECTIONS

English Huguenot silver may be seen at the following:

London: Victoria and Albert Museum
Oxford: Ashmolean Museum

FURTHER READING

Silver by Gerald Taylor, London, 1965.
Huguenot Silver in England, 1688–1727 by J. F. Hayward, London, 1959.
Huguenot Goldsmiths in England and Ireland by Joan Evans, London, 1933.

DWIGHT AND THE ELERS

Mavis Bimson

John Dwight and the brothers Elers were pioneers of the ceramic arts in England. While Dwight strove to imitate the fine white wares of China, John and David Elers introduced to the Staffordshire potteries fine earthenware, not dissimilar to the red ware of Meissen.

Museum Photo

Fig. 1 **Portrait bust of Dwight's daughter,** *1673. (Victoria and Albert Museum, London.)*

Fig. 2 **John Dwight's signature.** *(Shepherd's Bush Library, Hammersmith.)*

Almost three hundred years ago, on 23 April 1672, John Dwight was granted a patent for the manufacture of 'transparent earthenware commonly known by the names of Porcelaine or China and Persian ware', and also for 'Stoneware vulgarly called Cologne Ware'. This date marks the beginning of the successful development of English ceramics beyond the lead-glazed, relatively low-fired wares which reached the peak of their development in the polychrome delft of the sixteenth and seventeenth centuries. The technical importance of hard-paste porcelains and stonewares lies in the fact that they are vitreous, non-porous ceramics with stable lead-free glazes and are thus particularly useful for the storage of liquids, having the virtues of glass without its fragility.

John Dwight was born in Gloucestershire in about 1640; he studied at Oxford and became an ecclesiastical lawyer, and, while acting as Registrar and Secretary to the Bishop of Chester at Wigan, carried out experimental work on stoneware, using clay from the cannel coal pits at Haigh. Having gained his patent, and, incidentally, quarrelled with the reigning Bishop of Chester, Dwight set up his manufactory in Fulham some time before 1673. In July 1673 a commentator, probably Sir John Colladon, wrote: 'I have learned for certain that the secret of the master potter at Fulham is a white transparent stone and a little fine white sand. Mr. Parker who works with him, described this material to me, which does in fact make fine porcelain but they have not yet been able to find the way to prevent the formation of blisters, like the blisters on leather, during the firing. He says that it is for lack of a fire that is hard and clear enough, for several pieces were found blackened. He leaves them forty-eight hours in firing and that he has not yet been able to do this in such a way that the pots are fired throughout without blistering . . . He says that several pieces melted into liquid'.

It seems likely that Dwight never in fact succeeded in making a true hard-paste porcelain, chiefly because he lacked knowledge of the essential ingredient, china-stone. However, there is no doubt about the quality of the stoneware he made at this period; the scientist Robert Hooke wrote in February 1673/4: 'Saw Mr. Dwight's English China, Dr. Willis his head, A little boye with a hauke on his fist, Severall little Jarrs of severall colours all exceeding hard as a flint, very light, of very good shape. The performance very admirable and outdoing any European potters'.

The death of Dwight's daughter Lydia occurred at about this time; her touching portrait in white stoneware bears the inscription 'Lydia Dwight dyd

March 3 1673' (Fig. 1). Unfortunately it is not known who modelled this or any of Dwight's sculptures. It is considered by some that they were his own work, but his contemporary Dr. Plot wrote: 'He hath also caused to be modelled statues of figures of the said transparent earth', and the variation in styles makes it extremely likely that more than one hand was involved (Figs. 3 and 10).

There was a family tradition, reported by Chaffers, that Dwight buried 'all his models, tools and moulds connected with this branch of the manufactory in some secret place on the premises at Fulham, observing that the production of such matters was expensive and unremunerative, and in order that his successors should not be tempted to perpetuate this part of the business, he put it out of their power, by concealing the means'. A pot containing some of the metal stamps used in the production of Dwight's fine stoneware was discovered buried at Fulham. Whatever the truth of this tradition, however, there is little doubt that the commercial success of the Fulham pottery was founded on the production of brown stoneware 'vulgarly called Cologne Ware'.

Stone-bottles by Dwight found in a bricked-up kiln

In his *History of Oxfordshire*, Dr. Plot wrote: 'Let it suffice for things of this nature (i.e., stoneware) that the ingenious John Dwight formerly M.A. of Christ Church College, Oxon., hath set up a manufacture of the same, which (by methods and contrivances of his own, altogether unlike those used by the Germans), in three or four years time, he hath brought it to greater perfection than it has attained where it hath been used for many ages, insomuch that the Company of Glass-Sellers of London, who are the dealers for that commodity, have contracted with the inventor to buy only of his English manufacture and refuse the foreign'. There are actually two agreements with the Glass-Sellers Company, the first dated 25 March, 1676, between the Company and John Dwight and his partner Windsor Sandys, and the second dated 1 May, 1677, between the Company and John Dwight alone; they are now preserved among the papers of the Glass-Sellers' Company in the Guildhall Library.

Several examples of Dwight's stone-bottles were found in a bricked-up kiln on the Fulham site and it may be noted that they are of much better quality than the debased contemporary German examples; the rims are neatly turned and the motifs are well moulded and neatly applied. The same characteristics must be looked for when attempting to identify Dwight's undecorated bottles; these are not common, probably because the stone-bottle was being quickly replaced by the glass wine-bottle at this date. The first patent was granted for a 'term' of fourteen years, but in 1684 Dwight rather surprisingly obtained a second patent; in 1693 he initiated a lengthy series of actions in the Court of Chancery against potters, whom he accused of infringing this later patent. It is clear from their wording that 'brown stone mugs' had become the chief article of manufacture.

Among the potters named in these lawsuits were the brothers Elers; they were both younger men than Dwight, David the elder being born in Amsterdam on 13 June, 1656, and John Philip at Utrecht on 7 September, 1664. According to a family history, John Philip was a godson of the Elector of Maintz and Queen Christina of Sweden; he became interested in chemistry and was associated with the scientist Joachim Becker. Like many eighteenth-century porcelain-makers, the brothers were silversmiths by profession.

It is often said that the Elers brothers were among the Dutch who came to England in the wake of William of Orange, soon after the Great Rebellion of 1688; David Elers himself stated in an affidavit that he had lived in Cologne for some time and there learned the technique of making Cologne ware, and that in about 1690 he and his brother had commenced to manufacture 'brown mugs and red teapots' in England. Their movements between 1690 and 1700, when they were declared bankrupt and ceased working as potters, are still not completely clear, though contemporary references show that for several years they manufactured

Fig. 3 ***Portrait bust*** *of Prince Rupert modelled from an engraving and made at Dwight's pottery at Fulham, late seventeenth century. White stoneware.*
Dwight is known to have made several life-size portrait busts. This is, however, the only surviving example that has come to light. It came from the collection of his family. (British Museum, London.)

Figs. 4 and 5 ***Two Mugs,*** *or pots, probably by the Elers brothers, late seventeenth century. Red stoneware.*
The sprig decoration is in imitation of Chinese prunus blossom.
(Victoria and Albert Museum.)

3

Museum Photo

4

Museum Photo

5

Museum Photo

6

Museum Photo

Fig. 6 ***Teapot***, *late seventeenth or early eighteenth century. Red stoneware with gilding and* chinoiserie *decoration. This type of work was inspired by the stoneware of the Elers. (Victoria and Albert Museum.)*

Fig. 7 ***Bottle*** *made at the Fulham pottery by Dwight, late seventeenth century. Brown stoneware with a band of marbled decoration and applied motifs many of which represent birds and snails in white stoneware.* (Victoria and Albert Museum.)

Fig. 8 ***Mug*** *from Dwight's pottery at Fulham, late seventeenth century. White stoneware in a silver mount, decorated with splashes of colour. (Victoria and Albert Museum.)*

7

K. Haddle

8

K. Haddle

Dwight
and the Brothers Elers

10

Fig. 9 **Portrait bust**, *said to represent Charles II, made at Dwight's Fulham pottery, late seventeenth century. White stoneware.*
Unlike the Prince Rupert which is of much higher quality, this bust is only a few inches high. (Victoria and Albert Museum.)

Fig. 10 **Neptune** *made at Dwight's pottery, possibly by an Italian after a bronze original, late seventeenth century. Brown stoneware.*
This piece belongs to a series of classical figures which may have originally formed a table centrepiece. Only four now survive; this Neptune, a Mars and a Meleager, both in the British Museum, and a Jupiter in the City Museum, Liverpool. (Victoria and Albert Museum.)

Museum Photo

9

Museum Photo

their red stoneware in Staffordshire near Newcastle-under-Lyme.

It was a family tradition that they settled in Staffordshire immediately after arriving in England, and as early as 1691 the Mayor of Newcastle-under-Lyme ordered that 'some of Mr. David Elers' earthenware to the vallew of three pounds or thereabouts' be presented to a judge coming from the Lancaster Assizes. However, in the Dwight lawsuit of 1693, John and David Elers are described as 'of Fulham'; and in the same year, John Houghton wrote: 'there is found near Faux-Hall in Surrey a sort of Clay used to make all sorts of Tea Pots, well approved of by most Toy-Shops about the Exchange, and are hardly discerned from China, and other Pots from beyond the Sea, being very exact in Colour, Strength, and Shape, and lately applied to this by two Dutch Brothers whose names are Eelers', whereas Dr. Martin Lister, writing on the subject of red clays, notes: 'I have this to add, that this clay, Haematites, is as good, if not better, than that which is brought from the East Indies. Witness the teapots now to be sold at the potters in the Poultry in Cheapside, which, not only for art, but for beautiful colour too, are far beyond any we have from China; these are made from the English Haematites in Staffordshire, as I take it, by two Dutchmen, incomparable artists'.

Celia Fiennes attempted to visit their pottery some time about 1698 but unfortunately was unsuccessful. 'I went to this NewCastle in Staffordshire to see the makeing of ye fine tea potts. Cups and saucers of ye fine red Earth in imitation and as Curious as y^{t} wch Comes from China, but was defeated in my design, they Comeing to an End of their Clay they made use of for y^{t} sort of ware, and therefore was remov'd to some other place where they were not settled at their work so Could not see it . . .'

It is possible that the Elers had already left Staffordshire, for in 1698 Lister noted that 'they were not long since at Hammersmith' and at the time of their bankruptcy they were described as 'late of Foxhall in Surrey'. A possible explanation of this rather confusing evidence is that for some time they made stoneware both in London and in Staffordshire, besides having a shop, and perhaps a home, in London.

The fine red teapots mentioned in these accounts were of a dense unglazed red stoneware made in imitation of the stoneware teapots of Yi-hsing; so far only a few fragments of wasters (flawed pieces) have been recovered from the Elers' pottery at Bradwell Wood, and, since they had no recognised mark, the identification of 'Elers ware' can only be based on stylistic considerations. Any piece of fine quality English seventeenth-century red stoneware bearing applied motifs that cannot be associated with Dwight, may be considered as probably made by the Elers. (It should be noted that the greater part of the red stoneware labelled as Elers in books and museum collections belongs to the eighteenth century and is far too late in date to have any connection with them.) (Fig. 6.)

The importance of the Elers brothers does not lie in any technical or artistic originality, but in the fact that they introduced the concept of fine earthenwares to the potters of Staffordshire. This was acknowledged in a letter written over seventy years later by Josiah Wedgwood, who summed the matter up thus: 'the improvement introduc'd by Mr. E. was the refining our common red clay, by sifting and making it into Tea and Coffee Ware in imitation of the Chinese Red Porcelaine by casting it in plaister moulds, and turning it on the outside upon Lathes, and ornamenting it with the Tea branch in relief, in imitation of the Chinese manner of ornamenting this ware. For these improvements, and very great ones they were for the time, we are indebted to the very ingenious Messrs. Elers, and I shall gladly contribute all in my power to honour their memories, and transmit to posterity the knowledge of the obligations we owe them . . .'

MUSEUMS AND COLLECTIONS

The pottery of Dwight and the Elers brothers may be seen at the following:

Cambridge: Fitzwilliam Museum
London: British Museum
Victoria and Albert Museum

FURTHER READING

'John Dwight' by M. Bimson in *English Ceramic Circle Transactions*, Vol 5, No. 2, London, 1960.
European Ceramic Art by W. B. Honey, London, 1952.
'Elers Ware' by W. B. Honey in *English Ceramic Circle Transactions*, Vol 1, No. 2, London, 1934.
The Ceramic Art of Great Britain by L. Jewitt, London, 1878.

Collector's Corner

doing your own furniture repairs

You can get a great deal of fun and pleasure from cleaning and fixing a loose handle, putting in a new drawer stop, or stripping off varnish and rewaxing. If you are inexperienced at these things, start on the very simple jobs first. Far better to learn gradually than be overenthusiastic and spoil what wasn't too bad a piece. The best advice is, if in doubt, don't do it yourself.

If in doubt, ask a specialist. There is sure to be an antique dealer, or an upholsterer or cabinetmaker with knowledge of repairing antiques, who can help you—even in the smallest of towns. But to have repairs done by competent craftsmen is not cheap, for they take time and skill. So you have to decide whether your piece of furniture is really worth elaborate repairs. Only you can decide. Don't over-capitalise, unless it is of great sentimental value or you have a signed warrant from the Queen's own hand to prove that Elizabeth I did sit on your chair.

If it is in a terrible state and the experts agree that it is an important piece, look at the photographs of the veneered chest of drawers on page 494 before and after repair and take heart.

I have put my tips and suggestions under headings so that you can find them quickly and easily. You might tackle one or two jobs on the same piece of furniture roughly in the order of my sections.

How to Treat Woodworm

More correctly, the woodworm should be called the furniture beetle. Two of the beetles' favourite woods are beech and walnut, and they are very partial to pine as well. In oak they only attack the sapwood. The female beetle lays her eggs in the cracks and crevices of furniture. When the grub hatches out, it feeds on the wood, making a continuous hole about 1/16 inch in diameter. After about two years the grub turns into a pupa which, after another few weeks, becomes a beetle. This bites its way out of the wood; the holes we see are the flight holes through which the beetle has left the wood. Signs of active woodworm are holes which appear newly bored and very fine wood dust.

Rentokil and Cuprinol are well known treatments for woodworm. If the infestation appears very extensive you can brush the liquid over the wood; if the holes are few, you can squirt it into them individually. If a table leg has become a mass of worm holes and the wood is very weak, soak it well with insecticide and allow it to dry out thoroughly. The leg can now be very considerably strengthened by pouring or injecting thin polyester resin (you could use the Isopon economy glass fibre kit for this) into the crumbling wood. After the resin has set hard, brush in a wax polish which matches the wood.

Repairing Joints

Never use metal plates, nails, or screws in an attempt to repair a loose or broken joint. You will only do more harm than good. Joints which have come apart and need regluing must first be well and carefully cleaned. You must remove as much of the old glue as possible with hot water.

Scotch glue was the traditional adhesive used for furniture, but is rather too much trouble for the odd small repair. Cascamite is a casein glue in powder form which is mixed with water, but becomes water-resistant when set. Care must be taken not to get it on to any visible faces of the wood. Aerolite is a quicker-drying adhesive, and consists of powder and a liquid hardener which have to be mixed together just before use.

The most important part of making a strong joint is to ensure that the parts are held very firmly together until the adhesive is completely set. If the underframe of a Windsor-type chair has come loose, a tourniquet is a simple and effective way of pulling and holding the joints together until the glue is set. Place pads of cloth round the legs so that the wood is not bruised (see **Fig. 1**). If a split table-top or -leaf has to be glued together an improvised clamp can be made, as shown in **Fig. 2.**

Warping

A table-top, door or shelf becomes warped if moisture gets into one side. Because this causes the wood to expand on that side, it forces the board into a convex shape. Try drying out this side and see if the wood flattens out. If it does not, damp the concave side. It will take at least a couple of days. Make sure the board is resting on strips of wood so that air can circulate (see **Fig. 3** overleaf). Warping usually occurs when only one side of

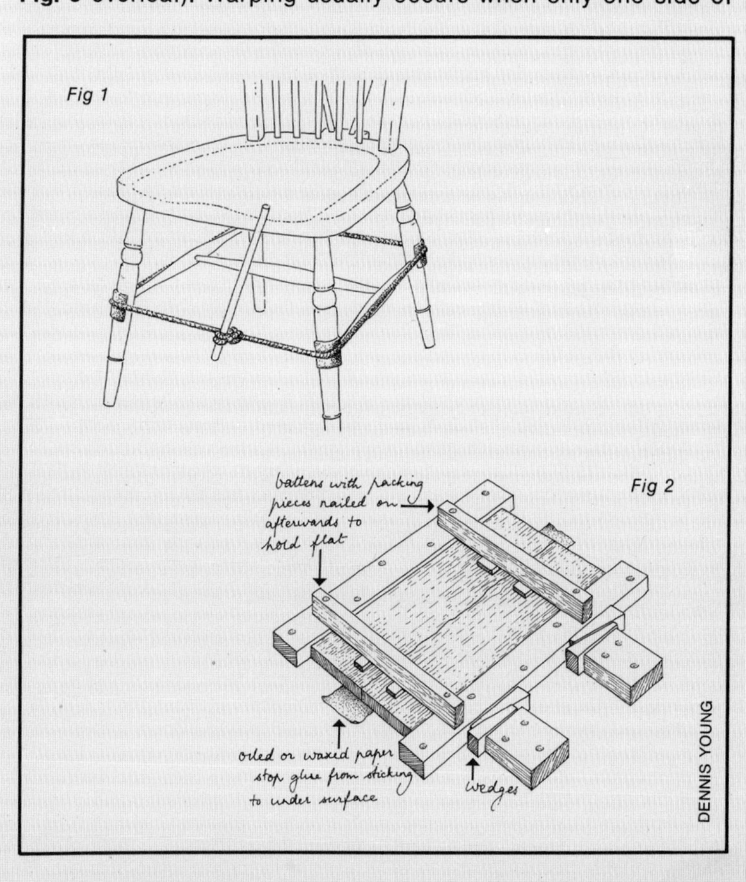

BEFORE **A complete ruin? This north Italian chest of drawers (c. 1750) was barely recognisable.**

AFTER **Only experts could have achieved this miraculous transformation. They are C. Wright and J. Kitchin.**

the board is sealed by wax or polish; the unsealed side allows moisture to get in. So when your table-top, door or shelf is flat again, make sure that both sides are equally sealed.

Stripping and Waxing

The best way to strip off thick coats of paint and varnish in the home is to use a proprietary paint stripper. Be careful not to roughen the wood when scraping off the 'goo'.

One of the best methods of removing dirt and varnish which is beginning to powder is to use steel wool and wax polish. First, get the worst of the dirt off with ammonia and warm water, dry off with a cloth and then leave until all dampness has gone. Now, with pads of '00' or the finer still '000' steel wool and generous amounts of wax polish, rub away at the old varnish. (Most domestic packets contain '1' or '0' pads. Finer grades can be obtained from most shops which sell paint and decorators' materials.) With patience and constant changing of the steel wool pad when it becomes gummed up, the colour and texture of the wood underneath will be exposed. When all the varnish is off, wipe down with waxed polish thinned with turpentine until the furniture is completely clean. Allow to dry and then rub over with furniture cream. Let this dry before polishing with a dry, soft cloth.

Loose and Blistered Veneers

When a piece of veneer is loose, it is best to lift it off completely, though you must do this gently. If part of a long strip is loose, break that part off. Clean off the old glue with hot water, taking care not to get any on to the polished surfaces. When dry, give a thin coat of Seccotine to the back of the veneer and on to the place where it has to go. Press the veneer into position, wipe off any surplus, cover with a piece of waxed or oiled paper and put under heavy pressure until the glue is set.

If a small piece of veneer has bubbled up or blistered, try ironing it down. Put a sheet of blotting paper over the blister and press down with a moderately hot iron. Keep taking a look at the blister and when it is flattened out, leave the iron on it until cold. The reason for this is that Scotch glue melts under heat, so that the pressure must be kept on until it has set again.

Scratches and Bruises

Fairly shallow scratches in a French-polished surface can be filled with beeswax which has been melted with a little rosin to make it harder. A little powder colour (children's tempera colour) may need to be added to match the rest of the wood. When cold, press this mixture into the scratch with a blunt knife with no rough edges, smooth off and then lightly wax the whole surface with a furniture cream and polish. Alternatively, children's coloured wax crayons can be melted together to get the right colour and then dripped into the scratch. After this remove the surplus and polish as above. If the scratch is deep and the light colour of the raw wood is showing, tone this down with a water stain of a matching colour, then proceed as above. (You must use a water stain, not a spirit stain. Water stains can be obtained from shops selling paint and decorators' materials. Alternatively you may use a water-based fabric dye.)

I have found shoe polish of the right colour of great help in disguising a scratch in mahogany or oak.

For bruises in French polish, there is little that can be done, but for a wax-finished piece of furniture try this method. Remove the wax over the bruise and damp with water, then lay a hot knife or the tip of an iron on the depression. Allow to dry and rub with '000' steel wool and wax. Finally polish the whole surface. If some of the colour has gone from the area of the bruise, tint it to the colour of the surrounding wood with water stain after having smoothed the wood with '000' steel wool only. Allow it to dry before washing and finally polishing.

Sticky Drawers

If a drawer is sticking, it is probably damp. Take the drawer out and allow it to dry in a warm room before rubbing the runners and top edges of the drawer sides with a candle or paraffin wax. Again, if a drawer does not run in and out evenly, the drawer guides are probably worn or have come off. Take out the drawer and look (see **Fig. 4**). The old guides may be good enough to glue back in position, or new ones may be needed. If the drawer goes in too far, the drawer stop has come away. Either it needs gluing or pinning back in position, or new ones will have to be made.

Iron Locks and Hinges

To remove rust and corrosion use penetrating oil and a rust remover and inhibitor such as Jenolite, but take care not to get this on to the wood.

If screws need to be removed and will not budge with the screwdriver, try gently tapping the screwdriver with a hammer to loosen the rust. Should this fail, allow some lubricating oil to lie on the screwhead for an hour or so, then hold a red-hot, pointed piece of metal on the centre of the screwhead for about half a minute. When the screw cools it should come out easily.

Handles and Knobs

A woodturner will make copies of wooden knobs if you take one of the original ones along as a pattern.

To clean brass handles, first remove them from the piece of furniture. They are usually held on by nuts on the inside of the door or drawer. Remove the dirt and grease with ammonia and water, then clean with a mixture of salt and vinegar. Wash well in clear, warm water and dry. Polish with a soft cloth and a few drops of sweet oil.

Cleaning Ormolu

Remove the ormolu from the furniture, taking care to put the nuts back on to the screws if this method of fixing is used (they are often not interchangeable). Start cleaning with a very weak solution of ammonia and water, increasing the strength until the ormolu is clean, then wash it well in clear water and rub it dry. Never use metal polish on ormolu.

Chair Cane Work

Caned chair seats and backs can be cleaned by gently scrubbing with a nailbrush using hot soapy water. Finally rinse with clean water and allow to dry out of doors, though not in strong sunlight. You will find that the caning tightens up. If you thinly brush matt-clear polyurethane over both sides of the caning, you will strengthen it considerably.

Leather Tops

First stick down loose pieces with Seccotine, then clean off dirt with soapy water, taking care not to get any on to the polished wood surroundings. Allow to dry and finish with a proprietary leather dressing such as Hide Food or Sheerwax. Properts' Saddle Soap, applied with a soft cloth pad, is very good for both cleaning and feeding leather tabletops and desk tops.

DENNIS YOUNG

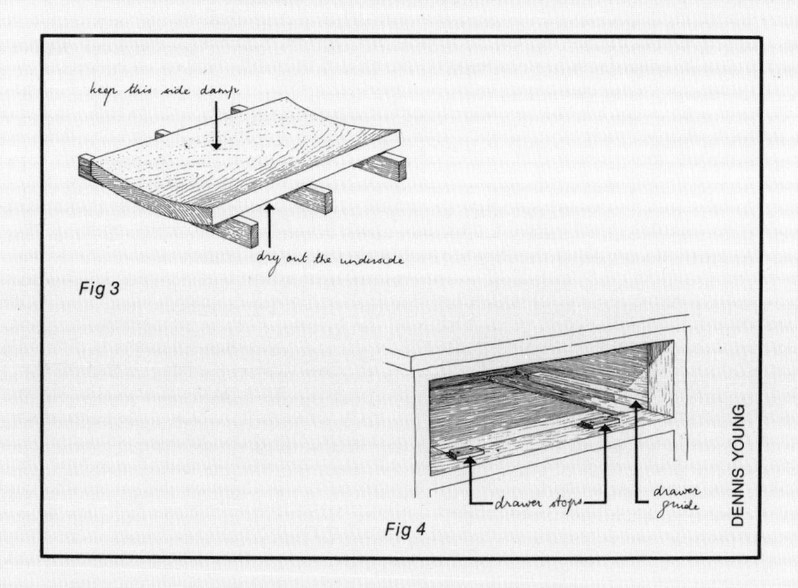

Fig 3

Fig 4

A BUYER'S GUIDE TO ELIZABETHAN FURNITURE

Oak is one of the most commonly found woods in Europe, Asia and America. It grows slowly, but yields a timber which is hard, heavy and very tough. For these reasons, it has been used for centuries throughout the world for furniture, houses and shipbuilding.

In England, oak has been used since gothic times, but has always been scarce; in the early seventeenth century so much was required for the building of ships that laws had to be passed limiting its domestic use. In the eighteenth and nineteenth centuries oak was imported from the Baltic for use in high-quality furniture.

There are several different species of oak. All are coloured a yellowish white and have a similar grain. This grain is more or less apparent depending on the method of sawing used. The most economical is to cut the log lengthwise, but this does not bring out the pattern, and causes the planks to warp. Less warping occurs if the log is sawn towards its centre. This method, known as quartersawing, is wasteful, but it reveals the distinctive grain with its yellow streaks called medullary rays. Because quartersawn wood tended to remain straight, it was used for wagon shafts, and became known in the Netherlands as 'Wagenschott' oak. This name returned to England as 'wainscot', which has described the high-quality oak used for panelling and furniture.

Oak is easily identifiable by its characteristic patterning of radial cracks with the medullary rays. These appear as wide yellow flecks or as thin parallel flashes of a darker colour, and are slightly raised due to the uneven shrinking of the wood as it ages.

There are three main points to watch out for when buying antique oak: texture, patination and cut. Fakers aware of the uneven texture of oak sometimes use acid and rotary wire brushes; these have much the same effect as time, since they wear down the softer parts of the wood and leave the harder flecks slightly raised. Fortunately, this form of faking is quite rare.

Patination comes naturally with time and has a deep shine which is very difficult to reproduce. It is caused by a build-up of polish such as bees-wax and turpentine which is still an excellent polish for old furniture. Light, honey-coloured patination is easier to fake than the darker colours, and should be regarded with more suspicion.

The other major factor to watch when inspecting the wood of a piece of antique furniture is the cut. Saws were common by the sixteenth century, but adzes were still used right up to the seventeenth, and their characteristic marks are often found on the backs of panels. Their absence is not a sure sign of a fake, but their presence is encouraging to the wary buyer.

When chairs were mostly thrones: this early manuscript illustration depicts Louise of Savoy, mother of Francis I, King of France 1515-47.

The advance of comfort

The aim of this article is not to help you to know all the styles of English upholstered furniture, but rather to outline the way in which chair shapes developed and changed. As you look at chairs in antique shops, museums, country houses and in your own and other people's homes, you start wondering why—why that chair is that particular shape and size, who it was made for and what materials went into its making.

Changing social conditions

The story of the development of upholstered furniture during the last 500 years is a very fascinating one. For one reason, it clearly traces changing social conditions and ways of life. One sees the evolution of more comfortable ways of sitting through new methods of construction and new materials. One also recognises the problems brought by changes in fashion: the narrow, armless chairs at the end of the sixteenth century were to accommodate the wide hooped skirts of the period, and the comfortable, fully-upholstered chairs of the 1870's were provided with a hole at the back to allow for ladies' bustles.

Chairs the exception

During medieval times chairs were a status symbol. Only the most important person of the household, court or assembly would be seated on a chair—or one might prefer to call it a throne. Everyone else would have to make do with stools, benches or cushions on the floor. A memory of this era survives: our continued use of the word 'chairman' is a relic of this age-old custom.

The two main types of chair during the sixteenth century were the framed-up box chair and the X-framed chair (sometimes called a Hamlet chair today). On these appeared the early forms of upholstery. On the box chair *(drawing 1)* the upholstery took the form of a loose cushion. This type of chair was made by joiners with the same methods of construction as they employed for cabinet furniture and wall panelling. Fixed upholstery began on X-framed chairs, in the form of padded arms *(drawing 2).* The chair illustrated is rigid, but the earliest examples could be folded. By the beginning of the seventeenth century the simple folding chair had become elaborately and richly upholstered *(drawing 3).* The whole of the framework is covered in velvet and decorated with close gilt nailing and fringes; the deeply upholstered seat platform, stuffed with hair and wool, supports a matching cushion filled with down. These chairs are the earliest examples of fixed, fully upholstered chairs in Britain.

Smaller-scale living

The seventeenth century saw many changes in living habits. The communal life of the great hall was replaced by greater privacy and houses had more and smaller rooms, a fact which was reflected in the scaling down of furniture. The chair in *drawing 4* is of similar oak, framed-up construction to that in *drawing 1* but the panels have been left out and fabric stretched over the seat and back frames to give a little more comfort. Often the covering fabric was of knotted wool called Turkey work, placed over a linen base.

It is from the two chairs in *drawings 3* and *4* that all subsequent upholstered chairs, made with what we might call traditional construction techniques, developed. Similarly, the forerunner of our dining chair was the so-called Farthingale chair (a name given in Victorian times) which appeared in the later part of the sixteenth century. Both seat and back were padded, usually with sheep's wool, horsehair and straw; feathers and down were used for loose cushions.

Peculiarly English chair

When the monarchy was restored in 1660, Charles II brought many new ideas and innovations from Europe, including a richness and extravagance to court life. The upholstered furniture of the period was rich with carving and colour, and comfort was not forgotten. *Drawing 5* shows a typical armchair and, although one can still detect the lines of the framed-up chair, these have been embellished with twist turning on the legs and arm stumps, and elaborate carving on the front stretcher rail. This chair has a simple type of ratchet so that the angle of the back can be adjusted. It is an early example of the wing chair which was to be so popular throughout the eighteenth century. I always like to think that the wing chair was especially designed for the English home. For you can sit in it, sheltered from draughts on three sides, and toast on the fourth in front of a roaring log fire.

The Queen Anne wing-back chair represents a turning point in the development of English upholstered chairs. Here for the first time is the feeling that the frame has been designed in conjunction with the upholstery and not, as in earlier chairs, that the padding was added as an afterthought *(drawing 6)*. The wooden frame has been designed to give a soft flowing line which follows through the whole chair, including the cabriole legs with their typical shell carving. The seat is wide and the arms set back in order to accommodate the wide skirts of the ladies and the full coats of the gentlemen.

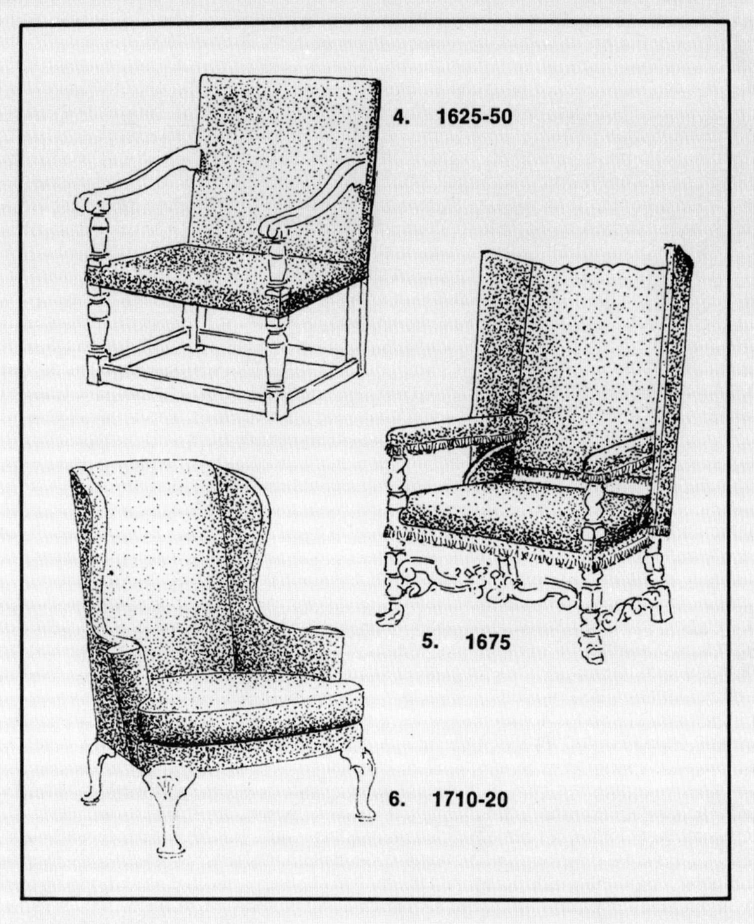
4. 1625-50
5. 1675
6. 1710-20

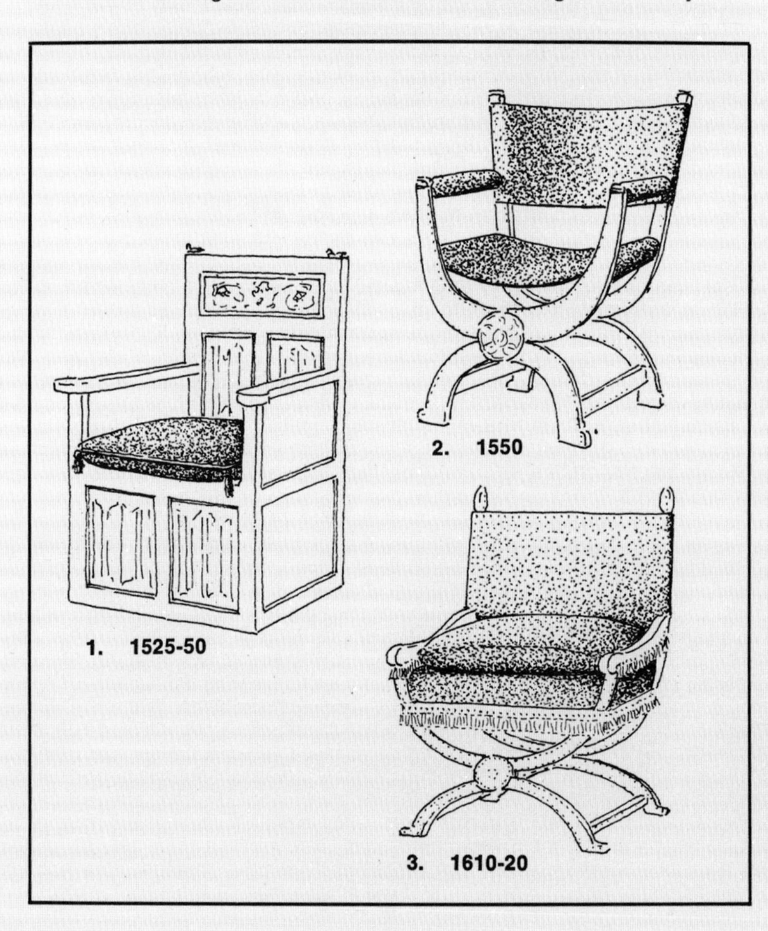
1. 1525-50
2. 1550
3. 1610-20

By the middle of the eighteenth century a strong French influence could be seen in many of the upholstered chairs *(see drawing 7)*. From now until the beginning of the nineteenth century the range of upholstered chairs includes the designs of such men as Chippendale, Hepplewhite, Sheraton and Adam. But, although the range was very wide, there were no major developments in chair construction or upholstery and the wing armchair was to remain popular for comfortable sitting. The superb lines of these chairs of the beginning of the century were rarely matched.

Nineteenth-century comfort

Drawing 8 illustrates the lines followed in both chairs and sofas at the beginning of the nineteenth century, although many of the chairs of this period were much heavier in appearance than the one I have drawn. The Regency period is probably better known for the elegant sofas which it produced and which fetch such high prices today.

In the 1820s Samuel Pratt invented and patented coil springs and by the 1840s sprung upholstery was being used in all types of chair. *Drawing 9* shows a typical sprung chair of the middle of the nineteenth century. The introduction of coil springs gave us what is known as deep upholstery, which became best known in the deep easy chairs first introduced into gentlemen's clubs in Piccadilly and St. James's.

To learn a little more about upholstered chairs in the nineteenth century, browse through some old bound copies of *Punch*, a wonderful source for dating chairs—and other furniture as well.

True craftsmanship

The skill of the upholsterer during the middle of the nineteenth century was never surpassed, for there was true craftsmanship in the way in which steel springs, horsehair and cotton linters were modelled and worked on to the wooden, or sometimes iron, frames to give deep comfortable chairs, even though many of them lacked the subtlety of the line of the eighteenth century.

DENNIS YOUNG

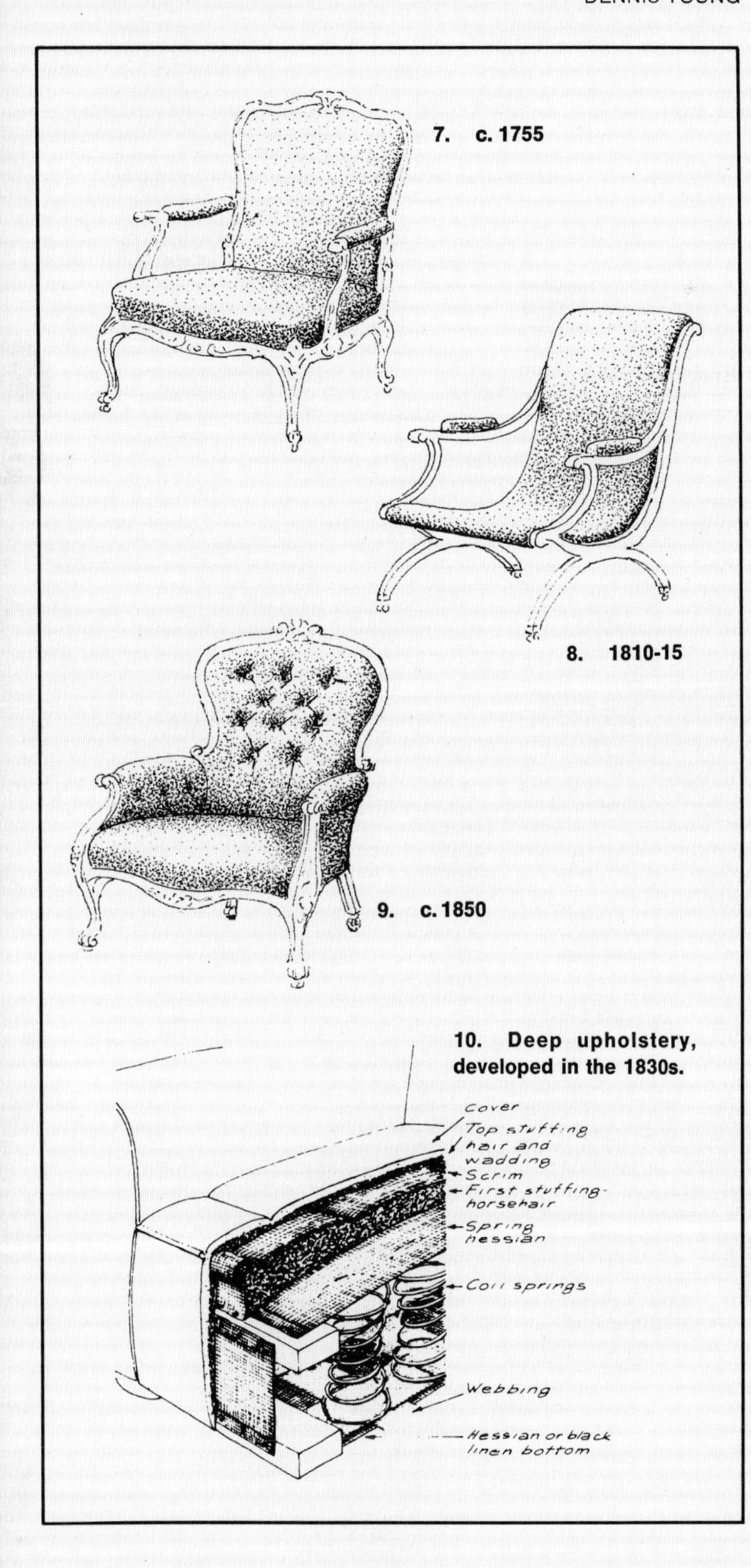

7. c. 1755

8. 1810-15

9. c. 1850

10. Deep upholstery, developed in the 1830s.

Market Trends

17TH CENTURY ANTIQUES

It is usually the less fine Mortlake tapestries of the later seventeenth century which come on the market, and many of these need urgent restoration. However, at Sotheby's in February 1969 two early tapestries, one showing *St. Paul preaching at Athens* from *The Acts of the Apostles* series after the Raphael cartoon, the other of *The Beautiful Gate,* also after Raphael, were sold for £850 and £420 respectively. Not high prices, but both had cut-down lower borders, the colours were faded and their condition required attention. In general, there is considerable fluctuation in prices; for instance, the same eight panels dating from the mid-century depicting *The Acts of the Apostles* and woven with the arms of the Earls of Winchelsea and Nottingham made £1,732 in June 1947 and £997 in March 1953, both at Christie's. A popular representation in several branches of the applied arts is that of *The Months.* Five late seventeenth-century panels with borders of fruit and flowers and showing a strong Netherlandish influence—they derive from the Lucas' tapestries attributed to Bernard van Orley—made £5,800 at Sotheby's in December 1969. Prices have shown a modest increase during the last decade and it is unlikely that any dramatic change in this will occur until all prospective purchasers are confident that a tapestry can be efficiently and relatively quickly repaired, which is not true today.

Furniture

In May 1936, an elaborate oak marquetry and parquetry buffet carved with grotesque masks and strap-work fetched £320 at Christie's; three years ago a similar piece inlaid with scrolling foliage panels and dated 1615 made only 500 guineas. It is only during the last two years or so that there has been a serious renewal of interest in Stuart and Commonwealth furniture; its appeal has been recognised and increases in price are beginning to vindicate the years of comparative neglect. A Caroline oak box carved with concentric circles, trellis work and flower heads —a relatively unimportant item—came up at Sotheby's in December 1969 and fetched £240; in the same sale, a fine James I oak cupboard boldly carved with gadrooning, flutes and foliage made £2,800. A month earlier at Christie's an elegant Charles I draw-leaf table with baluster supports and lightly carved frieze was sold for 600 guineas, a price one would expect to be noticeably bettered now.

Silver

Many readers will know that the silver market has fallen considerably since April 1969 and in particular that it affected the most ordinary and extensively produced examples of the eighteenth century, such as candlesticks and coffee pots. One reason for this is that they are plentiful. This does not apply to plate

A Charles I wine cup, 4¼ inches high, 1635, sold at Christie's in 1965 for £2,300.

of the seventeenth century with the exception of spoons; it has long attracted the discerning and perhaps more academic collector. Not that all examples have shown large price increases; the wine cup illustrated would probably fetch little more today, but at least seventeenth-century silver has maintained its value and, due to scarcity and increasing interest, will inevitably continue to do so. TOM MILNES GASKELL

STUART NEEDLEWORK, CRYSTAL AND GLASS

Here is one of the applied arts that few would choose to laboriously reproduce and sell as an original. Indeed, few would be able to do so. The attraction of Stuart needlework has not recently been discovered; its appeal has spread gradually to a wider audience which explains the steady increase in prices over the past decade. Caskets appear irregularly but not infrequently on the market and remain relatively numerous. A Charles II example (Sotheby's, March 1959) depicting *Solomon and the Queen of Sheba* with additional figures of *Justice, Faith, Hope* and *Charity,* and dated 1662, fetched £360. In the same sale, a toilet mirror with stumpwork decoration portraying biblical figures, including *Delilah* and *Jael,* made £320. More recently (July 1970), a dazzling late sixteenth-century *petit point* needlework picture of a monarch, presumed to be *Elizabeth I, receiving an Ambassador in a Formal Garden,* was sold for £1,300.

Crystal

The sheer grandness of a fine translucent crystal, a piece of Sieburg pottery or Ming porcelain, mounted in silver or silver-gilt, is hard to surpass; the splendour of their contrasting textures and tones give them an imposing quality which is unique. As long ago as November 1949, a crystal cup of 1573 with chased caryatid figures enclosing the bowl, and lavishly decorated with flowers and fruit, made £2,000 at Sotheby's. In the same year at Christie's, a magnificent ostrich cup (the egg itself a replacement) made in London in 1584, with dolphin scroll brackets to the stem, a baluster finial springing from a fluted calyx and engraved with a contemporary coat of arms, was sold for £4,400. Naturally not all mounted pieces will command this kind of price. A James I blue and white porcelain ewer, the mounts bearing no hallmarks, realised £500 at Christie's in May 1965, although its incomparably finer companion, struck with a maker's mark only, made £1,850. Prices are influenced according to whether a piece is hallmarked or not and, if unmarked, whether it is of Continental or English origin. An elegant unmarked mother-of-pearl bowl with plain staves and scalloped mounts (illustrated in J. Banister's article, **Fig. 4**) was sold for £500 by Christie's in February 1966.

Glass

Careful followers of the Times-Sotheby Index will know that early glass has appreciated by 6.88 times since 1951 as of August 1970. But only a fraction of this early glass was pre-Ravenscroft, and it is a rare event, and causes considerable excitement, when a piece appears on the market. In June 1963 a commemorative bowl and a similar companion piece were offered at Christie's. The bowls also have the distinction of being the only known examples of diamond point engraving on Ravenscroft glass. They realised £3,600 and £3,200 respectively. However, less historic, humble pieces such as wine glasses and flasks, are within the reach of many. A pear-shaped flask, decorated with gadrooning and four applied raspberry medallions, 5½ inches high, was sold in July 1954 for £30. TOM MILNES GASKELL

A silver-mounted serpentine tankard, maker's mark TP in monogram, 1637, 6¾ inches high, was sold at Christie's in November 1961 for £420.

RESTORATION ANTIQUES / by Tom Milnes Gaskell

The obvious spontaneity and lack of pretension of English delftware, crudely potted as it is, have made it a natural area for the collector who is concerned neither with quality nor with undue refinement. While there is such a premium on all articles of excellent workmanship, it is still possible to buy attractive delft pieces for a modest sum. Only three years ago (in October 1967) an attractive blue-dash tulip charger painted with three stylised flowers made a mere 80 gns. at Christie's and a Bristol delft Adam and Eve charger—a popular subject—was sold for 140 gns. In March 1965 at Sotheby's a very rare Lambeth jug and dish of considerable elegance, dated 1686 and painted with a cartouche of griffins, swags and tassels, realised only £155. But this has been noticed over the last two or three years and consequently prices have risen steeply. A fine Dublin delft bowl painted with a church and houses around a lake brought 600 gns. at Sotheby's in October 1968 and a London delft blue and white standing salt, with scroll brackets to the rim and dated 1675, made 700 gns. However, considerable quantities of delftware still exist, in particular chargers which were produced in prodigious quantities. Two blue-dash chargers, painted with Prince George, consort to Queen Anne, and The Fall of Man, made 350 and 480 gns. respectively at Christie's in May 1969. Less significant examples than these are also available. For instance, a Bristol polychrome blue-dash oak leaf charger sold for 130 gns. at Sotheby's in June 1970.

Musical instruments

It is the name of Antonio Stradivari that comes first to mind when writing of early eighteenth-century musical instruments. He probably produced the finest violins ever made. Sotheby's sold one in May 1964 for £8,000; two years earlier another had realised £3,300. They were extensively reproduced during the later years of the nineteenth century, many bearing false signature labels. Genuine Stradivari violins will always remain sought after by professional musicians as well as by collectors of musical instruments. It was a rare occasion when a field trumpet of brass with silver mounts (see illustration) came on the market. It was called the Luck of Woodsome Hall, signed by Simon Beale and dated 1667: Beale was state trumpeter to Cromwell and Charles II. Christie's sold this for £1,600 in October 1967.

***Below:** This field trumpet, made in 1667, fetched £1,600 in October 1967.*

Restoration furniture

Walnut furniture of the Restoration period has long been in demand. Eight walnut chairs of farthingale type, upholstered in tapestry, realised 2,200 gns at Christie's in May 1969. The appeal and simplicity of walnut is obvious and it lends itself to today's taste. There is the additional advantage that much of this type of furniture will fit into relatively small houses. Six oak chairs with spiral twist and square uprights made £1,800 at Sotheby's in December 1969 and, in the same sale, a small but attractive gate-leg table fetched £1,150.